The Secrets of Mary

ALSO BY JANICE T. CONNELL

Queen of the Cosmos

The Visions of the Children

Triumph of the Immaculate Heart

Angel Power

Meetings with Mary

Praying with Mary

Prayer Power

Queen of Angels

Faith of Our Founding Father

The Spiritual Journey of George Washington

THE *Secrets*

OF *Mary*

GIFTS FROM THE BLESSED MOTHER

JANICE T. CONNELL

ST. MARTIN'S PRESS
NEW YORK

Book design by Ellen Cipriano

Library of Congress Cataloging-in-Publication Data

Connell, Janice T.
    The secrets of Mary : gifts from the Blessed Mother / Janice T. Connell.—1st ed.
        p. cm.
    Includes bibliographical references.
    ISBN 978-0-312-38541-5
    1. Mary, Blessed Virgin, Saint—Apparitions and miracles.   I. Title.
    BT650.C66 2009
    232.91'7—dc22

                                                            2009017120

First Edition: October 2009

10   9   8   7   6   5   4   3   2   1

Declaration

Bible quotes are from The Holy Bible Douay Rheims Version, Revised by Bishop Richard Challoner, A.D. 1749–1752, published by Tan Books and Publishers, Inc., Rockford, Illinois, 61105.

Certain theological concepts are written by the author in poetic form in the first person: the book has been edited for theological accuracy in Rome by Robert Faricy, S.J., S.T.D. and in Washington, D.C., by Thomas King, S.J., S.T.D.

This book contains stories, quotations, and teachings from Sacred Scripture, the Doctors of the Church, saints, and experts of vast spiritual disciplines, historical records, art, history, and music. The Divine Mercy revelation and the writings of Saint Faustina herein are used with permission and excerpted from the diary of Sister M. Faustina Kowalska, *Divine Mercy in My Soul,* copyright © 1987, Congregation of Marians of the Immaculate Conception; all world rights reserved. Heartfelt thanks for help and prayers over the years. The expertise and generosity of Thomas Thompson, S.M., director of the Marian Library, International Marian Research Institute, and his colleagues were helpful in preparing this book. Research was made available in Rome by Robert Faricy, S.J., and Joseph Fox, O.P.; in Saint Petersburg, Russia, by Archpriest Victor Potapov; in Spain by Joseph Dempsey, J.R.; at Lourdes by M. Jenkins Cromwell, J.R.; in Malta by Peter Hutley; in Asia by the late Jamie Cardinal Sin; in Eastern Europe by the late Czech bishop Pavel Hnilica; at Fatima by the late John Haffert; at Medjugorje by Tomislav Pervan, OFM; in Washington, D.C., by the late Monsignor Joseph Murphy, the late William Most, and Monsignor Roger C. Roensch; and in the Holy Land and Washington, D.C., by Thomas M. King, S.J. Heartfelt thanks. May their graciousness and generosity bear sweet fruit for the Kingdom of Mary's Son.

Our Lady, Queen of Peace

Little heirs of the Kingdom of Love,
Treasure my secrets.
Persevere for Jesus comes soon.
Those who recognize Him
and
follow Him to the Promised Land
are being prepared
now in the holocaust of Satan's last stand.
His days of reign are drawing to an end.

My Son Jesus longs for all our Father's children to know
my Mother's Heart, overflowing with love for
all His beloved sons and daughters.
Come little ones into my Immaculate Heart.
I am with you in a most special presence in these times.

Our Father is blessing you with many rewards for
He appreciates faithfulness my little children.
Praise our Father.
Praise Him with greater love and gratitude.
You have nothing to fear my little ones.
He longs for the return of His children.
All your sacrifices in the name of obedience to
God's plan in the world
are very great gifts that bless my name
in the world.
Please protect the sacredness of the gift of my apparitions.

You come to earth to acquire virtues that enable you to
be happy in eternal life.
Each of you is so much more than your corporeal substance
That you will rejoice for all eternity in my presence

As we praise and thank our Father for
His great love for each of us.

Allow me to take you to Jesus now dear little children.
He has much to teach you in these final days.
Find Him in the quiet of your hearts.
He is everywhere that you go.
The cosmos cannot contain Him.
Jesus is Heaven.
Peace little children.
Come with me now in peace to Jesus.
He awaits you.

Contents

Part Two: Queen of Prophets:
SUPERNATURAL HOPE / 89

Part Three: Gate of Heaven:
SUPERNATURAL LOVE / 173

Author's Note

Dear Reader,

Thank you for responding to the call deep within your soul to draw nearer our Blessed Mother. We can never thank God enough for this privilege we share. If you want to be very happy, make of your heart a small chapel. Enter into the silence of your heart and its longings as you read this book about our Blessed Mother's spiritual secrets and the wonderful gifts she has for us. Read as the Holy Spirit directs you and you are sure to find what God desires you to know now. Jesus Christ, God Incarnate, was born of Mary, lived on earth for thirty-three years and died for us that we might have this blessing. If you allow prayerful reading of this book to be your special time each day with Mary, daughter of the Father, mother of the Son, and spouse of the Holy Spirit, riches that pass all understanding will be yours. Read it many times in small doses that you may drink deep of the Empyrean Springs.

I am praying with our Blessed Mother for you and hope that you will pray with Mary for me. Indeed, the church is a supernatural reality beyond its structures, nations, and the earth. We are the church. God bless you.

—JANICE T. CONNELL, J.D., D.M.
May 31, 2009

Pope John Paul II celebrating Mass in Saint Peters, Rome

"Today we wish to entrust to you {Mary} the future that awaits us,
and we ask you to be with us on our way.
We are the men and women of an extraordinary time,
exhilarating yet full of contradictions.

"Humanity now has instruments of unprecedented power:
we can turn this world into a garden,
or reduce it to a pile of rubble.
We have devised the astounding capacity
to intervene in the very well-springs of life:
man can use this power for good, within the bounds of the moral law,
or he can succumb to the short-sighted pride
of a science which accepts no limits,
but tramples on the respect due to every human being.

"Today as never before in the past,
humanity stands at a crossroads.
And once again, O Virgin Most Holy,
salvation lies fully and uniquely in Jesus, your Son."[1]

—Pope John Paul II

Acknowledgments

Mary's children throughout the world, who personally helped me on this project for the glory of God and, in their humility, are known to Him alone. Their commitment and generosity bring the love of the Blessed Mother to the four corners of the earth.

Devotees of Mary throughout the world prayed this book into being.

My family and especially my husband whose collaboration is reflected throughout this book, our beloved children and dear grandchildren; their devotion to Our Lady continues to inspire and intrigue. Without them, it is probable that this book, written over a lifetime, would not be.

Much gratitude to Robert Faricy, S.J., who graciously edited this book for theological accuracy and wrote the foreword.

The expertise of the late Thomas M. King, S.J., whose loving dedication to Mary inspired this work, is gratefully acknowledged.

Donald Wuerl, S.T.D.; Thomas Olmsted, S.T.D.; Robert Faricy, S.J., S.T.D.; Thomas King, S.J., Ph.D.; Michael Scanlan, T.O.R., J.D.; Roderick Jones, O.S.B.; the late Adrian van Kaam, C.S.Sp., and Susan Muto, Ph.D. for their committed devotion to the Mother of God, and for their discernment, scholarship, and encouragement, all of which find expression in this book.

Alyse Diamond and Matthew Shear, and all my St. Martin's Press colleagues for their belief in this project, and their expertise.

Ronald Goldfarb, Esq., for his assistance.

The Sisters of Our Lady of Mount Carmel who mobilized Herculean prayer support on behalf of this book. I am especially grateful for the guidance and encouragement of the late Mother Teresa Margaret of Lafayette, Louisiana.

The Sisters of Georgetown Visitation Convent, especially the late

Sister Mary Theresa Burns. They formed me as a teenager and trained me in the ways of Our Lady.

My professional colleagues throughout the world who have inspired me to continue on this project during many decades.

My classmates and faculty at Georgetown University School of Foreign Service, the University of Pittsburgh Graduate School of Public and International Affairs, and Duquesne University School of Law who courageously illumined for me the value of geopolitical humility in a world of power politics, the nonnegotiable necessity of mutually beneficial global cooperation, and the moral imperative for each of us to make the next generation better.

I deeply appreciate those heroic ones who have gone before us, are with us now, and who will rise in the future to defend the integrity of the holy Mother of God.

This book was consecrated to God at the site of the Archangel Gabriel's visit to Mary at Nazareth in the Grotto of the Annunciation in the Holy Land. Special thanks to Jesuits Thomas King, Brendan Hurley, Thomas Stahl, Josef Kadlec, Daniel O'Connell, the late Harold Bradley, and to Benedictine Roderick Jones.

The Secrets of Mary is dedicated to everyone on earth, Mary's spiritual children, with great thanks to our Blessed Mother Mary who gave us Jesus Christ our Savior.

Any errors or omissions are unintentional and will be promptly remedied upon proper notification.

Finally, and most important of all, I pray the Lord Jesus will bless this book and all those it touches with deep, abiding, fruitful trust in His Blessed Mother, the Queen of Peace.

Introduction

Jesus said: "*Ask and it shall be given to you: seek, and you shall find: knock and it shall be opened to you. For everyone that asketh, receiveth: and he that seeketh, findeth: and to him that knocketh, it shall be opened. Or what man is there among you, of whom if his son shall ask for bread, will he reach him a stone? Or if he shall ask him a fish, will he reach him a serpent? If you then being evil, know how to give good gifts to your children: how much more will your Father, who is in heaven, give good things to them that ask?*"[1]

The twenty-first century is a time of immense spiritual opportunity. Life is changing for everyone in most regions of the world. Places steeped in ancient customs and superstitions as well as technologically advanced regions of commerce and industry are experiencing the bountiful gifts of Mary. Our challenge is to appropriate Mary's prophetic wisdom into our personal lives. Jesus' Blessed Mother is our spiritual mother.[2] She is our most loving advocate with Him because He said so.[3] The Mother of our Savior cooperates uniquely in the work of our Redemption.[4] Consciously or subconsciously we all seek our Spiritual Mother.

A serious warning: Mary is *not* a medium or spiritualist. Mother of the Redeemer, she is first among the communion of saints. Assumed into Heaven body and soul,[5] Mary inaugurated the assumption of all humanity in God. Her presence in these times foreshadows the mystical dimension of our own eternal destiny.[6]

This is the time of our heavenly visitation. We intuitively turn to God however we know that unknowable word. God loves us, each of us on the earth, unconditionally and completely. He knows we need perfect mother love. Jesus Christ gave us His own Mother. In our depths, we do cling to her. Becoming aware of our Blessed Mother allows us to experience renewal, enlightenment, peace, and prosperity. God's immeasurable love for us becomes a living reality. Awareness of how infinitely loved we are fulfills the deepest longings of our body, mind, and spirit. God has always loved us totally and will always love us, no matter what we think or say or do. We need to know that. We belong to God. It is up to us to discover the absolute, immutable reality that God is love and His love includes each of us. God wills only the best for all of us.

Mary is a vital part of our ongoing spiritual development. God, knowing how profoundly we need our Spiritual Mother's unconditional love, gives us Mary in a new and beautiful way in these times. She reflects perfectly the feminine attributes of God. Mary among us reveals cherished secrets of divine love. Hidden in those secrets are glorious gifts for us from the depths of the Heart of God. We need such heavenly help in these times of global economic crisis, climate change, and war.

Mary is not divine. She is one of us in all things but sin. She was created to be the Mother of the Savior. Consequently, though she was conceived by natural means through Joachim her father in her mother Anne's womb, Mary's conception was different from that of any other creature. By God's mercy upon all of us, she was created totally without any stain of original sin, and filled with divine grace from the first moment of her being.[7] That is what Mary's "Immaculate Conception" really means.[8]

God created Mary without any imperfection to bear the Second Person of the Holy Trinity made flesh, her human son Jesus Christ. The Babe of Bethlehem, Mary's Son Jesus, bone of her bone and flesh of her flesh, the Incarnate Word *is* "*the only-begotten son of God, begotten of the Father before all worlds, God of God, Light of Light, Very God of Very God, begotten not made, being of one substance with the Father by whom all things were made; who for us, and for our salvation, came down from heaven, and was incarnate by the Holy Spirit of the Virgin Mary, and was made man.*"[9] Though He needed nothing, Jesus allowed Mary and her husband, Joseph, to love Him, serve Him, bless Him, and praise Him. It is good for us to do as they did.

Jesus Christ the Savior is impossible to comprehend with our mere human intellects.[10] Jesus our Redeemer cannot be understood by human means.[11] The fact that He is true God and true man at the same time is a matter of faith. His love for each one of us is eternal. It is unchanging. Mary's son is the Savior of all our dreams and hopes. He alone can make all we cherish new and bright and enduringly wonderful. As we grow in ability to treasure our eternal life, we bow in awe before the mystery of Christ's amazing, unmerited gifts to us. Jesus assures all of us: *"You have not chosen me, but I have chosen you . . . that whatever you ask of the Father in my name, he may give it to you."*[12]

His human Mother Mary's role in the divine distribution of grace and her intersession on our behalf is at the same time a matter of faith and an empirical fact.[13] Mary, His Mother is God's marvelous blessing for each of us, of all faiths, backgrounds, beliefs, and needs. Our Blessed Mother, totally steeped in the merits of her Divine Son, of course has a unique relationship with the Redeemer as He has with her.[14] At the very minimum, He is duty bound under His own Fourth Commandment to honor His Mother perfectly.[15] God commanded us through Moses: *"Honor your father and mother, as the LORD, your God, has commanded you, that you may have a long life and prosperity in the land which the Lord, your God, is giving you."*[16] Christ honors His Mother's children because He honors her. Mary knows God's will and is the most perfect adherent to His ways. Her decisions mirror His will perfectly.

We are wise to draw nearer Mary our Spiritual Mother.[17] Jesus is always with her. No one knows Christ as she does. Jesus allowed Himself to be totally dependent upon her. Christ offered His Blessed Mother Mary to us.[18] No one *must* accept a gift. Should we acquire the wisdom to allow Christ's Blessed Mother to care for us as her own dear children, we will truly want for nothing.[19]

Mary's gifts to us flow from her singular participation in the mystery of God. The Blessed Mother during her life on earth *"kept all these things reflecting on them in her heart."*[20] She has glorious, truly beautiful, godly gifts to share with her beloved spiritual children.[21] Jesus' Mother is a most sublime mystery of beauty and charity. She is Spiritual Mother of the human race—the "New Eve" because God made her so. Through the mercy of God, Mary Most Holy is extraordinarily and supernaturally involved in human affairs, especially in these last times.[22]

Mary's apparitions to us flow from God's divine covenant with humanity hidden in nature. That covenant is eternal.[23] Nature offers symbols to every generation of God's protective relationship with His people.[24] Mary's presence assures us that there truly is life beyond death.[25]

Mary, the best of mothers wants us to be exquisitely happy. She shows us how to quiet our five senses, allow ourselves to courageously enter into all life around us, both spiritually and materially. Mary nurtures within us the skill to communicate with God, to truly pray well and to hear the silent pulsations of God deep within our soul. Our Blessed Mother, whom all generations call blessed, illumines for us the presence of God in us, around us, and always with us.[26] She is a resplendent beacon: Mary is here to guide *all* of us, everywhere, into the celestial realms where all is serene. We are *all* capable of becoming Mary's children. *Everyone* is included.

Often circumstances force us into deep prayer when there are no obvious human answers to pressing problems. Perhaps that is why global tribulation is foretold in the Scriptures. In prayer, and through prayer, people *do* find godly solutions to all difficulties. Mary, transcending the thick fog of wars, sorrow, sickness, and death surrounding the earth, reveals dazzling gifts of happiness and joy that radiate from the Spirit of Divine Love.

Mary, Heaven's feminine voice, is our eternal Mother Most Loving. She, holding keys to the Heart of Christ, is exquisitely humble. Consequently, Mary does not interrupt our lives uninvited.[27] Known as the "Seat of Wisdom," our Blessed Mother never disappoints anyone who seeks her help and protection. Few know our Blessed Mother well. All of us search for her, either knowingly or unknowingly. If we allow Mary, our Mother Most Faithful, to enter into our thoughts, and respond to her dazzling wisdom, she ever so graciously communicates celestial secrets of eternal happiness to us. Secrets, of course, imply a deep level of intimacy between the secret bearer and the secret receiver. To be a spiritual companion of the Blessed Mother is to find the fastest, easiest, and safest route into the very Heart of God.

The bloody twentieth century saw three prophetic global secrets revealed by Christ's Mother to three young children in the remote mountains of Fatima, Portugal, in 1917. In that place, Mary, Queen of Prophets, foretold not only opportunities and blessings of technological innovation, but also revealed possibilities of global geopolitical intrigue, war, holocaust, assassinations, annihilation of nations, and a reign of terror. Too few knew of Our Lady of Fatima's urgent calls to the whole world with geostrategic, spiritual messages for everyone. We may never know if the twentieth century yielded a worst-case scenario: all people were impacted in some way by its bloodshed.[28]

If we could only grasp, as the visionaries at Fatima knew by prophetic vision, the value of faith, we would rejoice forever that we have been chosen to become aware of Mary's ways. Her faith shows us how to overcome evil both retrospectively and prospectively. The salutary efforts of the visionaries of Fatima were heroic; unfortunately, few were informed of Mary's Fatima apparitions and her global requests.

Times have changed. Mary is now recognized internationally as everyone's Spiritual Mother. Each person on earth is Our Lady's child. Some know that. Many do not. Technology allows instantaneous information anywhere and everywhere. Billions around the globe *are* responding to her calls. Consequently, we can expect great blessings. God is never outdone in generosity.

The Blessed Mother, House of Gold, gave wonderful guidance at Fatima about global opportunities for peace and reconciliation of nations; she identified places of safety and protection during truly difficult times in the world. Few had access to that heaven-sent information. Hideous atrocities flowed from such ignorance. Again, in this age, our Blessed Mother fills the world with light and blessings. Now we all have access to her messages. In the end, Mary's Immaculate Heart *will* triumph and a period of peace *will* be given to us. Blessed are those who join Mary's team.

It is up to us to choose the blessings Mary brings or endure the curses she asks us to avoid. Mary is here to help us: she brings good things for the whole world. Many have eyes to see and ears to hear, thanks in large part to responsible media personnel.[29] The Vatican announced that from 1928 until 1975, thirty-two countries reported 232 authentic and alleged apparitions of the Blessed Virgin Mary.[30] The Church, slow to act and steeped in its two-thousand-year history, has officially recognized fifteen. Fortunately for the public, the media is not so constrained.[31]

Mary's secrets point to Saint Petersburg as the spiritual center of the Russian nation. Our Lady of Fatima promised that God will be greatly glorified by the Russian people. Children of Mary throughout the world have been praying specifically for their Russian brothers and sisters for nearly a century because Mary made that request at Fatima. Perhaps you are one of them. Recently, Medjugorje has become a prodigious spiritual oasis hidden in the mountains of Bosnia-Herzegovina where it is reported that Mary, Queen of Peace, has been appearing to six young people daily since June 24, 1981. After more than a quarter century, hundreds of millions of seekers have heard Mary's call from Cross Mountain at Medjugorje, and millions have made the pilgrimage to the shrine of Our Lady Queen of Peace. Of course, controversy surrounds that holy place.[32] Miracles are prolific there.

Our Lady reportedly told the visionaries at Medjugorje that her appearances to them are her final ones on earth: after certain secrets unfold she will (for as yet unknown reasons) have no need to appear on earth again in this way.[33] Three Medjugorje visionaries (Ivanka, Mirjana, and Jacov) claim they have been given ten secrets that allegedly involve the "final chapters in the history of the world."[34] Three other Medjugorje visionaries (Vicka, Ivan, and Marija) claim to have received nine secrets. People from all over the world, of every faith, race, and nation, have felt the call to come to Medjugorje. This spiritual invitation is so deeply infused into people's souls that war, political and spiritual intrigue, and difficulties of every sort have been no deterrent. Franciscans at Saint James Church in Medjugorje say Our Lady identifies herself there as Queen of Peace and asks everyone, of every faith and background, to become spiritual warriors for peace on earth. Hopefully, miracles will continue to abound at Medjugorje. Certain Vatican leaders have acknowledged the sweetest spiritual fruits on earth flow from that Marian shrine at this time.[35]

In the twenty-first century, Mary is appearing in many places, in many differing manifestations, to many, many people. Her loving voice calls God's children from the four winds of every faith, race, nation, and age to share in the heights and depths of divine love and mercy in these times.[36] Children of Mary throughout the world are awakening spiritually and responding to her heavenly invitation with love, commitment, prayer, personal sacrifice, spiritual fasting, and faithful dedication.[37]

Mary is ever so lovingly revealing the glories of the Kingdom of God. Everywhere people have eyes to see and ears to hear the signs of the times heralding Christ's promised reign of peace. Mary gently, yet persistently, continues to gather the scattered flock throughout the world. Amazingly, Mary's "little lambs" even include people who have never heard her Son's name. Now their spiritual mother is showing them the Way, the Truth, and the Light. Jesus the Lord is being revealed to us in a most loving, humble, and gentle way through His beloved Mother Mary.

Two thousand years ago or so, the Blessed Virgin listened to the will of God being disclosed to her by an Archangel named Gabriel. Her response—"Be it done unto me according thy word"—brought God in human flesh to earth. The Immaculate One, dazzling with love, welcomed God Incarnate, Jesus Christ the Savior of the human race, into her body and she became the actual Arc of the Covenant— the human tabernacle of the Most High God. The One whom galaxies cannot contain or penetrate became bone of Mary's bone and flesh of her flesh.[38]

Who can understand such mysteries? Truly blessed are those with Mary's faith. They hear the word of God and lovingly accept it as she did. When our own faith is weak, it is wise to cling to Mary whose tested faith is strong enough for each of us. After all, she is the best of mothers: her Immaculate Heart, "our life, our sweetness and our hope"[39] is our refuge, a priceless gift to us who would successfully climb the mountain of divinity.

This generation[40] is a special beneficiary of Mary's secrets. There are most certainly remedies to the sorrows of the ages and our Blessed Mother is bringing them to us now. Our Lady, Tower of Ivory, knows the most enlightened way for each of us to use our allotted time on earth profitably. And she, daughter of the Father, Mother of the Son, and Spouse of the Holy Spirit is so filled with unconditional love for us that it is her unique joy and privilege to help us each moment along the way.

We are *all* children of the One, True God. Though we differ in beliefs, race, gender, and nationalities, the mercy of God is glorious in these times. He who is mighty sends our Mother Most Loving to inspire, enlighten, ennoble, and unite us as the true family of God our Father. Billions throughout the world encounter Mary through the portal of faith. More hear her kind, gentle voice in the silence of their deepest longings. Mary shines forth to all people as a clear harbinger of light and beauty. Our Blessed Mother Most Loving is God's way of allowing all of us to experience the fulfillment of faith realized.

We *need* to know, love, and cling to our Spiritual Mother for we are spiritual beings enduring a physical experience. Though we are *on* the earth, we are not *of* the earth. Thousands upon thousands of celestial beings watch over us, pray for us, cheer us on.[41] The purpose of our earth lives—the opportunity to know God, love God, serve Him here—so as to live happily ever after in His Heavenly Kingdom, involves journeying to the place where Mary lives in the Heart of God. Eye has not seen, ear has not heard, nor has it entered into our minds the wonders that God has prepared for those who remain faithful to His statutes and ordinances.[42]

God, prodding us on, delicately chastises sons and daughters He loves: virtue untested is not virtue but only theory. Our limitations, and we all have them, are opportunities to practice all the virtues. Our Blessed Mother knows sweeter paths than we can find on our own amid the brambles of earth's difficulties. Jesus would not have shared His own dear Mother with us unless He was certain that we truly profit being children of Mary. Her secrets are sourced in the wisdom of the ages: they hold longings of the patriarchs and prophets, teachings and tradition of the Church, and mysteries of each human heart. Mary's secrets reveal effective opportunities for mutual understanding, respect, a better world for everyone. Mary, who is Queen of the Cosmos, bears amazing gifts from the highest celestial heights to share with all her children.

This is Mary's time. Under her protection and biblically her seed,[43] all of us—believers and unbelievers alike—are being called to hasten the glorious reign of The One the whole world awaits: Messiah, Savior of the human race, Wonder-Counselor, God-Hero, Father-Forever, Prince of Peace.[44]

Peace, joy, love, holiness, happiness, health, contentment, prosperity, sobriety, proximity of family and friends are lovely gifts the Blessed Mother especially enjoys bringing to her children. We all long for those gifts. For far too many centuries, too few have known their Spiritual Mother. Yet everyone seeks the wonderful gifts that Mary lavishes upon her spiritual children. Perhaps many do not know how to enter into relationship with her. Or perhaps some abandon this guiding Star of the Sea when waves of fear or indolence overtake spiritual reason. Be assured, those who experience the joy of Our Blessed Lady's bountiful generosity enter intimately into the mysteries of God's unfathomable love and generosity.

Certain things are quite clear. All of us were created to live eternally in the Kingdom of Love. Our most important job on earth is to find, choose, and remain on the path that brings us to the joys of Eternal Life. Mary knows the most delightful way: our Blessed Mother is here to take us by the hand along her secret passages into the Kingdom of Eternal Love. Blessed are those who belong to the lowly lady of Nazareth, lovely mother of the Savior. Such humility blinds the proud.[45]

If you desire to find the path of truth and beauty and kindness and happiness, you are welcome to share in the Secrets of Mary and receive gifts our Blessed Mother so bountifully distributes to her beloved spiritual children. Everyone is included in Mary's loving heart. Jesus reminded us: *"Amen, I say to you, unless you be converted, and become as little children, you shall not enter into the kingdom of heaven."*[46] Mary, our Spiritual Mother Most Prudent is supremely generous: she carries her trusting little children into the grandeur of God's rich creation, filled with prizes and surprises. The secrets of Mary are great gifts for these last times. If you want to believe you will be able to believe.

Those who honor their Blessed Mother
are the treasure of God's Providence.
They live on the Island of Beauty
where winds of myrrh
blow over the hills
and
scent the earth
with God's sweet mercy.

Divine Mercy Image, Saint Maxmillan Kolbe Church, near Warsaw, Poland

Serve My Mother dearest children of My Heart.
Serve her faithfully and fully.
Then you will know My ways, for I always serve her.
She is My gift and My bond with My children of the earth.
Paradise is her home.
I reserve the places in My Kingdom for her children.[1]

Sacred Heart of Jesus and Immaculate Heart of Mary

My dear little children,
You are hungry and thirsty for love.
I am inviting you to my home.
Spend fifteen minutes each day in my conscious presence.
I desire to speak to you of the glories of my Divine Son.
Should you accept my invitation, I shall bring you into my
Immaculate Heart.
There Jesus dwells in total glory.
Those who encounter Jesus in my Immaculate Heart know Him
through my knowledge.
Those who know Jesus through my knowledge acquire a taste of
Paradise now that lights their journey in the
remote lands of earth.
I am the Mother of True Life in God.
My heart is the resting place of God's elect.
My heart is your portal to Jesus.
Jesus is God. Jesus Alone is True Life.
All else is illusion. All else is death.
Draw nearer to me now little ones.
Allow me to open new doors for you in my heart
that your fullness may be complete.[1]

THE CANTICLE OF MARY

My soul doth magnify the Lord;
And my spirit hath rejoiced in God my Saviour,
Because He hath regarded the humility of His handmaid; for
behold from henceforth all generations shall call me blessed.
Because he that is mighty, hath done great things to me;
and holy is his name.
And his mercy is from generation unto generations, to them
that fear him. . . .
He has shewed might in his arm:
He has scattered the proud in the conceit of their heart.
He hath put down the mighty from their seat, and hath
exalted the humble.
He hath filled the hungry with good things; and the
rich he hath sent away empty.
He has received Israel his servant,
Being mindful of his mercy:
As he spoke to our fathers, to Abraham and to his seed forever.[1]

Foreword

Through this book Mary, the mother of Jesus, wants to tell us who she is. She wants us to know about her, and so to come to know her better.

Mary is the mother of Jesus who is the Son of God, one of the Divine Trinity, God. And Mary, his mother, is therefore, as Christians have professed since the beginnings of Christianity, the Mother of God. Not was, but *is* the Mother of God. The relationship is permanent. Mary was, is, and will always be the mother of Jesus Christ. Because Jesus, the greatest of all graces, has come to us first through Mary, and because her maternity of Jesus is an eternal relationship, all graces come to us through Mary who is the channel of grace.

She is our spiritual mother who nourishes us, feeds us, supports us, teaches us, helps us to grow and to mature in the spiritual life. Mary is mediatrix of grace. She is *not* mediatrix the way that our Savior Jesus is for He alone is our unique Mediator with the Father. Rather, Mary is the channel of grace because she is the mother of Jesus. We do not *have* to pray to Jesus through Mary. We *can* pray to Jesus through Mary.

Mary is in no way God, in no way divine; she is entirely a creature. But she is the mother of God, the mother of Jesus. And so we can ask her to intercede for us with Jesus, to put in a word for us so to speak, to pray for us.

What good does it do to pray to Mary, to ask her for help, to ask her to pray for us? A great deal! At the wedding feast of Cana, would Jesus have changed the water into wine if Mary had not wanted him to? He objected, and he added that the time was all wrong for such a thing. But he performed the miracle because His Mother asked him. Mary's prayer is powerful, and it can be powerful for us. Mary wants to be a mother to us.

Jesus died for each of us personally, to save us, as though each one of us was the only other person besides him who ever walked on earth. He loves us so much that he would do it again if that were necessary. When he was dying on the cross, he gave his mother to us as our mother. The apostle John, the disciple whom Jesus loved, stood in for each of us. So Jesus gave his mother, by giving her to John, to you and me. Mary is, in fact, our mother in the spiritual order, in the order of grace. As she is the mother of Jesus, she is mother of the life of Jesus in each of us, of the life of the Spirit in us. She nourishes and nurtures the divine life in us. She teaches us, and she prays for us. She takes care of us, intercedes for us with Jesus.

The wedding reception in the town of Cana in Galilee of Israel is a paradigm for each of us, a model as it were, that assures us that Mary wants to help us, intercedes for us, and that Jesus will honor His Mother by caring for us at her request.[1] Mary, with complete trust in Jesus, asked him to solve the problem at Cana. Jesus did what Mary asked, even though it did not at all seem an appropriate thing to do, and even though the timing was not by his choice, he began his public ministry by performing a miracle as a sign. Jesus acted not only because his mother asked him but also out of compassion for the bride and groom and their parents, helping them so that they would not be embarrassed at not having enough wine for the wedding feast.

PRAYER

Mary, my mother, you asked Jesus for a special favor at Cana and He did what you asked. Help me to know you better through this book, and to know that you pray for me, want to help me, and are my intercessor with Jesus. Amen

I have known Jan Connell, the author of this book, for many years. She is a person of total integrity who knows the Lord Jesus and His Mother, is a woman of deep prayer, prudent, faithful in her Christian beliefs and in her books and her lectures. In this book, she tells us valuable things about the Mother of Jesus that have created widespread global interest over many centuries. Those who read it will know the Lord Jesus and His Blessed Mother better.

ROBERT FARICY, S.J.
Professor Emeritus of Mystical Theology
Pontifical Gregorian University
Rome, Italy
December 25, 2008

The Secrets of Mary

The Annunciation—Nazareth

PART I

Mother Most Faithful

SUPERNATURAL FAITH

Jesus said: *"For what doth it profit a man, if he gain the whole world, and suffer the loss of his own soul? Or what exchange shall a man give for his soul? For the son of man shall come in the glory of his Father with his angels and then will he render to every man according to his works."*[1]

*U*ntold *millions* all over the world believe they are now living in biblical "End Times" and await the return of Jesus within their lifetime.[2] Some spiritual seekers are speculating the possibility that the imminent Second Coming of Christ and the arrival of the long-awaited Jewish Messiah are the same event. Certain military leaders even conjecture the Battle of Armageddon transpiring in the Middle East. Scientists warn of everything from global warming to extinction of the planet through environmental malfeasance or nuclear holocaust. Some expect the earth to be destroyed by a wayward comet. According to a recent poll, a majority of Americans are convinced that prophesies in the Book of Revelation are accurate.[3]

Philanthropists compete to share their wealth and know-how with the sick, poor, and illiterate of the earth. This is a noble, truly good use of assets, talent, and time. High-speed planes and telecommunications can now link every town, village, and hamlet in the world. Yet poor, hungry, unemployed, uninformed people still seek vengeance for their sorry lot, sometimes even joining misguided fanatics in violent terrorism. For many, the world is a tired, lonely, and heavily armed place.

The good news is that each one of us is begotten of Almighty God. Our Creator breathed our immortal souls into human bodies so that we can grow and prosper and learn about Him through the works of His Hand. Now, the gentle voice of the Blessed Mother of Jesus, born on earth more than two thousand years ago and transfigured in the Resurrected Christ, is quietly reawakening souls grown accustomed to sleeping in darkness for thousands of years.[4]

Never before has Mary been known to appear to an entire generation and speak to diverse people of every culture, belief, and continent as she does now.[5] Many are listening. The Blessed Virgin

Mary, as she has done from the beginning, reveals the Incarnation and omnipotence of God. There is a special brilliance to Mary's ubiquitous appearances in the world carrying secrets and gifts of the divinity. She knows Jesus uniquely: Christ all powerful, unconditionally loving, who is the object of our largely unconscious and underdeveloped love. Mary's sacred secrets, true gifts of God, bring profit to our souls, knowledge to our minds, health to our bodies, and valuable eternal currency. The Blessed Mother's spiritual blessings we *are* able to sow and reap vastly influence our personal perceptions about our immense, inestimable worth in God's loving providence.

We are animated from within. God dwells in each of us. Our Blessed Mother invites us to make little chapels of our bodies to honor His presence. Mary wants us to use the fire of love as our votive light. She asks us to use whatever personal freedom we have to maintain our bodies as sacred temples housing the great Lord of Heaven and earth.[6] We cannot love what we do not know. Our Spiritual Mother is here to help us know God in spirit and truth and learn who we really are. Mary shows us the earth: holy ground created by God as our sacred House of Prayer, growth, material and spiritual development.

Each of us on this planet is the offspring of God and the spiritual child of Mary. As such, all of us are worthy of respect, protection, and love. Although Sacred Texts, considered the inspired word of God have unified and divided religious groups for centuries, the Blessed Virgin Mary, totally clothed in God's Word, brings the healing balm of God's merciful love to extinguish the pain of separation and estrangement.[7] Mary blessedly belongs to all God's people. Her presence in these times is not just for a privileged few.

Our Blessed Mother, Eternal Temple of the Godhead, Venerable Treasure of Creation, Crown of Virginity, Support of the True Faith in which the people of the earth are enfolded, crosses the boundaries of separation and estrangement. Mary constantly reminds us that she is Spiritual Mother of the *entire* human family.[8] No one is excluded. Mary is not just the domain of Christians, or Europeans, or westerners. She, Mother of the Eternal Word, is the Eternal Mother of each of us. All generations call her blessed for the Almighty has done great things for her, and through her, for each of us.[9]

In this section you will find stories of simple seekers from long ago who dared to act on Mary's inspirations. Consequently, they became leaders whose lives continue to vastly enrich the world today. Their responses to life's opportunities offer us wonderful insights that can ennoble our personal lives and bring us enduring light and strength and goodness. The people you will read about in this section enjoyed an intimate relationship with Mary that offered them exquisite harmony with cosmic reality. Mary guided them into the realms of supernatural faith where union with almighty God occurs. Their stories can be our stories, too. Mary brings visionary enlightenment to us as we welcome her into our hearts and homes.[10] Sit at Mary's knee and listen with ears of faith to the call of God.

Dearest little ones, come to your Father's Heart.
Rest in My Heart. Never fear.
Trust My love. Trust My bounty. Trust My generosity.
Call to Me now dear children.
I hear all prayer. We are one oh My children.
Oh My holy people, how I long for you.
I am your Love. I am your Peace. I am your Joy.

Dear children of My Heart
Open the portal of Paradise through prayer.
Prayer leads to obedience to My call.
Preserve My earth.
Bless one another. Love one another. Serve one another.
How I love you My little ones.
My Heart cries out to each of you.

Each blade of grass is dear to Me, your Father.
Each fish I have made is beautiful.
Each leaf on the trees I have given you is precious to Me.
Watch My Face in the leaves and the flowers and the fishes and
the birds and the grain and the clear water.
Touch My flowers—touch My Face. Touch one another—touch Me.
How sacred is My earth—your House of Prayer.

How sacred are My children.
Help one another. Love one another. Feed one another.
Dress one another. Educate one another.
Free one another from bondage. Turn to Me. I hear all prayer.
I answer all prayer. I am Love. I am Life. I am Truth.
I am your Father. I am your Love. I am your Life.
Those who seek Me find Me.

My ways are joy. My ways are peace. My ways are love.
Listen to My beloved daughter Mary who trusts Me perfectly.
You must trust the power of Mary to understand My will.
She communicates My will in these times to My children
who accept the virtue of obedience.
You are the children of the covenant I have made with My people.
I am the Faithful One.

Pilgrim Statue of Our Lady of Fatima

Dear children of my Immaculate Heart
Embrace joy as your inheritance and gift.
Send joyful praises to God at every moment.
Cling to my Son. Sing to my Son.
Bless and praise His triumph.
You are the privileged ones for you know my Son.
Pray and fast for those who know Him not.
Do penance with your time.
Pray. Pray. Pray.
Praise God. Love God. Obey God.
Rejoice oh highly favored children of my Immaculate Heart.
I am your Mother Most Faithful.
Always tell others: "Never fear. The Blessed Mother is near."

CHAPTER 1

Mother of God

"{T}he angel Gabriel was sent from God into a city of Galilee, called Nazareth, to a virgin espoused to a man whose name was Joseph, of the House of David; and the virgin's name was Mary. And the angel being come in, said unto her: 'Hail full of grace, the Lord is with thee: blessed art thou among women.' Who having heard was troubled at his saying, and thought with herself what manner of salutation this should be. And the angel said to her: 'Fear not Mary, for thou hast found grace with God. Behold thou shalt conceive in thy womb and bring forth a son; and thou shalt call his name Jesus. He shall be great, and shall be called the Son of the Most High; and the Lord God shall give unto him the throne of David, his father; and he shall reign in the house of Jacob forever. And of his kingdom there shall be no end.' And Mary said to the angel: 'How shall this be done, because I know not man?' And the angel answering, said to her: 'The Holy Ghost shall come upon thee, and the power of the most High shall overshadow thee. And therefore the Holy which shall be born of thee shall be called the Son of God. And behold, thy cousin Elizabeth, she also hath conceived a son in her old age; and this is the sixth month with her that is called barren: Because no word shall be impossible with God.' And Mary said: 'Behold the handmaid of the Lord; be it done to me according to thy word.' And the angel departed from her."[1]

Approximately 80 percent of Americans believe that Jesus Christ was born of the Blessed Virgin Mary without a human father.[2] Mary is clearly unlike any other person. Recently a jovial Harvard faculty member mused: "And Jesus said at the pearly gate: 'Ah, Professor, I know you have met my father, but I don't believe you know my mother.'"[3]

Jesus wants us to know His Mother. To know her is to love her. To love her is to find the pearl of great price we all seek. Mary's "yes" to God's plan for the human race allowed Jesus, the Savior of the world, to be born into time and space as a full member of our species, yet mysteriously always "God from God and light from light."[4] The very cosmos is rooted in Christ. It came to be through Him and finds its fullness of perfection only in and through Him.[5] The fact that the Second Person of the Holy Trinity took human flesh and bone of Mary and become one of our species in the fullness of time is beyond the intellect and remains hidden in divine cosmic mystery we access only through the portal of faith.

If we have problems with such sublime concepts we can ask ourselves how vast is our wisdom, what galaxies have we made? Do we have sick eyes and tainted hands? If so, where do we find the paste of humility, how do we dress ourselves in sackcloth of compliance with God's way so that we may prosper?[6] Mary knows.

The Blessed Mother gives us amazing gifts. Our Lady's heavenly delights transform our sorrows and heal the pain of broken dreams. Mary is forever Mother of the Redeemer who ransomed each of us from eternal misfortune. Our Blessed Mother knows how valuable and vulnerable we are. Mary, our Eternal Mother, is faithful to us, even when we are not, or cannot be. She knows that when we fall we need her love, protection, and intercessory prayer even more. Our Spiritual Mother loves, each of us unconditionally, with the pure mother-love we all crave. Our Holy Mother Mary has precious divine graces of such grandeur to give us that we will never be able to thank God enough for her.

It is a joyful journey and a great privilege to travel back through history searching for threads of wisdom about our Blessed Mother that help us draw ever closer to her today.

MOTHER OF GOD: SAINT PATRICK, A.D. 400

Scholars are divided over facts surrounding the life of Saint Patrick. History and lure are more generous. In the modern day, few saints enjoy more reverence than this great son of Ireland. His devotees find expression for their admiration in everything from green beer on his feast day, March 17, to Irish ballads memorializing his feats of valor, big-city Saint Patrick's Day parades, and Hibernian societies in places far away from Ireland.

Few have loved the Holy Mother of God more, or worked more diligently for her Divine Son than the great Saint Patrick. Thanks in large measure to him, Mary is Queen Mother of people of Irish descent, wherever they may be. Saint Patrick was a mystic: his followers have remained faithful to the sacred beliefs he taught even through persecution, betrayal, hunger, shipwreck, political intrigue, war, poverty, addiction, disdain, degradation, and death. Love for the Holy Mother of God is as natural to a true Irishman as life itself.

Patrick was captured in Britain as a teenager and sold into slavery in Ireland. There he learned the Druid faith and language of his overlord, Druidical high priest and chieftain Milchu. Patrick's slave job was tending flocks: the young Christian captive prayed constantly on the slopes as he watched over the sheep. One such prayer remains and is recorded in Saint Patrick's "Confessio."

"The love of God, and His fear increased in me more and more, and the faith grew in me, and the Spirit was roused, so that, in a single day, I have said as many as a hundred prayers, and in the night nearly the same, so that whilst in the woods and on the mountain, even before the dawn, I was roused to prayer and felt no hurt from it, whether there was snow or ice or rain; nor was there any slothfulness in me, such as I see now, because the Spirit was then fervent within me."[7]

An angel summoned Patrick from the mountains and guided him to a ship that brought him home to Britain, and eventually on to Auxerre. There, Patrick studied under Saint Germain, was ordained a priest, and assigned back to Britain where he worked as a Christian missionary. Saint Patrick, strong, muscular, intelligent, perhaps even a genius, understood fully and treasured the teachings of the Council of Ephesus that declared the Blessed Virgin Mary forever among men the true "Mother of God."[8] Patrick, it is said, consecrated Ireland and all the sons and daughters of that great land to the Holy Mother of God forever.

Patrick's prayer life intensified and mystical experiences were vital in his work for the Kingdom of God. One of his more famous visions occurred by the Western Sea. Children of Ireland of every time and place appeared to him crying: "O holy youth, come back to Erin and walk once more among us." Appointed by the Pope as Apostle to Ireland, Patrick returned to the shores of Erin. Of course, the Druids took up arms against him and his fellow missionaries. But Patrick was more than a match for them.

Patrick quickly sought out his former Druid master and paid him the price of his freedom. Then he began his extraordinary work for Christ in the Pagan lands. Supernatural faith empowered Saint Patrick with divine gifts never before seen in those places. His first miracle in Ireland was performed as a tribute to the Holy Mother of God and the Divine Birth of her Son Jesus, the Savior. A chieftain, in full view of his army, drew his sword against Saint Patrick. But his arm became rigid as stone and continued so until he declared himself open to the faith that animated Saint Patrick. The Lord provided this strategy: as leaders were converted, their followers emulated their Christian piety.

Those who profess Saint Patrick's supernatural faith are all over the world. They are faithful children of Mary in every land.

MOTHER MOST RENOWN:
SAINT AUGUSTINE, SAINT MONICA, AND
SAINT PATRICIUS,[9] A.D. 450

Few souls have attained the spiritual heights that Saint Augustine experienced during his lifetime. Mary's supernatural faith, hope, and love are very much intertwined with this fourth-century doctor of the Church and his family who ascended to the heights of supernatural union with God through Mary's loving care. We all are invited to soar to the mountain of divinity that Augustine ascended in Christ through Mary. His legend, history, and famous writings illumine our own spiritual opportunities.

Augustine was born near present-day Tripoli. His mother, Monica, a beautiful woman,[10] was a devout Christian. Patricius, her husband, who was not a Christian, was a Roman citizen of high passion and difficult temperament. He was a member of the city council in Tagaste, a small town in the Roman province of Numidia. Youthful Augustine admired his affluent, passionate father and usually avoided his prayerful mother. Her spiritual practices were unattractive to this young man of dark ambition, pride-filled intellect, and lustful appetite. God, however, does not call just one member of a family. Saints do grow in clusters.

Patricius and Augustine were men of the world with no time to waste on what they considered abstract Christian notions. Though youthful Augustine did not share his mother's faith, many years later, after his extraordinary conversion, Augustine wrote of his Mother:

"She strove to win him (her husband) to you (God), speaking to him about you through her conduct, by which you made her beautiful, an object of reverent love, and a source of admiration to her husband. . . . She looked forward to seeing your mercy upon him, so that he would believe in you and be made chaste. . . . By her good services and by perseverance in patience and meekness, she also won over her mother-in-law. . . . wherever she could, she showed herself to be a great peacemaker between persons who were at odds and in disagreement. . . . Finally, toward the very

end of his earthly life, she gained her husband for you (God). . . .
whoever knew her greatly praised you (God), and honored you,
and loved you in her, because they recognized your presence in
her heart, for the fruit of her holy life bore witness to this."

Monica respected God's munificence in endowing His people
with the gift of freedom of choice. The more she prayed, the better
she was able to trust God's mercy on behalf of her husband and son.
Good example and prayerful perseverance were her kindest gifts to
them. She sincerely believed that God hears and answers all prayers.
She knew God's generosity is unmatched. Patricius accepted the reality of God at the end of his life; he was baptized in his final hours,
receiving the full Redemption of Jesus Christ. This gentle gift of
God's tender love filled him with newfound joy and peace. Patricius
departed this earth steeped in love and light. Though Augustine
witnessed his father's final light, he did not understand it.

Monica, now a widowed mother abandoned by a son steeped in
darkness and consumed with pleasure and pride-filled intellectual
pursuits, continued to pray with great fervor and trust. Augustine
craved the adulation of peers and hungrily indulged his appetites. He
actually thought he was enjoying his decadent lifestyle, and had little
time or patience for his mother. Monica, in the process of becoming a
woman of supernatural faith, realized the only human tragedy is the
loss of an immortal soul. She prayed for her son constantly, and for his
mistress of fifteen years and their son Adeodatus. She practiced speaking more to God about Augustine than to Augustine about God. In
his later years, Augustine would look back at his first thirty-three
years and write in his autobiography, "The Confessions."[11]

"The wicked [thinking of himself] who are without rest may go
their way and flee from you but you see them and pierce the
shadows. Behold, all things about them are beautiful, but they
themselves are vile. How have they done injury to you, and in
what way have they disfigured your sway, which is just and perfect from the heavens even down to the lowest depths? Whither
did they flee when they would flee from your face? Or where
would you not find them out? But they fled away so that they

might not see you who see them always, and that being blinded, they might stumble upon you, and thus be justly troubled, withdrawing themselves from your gentleness, stumbling against your righteousness, and falling upon your severity. In truth they do not know that you are everywhere, for no place can enclose you, and that you alone are present even with those who have set themselves far from you. . . . [B]ehold, you are there within their hearts . . . you O Lord who made them can remake them and give them consolation. Where was I when I sought you [in womanizing and drink and intellectual vanity]? You were before me, but I had departed even from myself."

Monica, the trusting mother of a wayward son, prayed with utmost confidence in God's merciful love for him. Augustine writes:

"She bewailed me as one dead, but yet destined to be brought back to life by you (God). In thought she put me before you on a bier, so that you (God) might say to a widow's son, 'Young man, I say to you, arise.' Then would he revive and begin to speak, and you would deliver him to his mother. Therefore, her heart did not pound in turbulent exultation when she heard that what she daily implored you with her tears to do was already done in so great a part. For although I had not yet attained to the truth, I had now been rescued from falsehood. Rather, she was all the more certain that You, who had promised the whole, would grant what still remained. Hence most calmly and with a heart filled with confidence, she replied to me how she believed in Christ that before she departed from this life she would see me a faithful Christian."

The Blessed Virgin Mary is the Mother of Consolation as well as the Mother of Sorrows. Her love for the poor and oppressed is coupled with her solidarity of love with the suffering. One day, when the sorrowful mother Monica was deep in prayer, lamenting the sinful structures of her son's life, Mary appeared to her, attired in black mourning dress, wearing a Cincture that shone with heavenly light. Monica knew in an instant that the Blessed Mother had come to her at God's bidding to reassure her of Christ's power to draw everything to Himself in transformative holiness. Is Mary's divine son not the Alpha and the Omega, the first and the last, the beginning and the end?[12]

In the motherly light of Mary's pure love, Monica entered into the depths of the Sacred Heart of Jesus. Ever present, ever ancient, yet ever new, His voice echoes throughout creation calling us all into the sweet chambers of divinity.

> *Experience My great love as you dwell in My Heart.*
> *My Heart is the place of refuge for My children of the*
> *earth for I am the Prince of Peace,*
> *I am the Lord of Lords, I am the Alpha and Omega.*
> *I am Peace. Peace. Only peace My child.*
> *I am Love. Love. Only love My child.*
> *Cherish My will. My will for those who are Mine.*

Monica rested in the quiet of Mary's heavenly gifts that flowed silently into the vast depths of her parched soul. She would always remember Mary's pure beauty: eternal youth and divine love merge in Christ's Blessed Mother.

"Daughter of mine, in this guise are you in future to clothe yourself; let this Cincture, [which I am handing to you] be to you a pledge of my love—this self-same Cincture that encircled the womb wherein the Word was made flesh; let it henceforward be yours, and wear it constantly. Never take it off; spread devotion to it far and wide. All who wear a Cincture like to this I shall esteem as my especial children. This Cincture is to become the wonder of the cosmos at a future day."[13]

Word spread quickly of Mary's magnificent visitation to Monica from the Empyrean shores of Paradise. None could dispute the joy that shone bright in her reverent demeanor. All could see Mary's resplendent, heaven-sent Cincture that Monica wore for the rest of her life. Even Augustine studied the Cincture. It made a profound impression upon him. Augustine knew his mother as only a child knows. Her descriptions of spiritual intimacy with Christ during Mary's appearance made an even greater impression upon him. Augustine was confronted with the majesty of the mystery of the Incarnation of the Word as he viewed the dazzling celestial Cincture given by Mary to his mother. "What is the human race that God should become one of us?" he wondered. Augustine's intellectual prowess, devoid of faith, led him to relentless searching for truth.

A tormented soul, Augustine sent his mistress away. But he promptly fell into the arms of another woman. He prayed: "God, grant me chastity and continence, but not yet." God is faithful, even when we are not. Augustine quite unexpectedly heard the mysterious, inexplicable voice of a small child calling to him: "Take and read [the sacred scripture]." Thoroughly startled, Augustine lunged for the nearby text and randomly opened to Paul's Epistle to the Romans 13:13–14: *"Let us walk honestly, as in the day: not in rioting and drunkenness, not in chambering and impurities, not in contention and envy: But put ye on the Lord Jesus Christ, and make not provision for the flesh in its concupisences."*

Monica continued to pray and fast for her spiritually dead son. Her two dear ordained friends, Ambrose, the Bishop of Milan, and Athenus, knew about Mary's apparition to Monica and her promise "I shall esteem as my special children those who choose to wear such a Cincture." Of course, these holy men quickly decided to gird themselves with black cinctures similar to the heaven-sent gift Monica wore.[14]

God works in wonderful ways. Ambrose's faith-filled understanding of the mysteries of the Incarnation of the Eternal Word began to impact the thinking and behavior of highly educated, thoroughly confused Augustine. Eventually Ambrose was instrumental in leading Augustine and his son Adeodatus to the baptismal font at Easter vigil in 387. The sacrament (of Baptism) had a powerful and highly noticeable effect upon Augustine's soul, spiritual life, and behavior. Day after day, he pursued the truths of his newfound faith with vigor and valor. Within the year, both Monica and Augustine's son, Adeodatus, died.

Augustine, now without family of his own, returned to North Africa. He gave his belongings to the poor and turned his family house into a monastery for himself and a few God-fearing men. He then wrote a most amazing monastic rule, outlining principles governing life in a religious community that is still followed today by untold thousands of men, women, and children all over the world. Augustinian Friars, cloistered Augustinian Sisters of Contemplative Life, Augustinian Religious Congregations, and Lay Fraternities continue to live the Rule of Saint Augustine.[15]

When Augustine finally encountered Jesus through supernatural faith, he was surprised to learn how meek and humble of heart Christ is. Augustine began to enter more profoundly into the vast interior chambers of his soul. Many years later, he wrote of the experience:

"I entered there, and by my soul's eye, such as it was, I saw above that same eye of my soul, above my mind, an unchangeable light. It was not this common light, plain to all flesh, nor a greater light, as it were, of the same kind, as though that light would shine many, many times more bright, and by its great power fill the whole universe. Not such was that light, but different, far different from all other lights. Nor was it above my mind, as oil is above water, or sky above earth. It was above my mind, because it made me, and I was beneath it, because I was made by it. He who knows the truth knows that light, and he who knows it knows eternity. Charity knows It. O Eternal Truth and True Love and Beloved Eternity! You are my God, I sigh to You by day and by night. When first I knew You, You lifted me up so that I might see that there was something to see, but that I was not yet able to see it. You beat back my feeble sight, sending down your beams most powerfully upon me, and I trembled with love and awe. I knew that I was far from You in a region of unlikeness, as though I heard Your Voice from on high: 'I am the food of grown men. Grow, and you shall feed upon Me. You will not change Me into yourself as you change food into your flesh, but you will be changed into Me.' "[16]

Augustine continued to journey deeper into the secret depths of the divine as the years of his earth life unfolded. Many consider his autobiography, *The Confessions of Saint Augustine,* the greatest spiritual autobiography of all time. Few people have experienced the interior light God allowed to Augustine. Even fewer have shared that knowledge. His treatise, *City of God*, continues to be one of the greatest spiritual masterpieces ever written.[17] Protestants, especially Calvinists and Lutherans, consider his teaching on salvation and grace to be the underpinnings of the Reformation. His work is of interest to Jewish scholars in the Kabala tradition. Augustine's penetration into the mystery of the Real Presence of Jesus Christ in the Eucharist continues to confound theologians and scientists in the twenty-first century.[18]

Augustine was ordained and became the Bishop of Hippo. The Roman Catholic Church, the Eastern Orthodox Church, and the Anglican Communion have canonized him a saint and consider Augustine an illustrious Doctor of the Church. Saint Augustine occupies a monumental position in the history of Christianity.[19]

Monica's faithful, hope-filled love, hidden in the ordinariness of marriage and family life, shines like a bright star in contemporary times. She was a woman of deep and passionate ardor for God's ways. Walking in the footsteps of the Mother of Jesus Christ, Monica discovered that love of any kind without faith is weak love. It is feeble. Love without faith and hope is a victim of fear. Love grounded in mere human faith and human hope is only disguised self-love. Disguised self-love is transitory, like all things of the earth. It is fragile and easily collapses. True love, grounded in faith in God's Word, hope in His promises, casts out all fear. True love is stronger than death: it lives forever.

Monica consciously modeled her life choices in harmony with Mary's virtues. Christ's Mother faced scorn, terror, and death all around her as she stood at the foot of the cross of her Divine Son. At every moment, Mary believed in the mission of her Son; she trusted God's loving, restorative, resurrection power completely and she loved the dying Savior with supernatural love beyond all telling. Monica—wife, mother, grandmother, and widow—would aspire to do no less. Her severely tested faith, perfected trust, and sacrificial love bore sweet spiritual fruit for all of us to enjoy.

Augustine profited greatly by his mother's prayers and example. He ultimately came to realize that we are too weak to find the truth by pure reason; consequently, we need the authority of Holy Scripture.

Holy Scripture, however, is not the food of proud intellects. Only the humble enter into the Empyrean Fields of God's love in the sacred word. Augustine sincerely longed for honors, wealth, and marriage, yet he sensed God's laughter in his pursuits.[20] Nothing he touched, apart from God, was sweet. Brilliant, urbane Augustine struggled spiritually for many years. Greed for temporal enjoyment debased him. This man of the world discovered slowly that he who loves danger perishes in it. Finally, Augustine came to the realization that no man can be happy unless God's grace grants him that gift.

By God's mercy, Monica's son began to see with the eyes of his soul that virtue and beauty must be embraced for their own sake. He wrote: "You [God] alone are rest. . . . You console us and you say to us, 'Run forward! I will bear you up, and I will bring you to the end, and there also will I bear you up.' "[21]

Augustine wrote of his spiritual journey:

"So I set about finding a way to gain the strength that was necessary for enjoying you [God]. And I could not find it until I embraced the mediator between God and man, the man Jesus Christ, who is over all things, God blessed forever, who was calling unto me and saying: "I am the way, the truth, and the life; and who brought into union with our nature that food which I lacked the strength to take: for the Word was made flesh that your wisdom, by which you created all things, might give suck to our soul's infancy. Late have I loved You, O Beauty so ancient and so new; late have I loved you! For behold you were within me, and I outside; and I sought You outside and in my ugliness fell upon those lovely things that you have made. You were with me, and I was not with you. I was kept from you by those things, yet had they not been in you, they would not have been at all. You called and cried to me and broke open my deafness: and you sent forth your beams and shone upon me and chased away my blindness: You breathed fragrance upon me, and I drew in my breath and do now pant for you: I tasted you, and now hunger and thirst for you: you touched me, and I burn with longing for your peace."

Monica, Patricius, and Augustine courageously traveled the path all families encounter on earth. They knew Mary's secrets better than most: mother, father, and son reaped gifts from the Blessed Mother and her Divine Son that we all may share. Saint Augustine, remembering the promise of Jesus Christ: "Behold I am with you always until the consummation of the world" said: "If he is with us, he speaks in us, he speaks concerning us, he speaks through us; and accordingly we speak in him and indeed we speak the truth because we speak in him. But when we want to speak in our own name and out of our own voice [and not Christ's] we remain in untruth."[22]

Untruth is the ultimate suffering. Augustine discovered: "In God's home there is an everlasting party. Melodies from that eternal party reach and delight the ears of the heart. The sweet strains of that celebration drift into the ears of those who still walk on earth and they are drawn to the refreshing springs of water that eternally flow in heaven."[23] To access the wonderful music that refreshes us on our journey to Paradise, we all are called to find places of solitude deep inside ourselves where we can be alone with God. Truth is the ultimate delight.

MOTHER MOST PURE:
SAINT ILDEFONSUS A.D. 675

Times were evil in the late seventh century. Sexual promiscuity proliferated. Consequently, a great heresy developed in Christendom disputing the perpetual virginity of the Blessed Virgin Mary. Archbishop Ildefonsus, abbot of a Benedictine Monastery near Toledo, Spain, saw the suffering that sexual ignorance distributed from its diseased claws. The abbot prayed for supernatural faith, hope, and love sufficient to transcend the darkness of the times. He fasted, studied much, and observed his flock. With prayerful discernment and immense guidance from the Holy Spirit, Ildefonsus wrote a treatise defending the perpetual Virginity of the Mother of Jesus[24] and exhorted the faithful to defend her integrity as a sign of their allegiance to the Eternal Word made flesh. He presented his treatise at a great Church Council,[25] where his defense of the perpetual virginity of the Blessed Virgin

Mary, before, during, and after the birth of Jesus Christ was accepted and promulgated throughout the Christian world.[26]

Sometime after the Church Council, Ildefonsus was deep in meditation in the cathedral. It was early spring in 657, the feast day of the Annunciation of the Blessed Virgin Mary. Ildefonsus quite suddenly saw our Blessed Mother seated on a throne near the high altar, surrounded by angels and saints. Ildefonsus was astounded to see in Mary's hands the treatise he had written. Was he dreaming or was our Blessed Mother really summoning him to approach her? His heart was pounding. The perspiration was pouring from his brow as he heard the angels encourage him to draw near the Mother of God. Inhaling deeply, Ildefonsus rose and approached the throne where Mary awaited him.

As he knelt, hot tears filled his eyes. Light surrounded him, so perfuse that he felt himself in another realm. Our Blessed Mother, Virgin Most Venerable, gently lifted Ildefonsus' consecrated hands and kissed them. Looking into the trembling abbot's eyes, the holy Mother of Jesus Christ humbly thanked her son's priest for defending her purity. One of the mighty angels stationed near Mary's throne stepped forward, holding a pure white garment. The Virgin Mother of the Incarnate Word accepted the garment from the hands of the angel. She then presented to Ildefonsus the spotless priest chasuble as a token of her gratitude. That heavenly vestment remains to this day a treasured heavenly relic in Orvieto.

The Chapel of the Sagrario in the Cathedral of Toledo is one of the great glories of Spain. Pilgrims flock to the site of Ildefonsus' apparition. They kneel and view the magnificent Virgin of the Sagrario statue, exquisitely adorned as a sign of the divine favor bestowed upon the site. A sense of awe pervades the atmosphere in the chapel. Many pilgrims claim to experience the presence of angels, or smell wildflowers or the scent of incense. A magnificent mosaic adorns the chapel wall depicting the Blessed Virgin presenting the heaven-sent chasuble to Saint Ildefonsus. Pilgrims touch the marble column that remains from the day and site where the Blessed Mother sat on the high altar. In that place, faith, hope, and love merge.

Abbot Ildefonsus responded to the difficulties of his era with the weapon of Truth. His treatise on the perpetual virginity of the Blessed

Virgin Mary brought light to the darkness of unrecognized lust. Every sin, lust included, brings suffering in one form or another. Suffering is a patient and relentless teacher. Christ is God's means to save us from our sins; eliminate sin's hideous effects. God is patient. God's love overcomes all iniquity with the sweet medicine of Truth.

Our Blessed Mother helps us to think of the mystery of how God, the source of all wisdom and knowledge and truth, is with us in her Son Jesus. Christ is truly God and truly man: Mary gave birth to Jesus who combines the human nature and the divine nature in one person.[27] When we grow weary of life's difficulties and vicissitudes, it is wise to humbly think about Jesus, the Second Person of the Holy Trinity, the One whom Mary conceived as man by the Holy Spirit, who truly became her son.[28] In that way, supernatural faith comes into play, supernatural hope is triggered, and supernatural love grows in us. The more we authentically strive to mirror God's ways as best we can, the more quickly we grow in His image and likeness planted deep in our souls, and live in the happiness of God's redeemed children. The great God of Abraham sent His Son into the world, clothed in Mary's flesh and blood to save us from sin, the contamination of evil. As we look to our heavenly origin and destiny, we are able to concentrate on the Heavenly Kingdom all around us.

Our Mother Most Faithful, who is truly Mother of God, asks us to rely upon God at all times. She reminds us that God sends His angels and saints to comfort and guide us while we dwell in our bodies on earth. If we speak fewer words and listen with our hearts, we can become aware of God's heavenly Kingdom all around us. After all, God allowed us to come to earth so that we might seek and find and enter into the heavenly Kingdom forever. God wants us to reside in His love and enjoy His providence. God's mercy leads us on. God's love speaks to our deepest longings.

MOTHER MOST VENERABLE:
SAINT DUNSTAN, A.D. 950

Toward the end of the tenth century, evil contaminated the Christian clergy. An English monk named Dunstan, son of an aristocrat from

Wessex, was surprisingly meek and humble of heart in spite of his noble lineage. His uncles were bishops of Wells and Winchester. From early childhood, he was dedicated to the Blessed Virgin Mary and his hero was the venerable Saint Patrick, Patron Saint of Ireland.[29]

Dunstan's prayerful mother, Cynethryth, was a devout believer, and while she awaited Dunstan's birth, she had a mysterious spiritual experience.

"She was in the church of Saint Mary on Candleday when all the lights were suddenly extinguished. Then the candle held by Cynethryth was as suddenly relighted, and all present lit their candles at this miraculous flame, thus foreshadowing that the boy [she expected to be born soon] would be the minister of eternal light to the Church of England."[30]

Cynethryth loved her infant son and frequently pondered the mystery of the Incarnation of the Word as she rocked her baby. How like Mary she felt as she cared for her helpless son. Though He needed nothing, Jesus allowed Mary and Joseph to love Him, serve Him, bless Him, praise Him. Cynethryth encouraged her husband to share her joy and wonder, and prayed for him to hold fast to the supernatural faith, hope, and love that inspired Saint Joseph. With much prayer and personal sacrifice, their ability to discern Jesus' presence in their lives deepened and grew, and their family joy increased.

As the years unfolded, Cynethryth and her husband pondered the love they experienced as a young parents. They cherished the wonder they experienced as they watched their child grow and change and mature. Their love was tested as they saw the foolishness of any action in their lives that was not Christ-centered. Cynethryth taught her young son that Jesus Christ loved him, redeemed him, and was always with him. Mother, father, and son entered into prayerful dialogue with Jesus in the Blessed Sacrament. They cherished His ways. They sought His blessing in family prayer.

When Dunstan became a teenager, he was taught by Irish monks at Glastonbury Abbey. Under their tutelage, he faced a near-death experience. Ever after, his unshakable faith and keen optimism were characteristics that endeared him to all. Following in his family's tradition, young Dunstan entered minor orders and served at Canterbury where yet another uncle, Athelm, was presiding archbishop.

Popular and handsome, and much delighted by feminine beauty, Dunstan seriously considered marriage. He enjoyed the companionship of intelligent, loving women and had a deep appreciation for the pleasures of matrimony. Consequently, Dunstan had serious reservations about his capacity to endure the rigors of celibacy. However, as his prayer life deepened, and his discernment grew, Dunstan understood God's calling to the priesthood. Knowing the Scriptures well, he wisely chose not to put God to the test.

After ordination in 943, temptation and worldly beguilements rooted in ecclesial privileges assailed the young cleric. Fearful of losing his soul, Dunstan retired to Glastonbury where he lived the ascetic life of a hermit. Of course, this life of penance was Dunstan's way of shedding his thick, worldly coat made of desires and appetites that destroy interior integrity. He lived in a small enclosure five feet long by two and a half feet deep. He prayed, fasted strictly, studied sacred scripture, and played praises to God on his harp. Legend is legion of Dunstan's fierce encounters with the devil during this time in his life.

Dunstan became renowned for his joyful practice of penance, prayer, and sacrifice on behalf of the people of his region. His friends stood by him, perhaps admiring his steadfast adherence to the sacred vocation of the priesthood. They knew what it had cost him to accept God's sacred calling. Those who admired him most called him Stan. In spite of his austere penances, or perhaps because of them, Stan had a wonderful sense of humor. His jolly laughter warmed even stony hearts grown cold with disdain.

Dunstan allowed God to work through him to raise the spiritual life of the clergy of England from the dregs of ignorance, laxity, exploitation, and corruption. Stan's ardor was great. Strong, with skillful hands and broad shoulders, he liked to work, and he found opportunities to express his understanding that loving work well done is true prayer. Lazy folks generally avoided him. Effeminate men despised him. History sees Stan as an early prototype of the revered Christian reformer Saint Francis of Assisi who would later be a momentous witness to Christ's ways of evangelical poverty in the world.

Dunstan influenced not only the lax clergy in England, but he greatly influenced the nobles and the king himself, exhorting all of them to a renewed commitment to holiness. Stan eventually inherited great wealth. He used the funds to foster a huge monastic revival in England faithful to the gospel of Jesus Christ. Where did he get such light and zeal? Stan liked to spend nights in various churches keeping vigil before the Blessed Sacrament. At that time, many in England had lost faith in the Real Presence of Jesus in the Holy Eucharist. Most frequently, Stan prayed throughout the night in Canterbury's church of Saints Peter and Paul, near the tomb of Saint Augustine.

The monks who shared community life with him attested that as Stan approached the chapel in the east part of the monastery in the darkness of the night, they would see the chapel suddenly fill with light. Some nights, Stan would actually hear angelic choirs singing hymns of Mary, Queen of Angels. Dunstan spoke lovingly of seeing our Blessed Mother kneeling in heavenly light before the tabernacle, offering all praise and blessing and adoration to her Divine Son Jesus.

The Blessed Virgin was surrounded by choirs of angels, he would say. The light around her was so pure, so pristine, so sweet that Stan could barely speak of its healing presence. His fellow monks, and even the laypeople who learned of Our Lady's presence during Stan's all-night prayer vigils before the Blessed Sacrament began to watch for the mysterious light. Quietly, the curious and the devout would creep into the chapel to witness the mystical phenomena that seemed attached to Monk Dunstan's prayerful eucharistic adoration. Electricity was an unknown in those times. What an experience it must have been for those who prayed in that divine light in an otherwise dark chapel. Eventually, the monks affectionately began to refer to the chapel as the "Lady Chapel" at Canterbury.

Dunstan's profound asceticism and miraculous spiritual gifts with which he was so abundantly endowed reminded English Christians of Christ's ways. His visions and apparitions of our Blessed Mother reawakened memories for many of their true homeland that had grown distant. Dunstan's life with our Blessed Mother taught others to respect their own spiritual refinement. There were, unfortunately, some who bore terrible resentment toward him, sourced in spiritual jealousy. Mary is always the Comforter of the Afflicted who suffer. She would console the brokenhearted:

Dear little children, rest serene upon the Heart of Jesus.
He too endured revolution.
His agony in the garden placed Him in the heart of all
pain, all suffering, all disobedience, all obstinacy, all
arrogance, all human appetites gone awry.
Trust Jesus. Be like Jesus.

Dunstan followed our Blessed Mother's gentle guidance. In spite of all the resentment his devout life spawned, he became Abbot of Glastonbury at the king's bidding because of a miracle. The story goes that:

"The king [Eadmund] rode out to hunt the stag in Mendip Forest. He became separated from his attendants and followed a stag at great speed on the direction of Cheddar Cliffs. The stag rushed blindly over the precipice and was followed by the hounds. Eadmund endeavored vainly to stop his horse; then seeing death to be imminent, he remembered his harsh treatment of Saint Dunstan and promised to make amends if his life was spared. At that moment his horse was stopped on the very edge of the cliff. Giving thanks to God, he returned forthwith to his palace, called for Saint Dunstan and bade him follow, then rode straight to Glastonbury. Entering the church, the king first knelt in prayer before the altar, then taking Saint Dunstan by the hand, he gave him the kiss of peace, led him to the abbot's throne, and seating him thereon, promised him all assistance in restoring divine worship and regular observance."[31]

Dunstan was aware that though God does not so will, He *allows* sickness, disability, all kinds of inconveniences and strange occurrences, even near-death experiences such as that of King Eadmund. Abbot Dunstan assured sincere seekers that God's will *is* realized in spite of us. Jesus restores harmony, integrity, wholeness. God's power shines, radiates throughout all creation. His cosmic presence is the reality. Jesus, the resurrected Christ, is the Savior of our Father's Kingdom.

Dunstan became effectively the prime minister of England.

His charity was so lavish that his stewards complained, fearing there would not be enough for them. He admonished them to be like Jesus and trust God totally.[32] He encouraged everyone to embrace supernatural faith and trust in God's loving providence. He taught his monks, often initially against their will, to embrace a true spirit of self-sacrifice. He enforced the law of celibacy, forbad simony (selling church positions for money), and ended the practice of clerics appointing relatives to offices within their jurisdiction. He built monasteries and required monks to actually live monastic rules; he required parish priests to be fully trained in the Christian faith, to actually serve their parishioners and teach them usable trades to improve their standard of living. He restored the clergy to their supernatural calling as sacramental servants of God's people.

Dunstan extolled the spiritual value of work well done. He himself worked as a blacksmith, painter, musician, and jeweler. A famous story tells of Dunstan nailing a horseshoe to the devil's hoof when he was asked to reshoe the devil's horse. This of course caused the devil great pain. Dunstan agreed to remove the shoe only after extracting from the devil his promise never to disturb a place where a horseshoe hangs over the door. To this day, the legend of the lucky horseshoe prevails.

Dunstan's influence was wide and noble. He supported scholars who came to England from all over Europe: encouraged officials and subjects to actualize good laws, endeavor to live under the rule of law for their own well-being, the glory of God, and the salvation of their souls. He built schools, defended the helpless, elderly, widows, and orphans, and enforced respect for purity. He constantly extolled the blessings of committed family values. Dunstan was a deep mystic. He had visions of the celestial kingdom that gave him wisdom far beyond his historical time.

Our Blessed Mother and the angels guided and comforted Dunstan in his quest to ennoble English-speaking people. Upon his death in May of 988, Dunstan was widely proclaimed a saint throughout England. He was formally canonized in 1029. Saint Dunstan has always been considered a most favorite saint of English-speaking people throughout the world. His life experiences help us to better grasp Mary's secrets: his path shows us how to receive Mary's exquisite gifts.

Mary asks us to cling to Jesus, drink deep of his presence, His ways, His love, His unity, His person-hood. We all endure suffering. We often know not what we do to others. When pain is great, our strength ebbs away in an abyss of unrequited longing. Deep, com-mitted prayer *does* bring us peace. Our Blessed Mother helps us to bless all that our Father allows in our lives. She assures us:

> *My dear little children of faith,*
> *trust God's love and gentleness.*
> *Be peace my little ones. All is well.*
> *Rest serene upon the Heart of Jesus.*
> *There alone is your strength and your joy.*
> *Peace, little ones. Seek and find only peace.*

Mary's son is the Savior of all our dreams and hopes. His call is to all people, for all times, places, and nations.

> *I come to all who call to Me,*
> *who give Me respite in the depths of their longings.*
> *I am the only life.*
> *Look only for Me. Then you will know peace.*
> *I am the Prince of Peace.*
> *Those of goodwill are those who obey My will.*
> *My will is truth.*
> *All else is illusion. All else is death.*
> *Peace.*
> *Only peace dearest children of My covenant of Eternal Life.*
> *Stay in My Heart My children.*
> *My blessings go with you.*

> *Listen with your hearts O lost sheep of*
> *the House of Israel.*

Be still. Be silent.
See Me in every circumstance of your lives.
Do not be so sorrowful, or so lonely.
Try harder to see Me everywhere.
You know I never leave you.
Please acknowledge Me. Speak to Me.
I made the world.
I sustain everything. I nurture everything.
You are not separate from Me.
I am here for you now if you want Me.
I want you to want Me in your lives in
every decision you make.
You are Mine. I redeemed you by My own blood.
I love you beyond your capacity to understand.

I love all My children.
My children do not grovel before Me.
I made each of you to be one with Me.
I am the light of your souls.
Live in My love always.
I never abandon any of My children.
It is through My love that you are free.
Be vigilant My children. Always pray for My help.
Stay in My will. I want you in heaven, but not yet.
There is much work to be done.
You must share with others.
Love My children. Encourage them. Teach them My ways.
Trust Me. Believe in Me. You are Mine.
Claim your birthright won for you by My beloved Jesus.
Allow My beloved daughter Mary to bring you to Jesus now.
Look to Him. Listen to Him. Cling to Him.
I AM WHO AM.

CHAPTER 2

Mother of Christ

Now this is how the birth of Jesus came about. When his mother Mary was betrothed to Joseph, but before they lived together, she was found with child through the Holy Spirit. Joseph, her husband, since he was a righteous man, yet unwilling to expose her to shame, decided to divorce her quietly. Such was his intention when, behold, an angel of the Lord appeared to him in a dream and said: "Joseph, son of David, do not be afraid to take Mary your wife into your home. For it is through the Holy Spirit that this child has been conceived in her. She will bear a son and you are to name him Jesus because he will save his people from their sins." All this took place to fulfill what the Lord had said through the prophet: "Behold, the virgin shall be with child and bear a son, and they shall name him Emmanuel," which means, "God is with us."[1]

Joseph responded to his angelic dream with supernatural faith. He believed what the angel said about his wife and her unborn child. With supernatural hope, he took Mary into his home, although he knew the child she was about to bear was not the fruit of his loins; he hoped against all hope that his putative son, conceived in Mary through the Holy Spirit, would indeed save his people from their sins as the angel had said. With supernatural love, Joseph named his little son Jesus and cared for the Christ Child and His sacred Mother Mary. Each of us is called by God to do no less.

MOTHER OF DIVINE GRACE:
SAINT NORBERT, A.D. 1080

History tells us there is nothing new under the sun. Many work today for the good of all, creating opportunities for cities, towns, and villages to offer personal satisfaction to inhabitants consonant with shared community development. A thousand years ago, monasteries serving families living in the surrounding villages were the beginning of such dreams. In this present day, high-speed communication and travel involve the world in shared responsibility for everything from natural resources, air, water, land use, even the planets and galaxies. Print, television, and the Internet give us access to information, including spiritual wonders as never before possible. We are in the process of growing into a global family.

Saint Norbert was an early pioneer who entered upon that path. His choices a thousand years ago still enrich people everywhere and his followers are all over the world.

Norbert was a relative of the emperor of Germany. The son of Heribert, Count of Gennep of the House of Lorraine, he was born near the village of Wesel, Germany, in 1080. Times were financially difficult for all but the wealthiest in Germany. As a young adult, Norbert was rich, handsome, and keen of intellect. Pleasure's slave, he placed high value on luxury, ease, entertainment, and recreation. Others were important to him but only if they provided him enjoyment or advancement. Dressed in finery he proudly admired, certain that he was superior to others and brilliantly handsome, Norbert was riding his exquisite and expensive horse to a gala ball at the Court of Henry V, emperor of Germany. Suddenly, with no warning at all, Norbert's magnificent stallion was struck by lightning. The dead horse fell to the ground leaving Norbert in a state of terror.

Shocked, confused, bitter, and thoroughly angry that his plans with the rich and famous were so abruptly interrupted, he cried out: "My God! What have You done to me?" He did not expect a reply as he was not aware of God's presence at all. Norbert tugged and pulled at his beautiful, beloved horse, hoping that somehow the animal was merely dazed. His frustration and anger mounted with each thought of the glittering gala at Court. He realized his mount must quickly rally if he was to arrive in time to receive the adulation, bows, and accolades his position demanded. Abruptly the air became still. The sun darkened. A chill penetrated Norbert like a sword. The voice of God echoed through the stunned courtier's soul:

"Turn away from evil and do good. Seek after peace and pursue it."

Norbert's involuntary nervous system quivered. In a split second of astonishment, Norbert knew he was in the presence of his Creator. His entire past unfolded before his eyes. He saw the lethal effects of every unloving action of his life until the end of time. "Mercy!" he moaned under the weight of his terrible, self-centered, narcissistic choices.

Humbled to the limits of his intellect, Norbert realized his body, with all its skills and machinations, was only a tool. Hovering over his fallen horse, he came face-to-face with the unpredictable finality of death. Norbert experienced uncomfortable shame and guilt. He could not intellectually comprehend his encounter with the reality of God's dominion over creation. He faced the issue everyone eventually experiences: was his life only a labyrinth with many avenues of deception? Surely there must be more, he hoped.

Nothing would ever be the same for handsome, glamorous, athletic, thoroughly worldly Norbert. He could not shake off his experience with God's ways. Death is a challenge only Jesus Christ has mastered. Norbert eventually withdrew from everyone and everything to seek wisdom at a monastery under the spiritual direction of Benedictine Abbot Cono, of Sieburg. His friends and relatives believed Norbert's sudden piety was just a passing phase, or even a reaction to the lightning strike that killed his horse.

However, at the monastery, certain prayerful monks listened to his story. Norbert told them the words of God *"Turn away from evil and do good. Seek after peace and pursue it."* These words would prove to be emblazoned on his soul for his entire life. Now the chastened young man with silk hands was an eager student. He sought with all his strength to learn lessons of the divine steeped in silence, prayer, and personal acts of penance and mortification.

Norbert trusted that he had experienced a spiritual rescue miracle he did not deserve. In seeking passing pleasurable pursuits, he had unwittingly but aggressively been driving himself into an abyss of nothingness. His appetite for earth's delights was strong. Norbert sometimes longed to be permanently free from his relentless quest for physical pleasure and worldly acclaim. He watched the monks at prayer and work. Was it possible, he wondered, for someone with his hubris, noble lineage, physical strength, and hearty appreciation for pleasure to obtain supreme intimacy with the Source of the Voice that struck him on the road to the Court Gala? He hoped disciplined hours of prayer and meditation would heal him of his relentless cravings.

The monastic path was arduous for clever Norbert. Old habits and customs are stubborn warriors. Under the disciplined guidance of spiritually savvy monks, Norbert persevered in his attempts to encounter the silent majesty of God. Eventually, when he least expected it, Norbert began to experience mysterious energy flowing from the Blessed Sacrament hidden in the chapel tabernacle of the monastery. The divine energy invigorated him so much that he spent every free moment in the chapel kneeling before the Blessed Sacrament. Aware of his disordered desires for ease, adulation, and pleasure, Norbert clung to the eucharistic presence of Jesus Christ in the Blessed Sacrament the way a nonswimmer clings to a life raft in heavy seas.

The purpose of Eucharistic Adoration is to bring the body into stillness before Jesus so that we can communicate spirit to Spirit. Each of us is the steward of our own body. After all, our body is a cavity that houses our soul during our sojourn on earth. We are encapsulated within our body on earth to use it to prove our love for God, to grow in authentic holiness. We will shed every worldly thing that is not for God, with God, in God, and that includes our bodies. These bodies of ours, after all, do have a built-in opalescence factor.

As Norbert grew in his ability to discipline his body, and to pray well, the presence of God throughout creation became more obvious to him. Fasting helped Norbert to grow in compassion for his own darkness: consequently he grew in his ability to forgive himself and, even more so, to forgive others. Norbert forced himself to embrace penance in his self-imposed hermitage. Gradually, he intuited majestic love in the sufferings of Christ. For him, the cross became a symbol of the seriousness of Christ's commitment to His own. Norbert gradually realized how far away in likeness to Christ he was. Often, he had pridefully scourged others, using his tongue as a whip. God's justice cleanses souls, but human justice all too often condemns. The more Norbert meditated on the passion of Christ, the more certain he was that God condemns no man. Rather, slaves to their disordered appetites, people condemn themselves and one another.

Resting in the depths of prayerful meditation, Norbert pondered divine powers vested by Christ in the priesthood. Jesus, knowing the difficulties of life on earth, promised to remain with us, and He chose to do so in the Holy Eucharist. A validly ordained priest, though an unworthy vessel, has Christ's authority, by the power of the Holy Spirit, to transubstantiate mere bread and wine into the Body and Blood, Soul and Divinity of the Savior. Valid Holy Eucharist is the food of eternal life.

As he was nearly thirty years old, Norbert wasn't certain he had the life span or personal qualities ordination to the priesthood would require. Yet he knew beyond any doubt that through the priesthood, Jesus Christ left His own Body and Blood to feed us the nourishment of eternal life.

The more he prayed, fasted, and served others with no thought of gain for himself except to be more like Christ, the more compassion Norbert began to experience for others, especially unbelievers. Who is poorer, after all, than those who do not know the love of God? Norbert had personal experience with the power of spiritual darkness to beget more darkness. He longed to bring the grace of Christ's Body and Blood to all God's children. Only as a validly ordained priest could Norbert feed God's starving children with Masses everywhere; he could offer Christ's Body and Blood to our Father for His people; let Christ's sacrifice spill on children of darkness. The call was great. Norbert was profoundly aware of his limitations.

Silence was now an urgent need for Norbert. Meditation on Christ's priesthood was difficult for him. He felt entirely unworthy of embracing the Christic dignity of ordination. He was aware that he did not know how to love himself and others, much less the Lord, properly. As Norbert worked in the garden one cool fall day, he inadvertently clutched poison ivy with his hands. Shortly thereafter, his hands became helpless and miserably uncomfortable. The poison ivy destroyed good tissue. So it is with sin, he reasoned: sin is poison for our souls; sin destroys the beauty of our souls. The realization frightened Norbert. Chastened and confused, Norbert prayed as if his very life depended upon God's mercy.

In the blink of an eye, Norbert saw the healing power of Christ's sacraments for human souls. "The sacraments of Jesus Christ are the balm that heals the poison of sin!" he suddenly exclaimed to monks working near him in the garden. Their reaction to his discoveries is not recorded.

Norbert pondered deeply whether God was truly calling him to the asceticism of vowed celibacy. He knew he wasn't doing well in the single life. He also knew, through deep prayer, that the sacrament of matrimony heals the sin of lust. It purifies the appetites of lust and greed and avarice and sloth. It heals self-love. Norbert discerned that he needed healing of all those difficulties, yet he feared his weaknesses would undermine his capacity to be a committed husband and father.

The sacrament of reconciliation builds endurance.[2] As the athlete must train, so also must those who would grow spiritually from the graces of the sacrament of reconciliation. The sacrament requires an ongoing awareness of the condition of one's soul in the light of grace. The true sacrament of reconciliation is painful, for sin is painful. Norbert availed himself of the great sacrament of reconciliation frequently. He was on a quest for Truth, and the light of Christ, poured out to him in the mysteries of the Church, brought him spiritual strength. Norbert continued to pray with all his heart. He turned to Mary, Mother of the Great High Priest, more frequently now. Her quiet, loving presence was his consolation.

When Norbert least expected, Christ revealed to him that true priests must become victims, with Christ, in the sacrament of reconciliation, to free God's people from the bondage of sin. God raises humble priests high on the cross with Jesus. Together, they destroy the bondage of our Father's children. Not one of the little ones entrusted to Christ by His Father is lost. True priests liberate, protect, and guard souls for God's Kingdom: nothing more, nothing less.

Norbert spent much time studying Scripture. He observed: "The word of God is fiery. It is inflamed with the fire of the Holy Spirit. It consumes vices and promotes virtue. It bestows wisdom on well disposed people and provides for them heavenly food."[3]

Norbert disciplined himself to make his life, thoughts, desires, words, ideas totally Christ-centered. In the rural area where he prayed, Norbert pondered the spiritual mysteries hidden in nature. He particularly loved the beauty of majestic trees. Made by God, they are perfectly obedient. Never do they deviate from what a tree is supposed to be. Not so for poor, fallen man. Norbert prayed to be as obedient to God's laws as are the trees. He knew what the church teaches: man is but dust empowered by God's hand, free only while the dust is activated by God. Death ends freedom. At that point, we are either with God or His enemy eternally.

As Norbert's faith, hope, and charity grew, so did his mystical life. He drew quite close to Mary in his thoughts, prayer life, and commitments. Norbert sought guidance from Mary who is forever Spouse of the Holy Spirit. Gradually, praying with Mary, he discovered treasures hidden in Sacred Scripture's divine light. The Bible teaches that almsgiving is a sin offering. To give to the less fortunate is to grow in love and joy. A joyful giver exudes God's joy; a sorrowful giver reveals his own greed. Norbert meticulously sold his estate and joyfully gave the proceeds to the poor. No resentments were his lot. Detachment from all that is not of God, for God, with God was his goal.

Norbert, like Mary at the foot of the cross, met anger and rebellion with love and forgiveness. He was learning that when we love in whatever way we can, we share God's peace and joy. When we forgive, beginning with ourselves, we bring His peace and joy into our hearts. Those who would not accept Norbert's love and forgiveness wandered away from him. Unfortunately, all of us from time to time reject not only God's love and forgiveness, but also the love and forgiveness of others. We, probably subconsciously, prefer our wounds, and nurse our wounds though we have no power to heal them. In forgiveness of all wrongs, we receive the balm of love and joy that heals all our hurts, frees our hearts, and brings God's peace to our souls longing for wholeness.

Clinging to Mary, Norbert was able to humble himself before God, the Source, the beginning, and the end of all that is, and was, and ever will be. Now he knew for certain that his well-being rested only in God. Norbert, with supernatural faith, finally had ears to hear Mary's Divine Son:

> *Come to Me My little ones.*
> *Come and rest in My Heart.*
> *There alone will you find the love you crave.*
> *There alone will you find rest.*

Filled with spiritual courage, Norbert sought and found a dwelling place of solitude, simplicity, and discernment. There, following Mary's guidance, Norbert and two companions quietly surrendered to the mystery of God's reality. They spent much of their time in silence and prayer. The process is similar for all of us. As our faith increases, and we become comfortable drawing near Mary, her celestial kindness enables us to better hear God's calls. We begin to perceive the Divine Voice deep in our souls. Even the mightiest must learn His ways for God speaks in the silence of mankind's longing. Mary's celestial gentleness calms restlessness: her grace is a diadem that brings peace to tortured souls. Her presence is an unequivocal assurance that God provides.

Eventually, in the forest of Coucy, Norbert found a small, abandoned chapel dedicated to Saint John the Baptist. This deep, marshy valley, Premontre, was filled with thorns and brushwood. It appealed to him whose soul longed to embrace the spirit of penance, not for the sake of penance itself, but to subdue the still heightened appetites that growled to him from the cravings of his senses. Every thorn and stick reminded Norbert of the pitiful condition of his soul. He spent many nights with Mary in prayer and adoration before the Blessed Sacrament. The rustic chapel became a refuge where Norbert actively sought spiritual freedom and light that only Christ can give.

Norbert humbly discerned a subtle, quiet invitation planted in the depths of his soul to found a Religious Order of men committed to serving Christ with a sincere spirit of loving asceticism. By now,

Norbert was aware that penance and self-sacrifice are a necessity for those whose appetites are wretched warriors that drive us far from the eternal shores of bliss. Longing to experience God's love, the cold, relentless darkness of the nights became a token of Norbert's spiritual desolation.

Day after day, he prayed, fasted, and served others as best he could. He willfully denied himself even the most meager pleasures. When Norbert reached the depths of the darkness of his own nothingness and felt certain annihilation mocking his all too feeble efforts, quite suddenly, without warning, a brilliant light blinded him. In that dazzling splendor, Norbert discerned the presence of Mary, the immaculate woman of Genesis 3:15. Time vanished. Our Blessed Mother's eternal tenderness and contagious love of God bathed his tormented spirit with unimaginable joy. Heaven's sacred consolation and encouragement were her gifts. She spoke to him of God's divine call and assured him of God's blessing for the Religious Order he had been pondering. Mary, Mother of Kindness Incarnate, most graciously asked Norbert to seek Pontifical confirmation of the Order in her name. As a memento of her visitation, our Blessed Mother gave Norbert a white priest's garment, requesting that members of his Religious Order wear a similar garment as a sign of her love and protection. Mary said the white garment symbolizes purity and holiness each human craves yet obtains only by determination and perseverance. No one knows where that garment is today, though in its time, Norbert's heaven-sent vestment was greatly venerated.

Several helpers worked with Norbert to build a monastery on the site of his apparition. One can only imagine the graces they received at that holy site. Thirteen men, desiring to live under his direction, joined Norbert there. They adapted the Rule of Saint Augustine to the severe austerity Norbert required of his followers. These monks who shared in Mary's secrets honored the privilege of our Blessed Mother's visitation by singing the divine praises every day of their lives in thanksgiving.

Norbert continued his practice of praying with Mary during night vigils in front of the Blessed Sacrament in the little chapel of Saint John the Baptist. Following her guidance, he meditated often on the mysteries of life and death, pondering the significance of sacred secrets hidden in our Blessed Mother's visitation. Mary led him to the heights of Scripture's wisdom: the quality of our eternal life is based entirely on the choices we make during our time on earth.

The spiritual stakes are high for all of us. Time is precious. Eternity is forever. In the silence of long nights of prayer with Mary, Norbert understood with supernatural knowledge that Jesus Christ, God from God, Light from Light, is truly present in validly transubstantiated Holy Eucharist just as surely as He was during His thirty-three years on earth. Christ has not left us orphans.

Supernatural understanding reveals celestial choirs of angels prostrate before the tabernacles of the world, doing homage to Christ the King of Kings. This Lord of lords so loves men that He dwells among us, disguised in a tiny wafer of bread, and ordinary wine that validly ordained priests consecrate by the power of the Holy Spirit. In that mystical moment of transubstantiation, bread and wine become the Body and Blood, Soul and Divinity of Jesus Christ. Norbert said frequently: "He who seldom receives Holy Communion because he is tepid and cold is like one who would say, 'I never approach the fire because I am cold.' "

"Mary the Mother of God is always in adoration before the Blessed Sacrament," Norbert explained to his followers. Those who desire the comforts of our Blessed Mother find her glorifying her Divine Son hidden in the Eucharist. The Holy Spirit of Love bound Norbert ever closer to the unseen world of adorers, empowering him with a zeal that attracted leaders and rulers to his path. His joy in wearing the white vestment given to him by the Mother of Christ was so contagious that many sought to emulate his attire.

Eventually, Norbert reluctantly became archbishop of Magdeburg in central Germany, a territory half pagan and half Christian. Disdaining the finery of clergy and aristocracy, especially the rich hierarchy and nobility, he continued to walk barefoot, even in the snow, and dressed in the shabbiest of outer garments, simply because he had spiritually grown to attribute no importance to things that pass away. Of course, he already had a heaven-sent garment. Bearing within his person a spark of Divine Life, he valued things of the earth only in so far as they brought glory to the Living God. Norbert was filled with supernatural faith, hope, and love.

Through his ascetic leadership, a powerful spirit of reform and renewal entered the Christian world of Europe. He courageously continued his work for the Church until his death on June 6, 1134, at Magdeburg. He was buried there at the Norbertine Abbey of Saint Mary. Miracles were prolific at that sacred place and pilgrims and seekers continued to visit his tomb over the centuries. In 1627, his remains were transported to the Abbey of Strahov, a suburb of Prague in Bohemia, now the Czech Republic. He is officially known as the Patron and Protector of Bohemia.[4]

Norbert held up the example of the first Christians gathered around Mary, whose community life, as described in Acts 2:42–47, was marked by the power of the Holy Spirit, the sharing of all things and the desire to serve God first by serving others in Christ's holy name. Today his religious order of men and women lead a vowed life following Christ by living in common, sharing all things in holy poverty, and dedicating themselves to ministering to God's people. Norbertines, as they have come to be known, have three abbeys in the United States, thirty in England, seven in Ireland, one in Northern Ireland, six in Scotland, one in Wales, eight in Germany, two in Austria, eight in Belgium, four in France, one in Cyprus, two in the Czech Republic, and one in Slovakia.

Norbert's sacred "yes" to his vocation finds expression nearly a thousand years later in the lives and ministries of his followers throughout the world. These vowed religious people strive to imitate the early Jerusalem Christian community in a shared life with Mary that is both ever ancient and ever new.

Norbert's path reveals that the same beguilements that entrapped him as a young man continue to lure us today. Amazing graces flow freely now as then. Mary's secrets of eternal happiness are for us, too. If we ask her properly, our Blessed Mother will take us by the hand and walk with us on the high road of tested human virtue. Mary knows wonderful sacred secrets that solve all our problems.[5] Her secrets are our gifts. She assures us:

I am your Mother of Perpetual Adoration.
I pray for you to the Heart of Jesus at every moment.
My prayers are your assurance of God's love.

My mother's heart, formed by Jesus before the world was
made, is your refuge from all the discord, lies and abuses of the world.
I love you. You can trust me. I do not disappoint.

MOTHER OF GOOD COUNSEL:
BLESSED GERARD, FATHER OF MODERN
WESTERN MEDICINE, A.D. 1099

At the close of the eleventh century, near the Church of the Holy Sepulchre in Jerusalem was the Benedictine Monastery of Santa Maria. Pilgrims from everywhere who made their way to the Holy Land were welcomed there. Many had become injured in battle. Others had succumbed to illnesses of the day. Far from home, pilgrims often had nowhere else to turn for help, especially as their strength and means were depleted.

Blessed Gerard, a true child of Mary from early childhood, was renowned for his humility and sanctity. This practical man, an active mystic, was the administrator of the monastery's hospice-infirmary. Under his leadership, the Sovereign Military and Hospitaller Order of Saint John (the Baptist) of Jerusalem, composed of Knights from many lands who were forced to take up arms to defend the hospice from attacks, became the first international religious order of the Catholic Church.[6] These Knights are regarded as the founders of modern hospital and ambulance work.[7]

Fra Gerard was imprisoned during one of the many battles in Jerusalem and severely tortured by enemies who claimed they believed he was hiding treasure in the hospice. Of course, Gerard considered each patient a cherished child of God, and as such, a true, invaluable treasure. His enemies were not interested in the sick. After his release, Gerard resumed his Hospitaller work, admitting the ill and afflicted of all backgrounds and economic means, both rich and poor, of every race, nationality, and religion.

When Godfrey de Boullion was elected ruler of Jerusalem in 1100, and given the title "Defender of the Holy Sepulcre," he became aware of the sacrificial work of Brother Gerard and rewarded him with donations of land and buildings for the expanding needs of the hospital. Gerard had eyes to see Christ hidden in the sorrows of the sick and poor in the area. Other men followed his example and gave up their military pursuits to serve with him at his expanding hospital. These Knights originally organized themselves into a Religious Order of Hospitallers, taking monastic vows of poverty, chastity, and obedience and dedicating their lives to the care of the sick and poor.

Gerard personally oversaw the formation of the Hospitaller Sisters of Saint John to care for the needs of sick women and children.[8] The Hospitallers and the Sisters chose the Rule of Saint Augustine, more flexible than that of the Benedictines, as a way of life for their work with the sick and the poor. The Order of Hospitallers was canonically approved by Pope Paschal II on February 15, 1113. This religious, military, and aristocratic order has served a dual function for nine hundred years, expressed in the Order's motto: "Defense of the Faith and Service of the Poor."

As sick or injured pilgrims were restored to some level of health by means of good medical care, they were necessarily dismissed from Hospice and took to the roads heading homeward to distant regions. Many discharged patients were poor, weak, and alone. Gerard seemed to perceive Christ's presence as he saw them go away to dangerous roads that led to their homelands. Perhaps he heard the Lord, deep in his soul as he watched them depart.

I came to My servant Gerard. He welcomed Me. He fed Me.
He blessed Me. Now he takes My food away.
Now he drives Me away for I am weak. I am hungry.
I am poor.
I am abandoned. No man shakes My hand. No man loves Me.
No man respects Me. I am confused. I am sad.
Where are My Father's servants?
Do you abandon Me, too?
Do you send Me away?

Thank you My son, My brother for I was happy for a
while in your care.
Now I go again to the highways for no one loves Me.

No one cares for Me.
I leave My blessings on you and yours for you took Me in
when no one had a place for Me.
No one understood My weakness.
No one saw Me for I am hidden. I am humble. I am God.
I live in the least of My children.
I live in the poorest of My children.
Now your sick and poor go to the roads again,
for they know My cross.
I live in them that all My little ones may glorify My Father.
Woe to those who see not the hour of My visitation.

Gerard, sensitive of heart and a man of quiet courage, sought assistance from the Pope and Christian Knights in Jerusalem to expand hospice services for needy travelers along the roads leading to and from the Holy Land. Over the years, Gerard and his associates started other Hospice-infirmaries as far away as southern France and Italy. He learned one of Mary's secrets well: each person on earth is a child of the Holy Trinity redeemed by Jesus and worthy of loving respect and care.

The needs of the sick and the poor were so great that Gerard continued to recruit consecrated helpers committed to sacrificial service of suffering humanity. Gerard and his followers promised to serve the Lord Jesus hidden in the sick and the poor. They worked tirelessly, endeavoring constantly to bring the loving kindness of Christ's mercy to the suffering. In 1170, as many as two thousand sick were being cared for in the wards of his hospital in Jerusalem: men, women, and children. Four doctors worked with him, assisted by Knights, and Serving Brothers and Sisters of Saint John.[9]

Such work is often grueling. Gerard spent many a night at the bedside of the suffering and dying. At such moments, Mary's strength was his consolation. Was she not Our Lady of Golgotha who walked to Calvary beside the Redeemer? Who would know better the ways of consolation for the suffering? Filled with such zeal and extraordinary efforts on behalf of the needy, Gerard was actually heralded as "Blessed" during his lifetime. He prayerfully referred to himself as "the servant of the sick and the poor" and "he stretched forth his arms into many lands to obtain what he needed to feed his own [sick and poor for whom he sacrificed his life]."[10]

Recognizing the call to holiness that is universal, and not just confined to monastic life, Gerard, sharing Mary's wisdom, was a visionary who recognized Christ's mysterious presence in all God's people. He encouraged others, by his example, to bring Christ's healing love to every situation. Over the centuries, Gerard's followers grew to include lay Religious members dedicated under the patronage of Our Lady of Philermos and Saint John the Baptist. One of the oldest institutions of Western and Christian civilization, Gerard's Order of Malta, officially known as the Sovereign Military Hospitaller Order of Saint John of Jerusalem of Rhodes and of Malta, operates throughout the world, tending to the needs of the poorest of the poor and sickest of the sick in poverty and disaster-stricken areas.

Blessed Gerard's tested love for Our Lady allowed him to be guided by her loving, maternal care for the sick and the poor. Though original members of his Order were Knights who gave up their swords to do Hospitaller work, within a generation, circumstances again forced the Knights to take up arms to defend pilgrims in the Holy Lands for two hundred years. After 1291, when Acre, the last great Christian holding in the Holy Land, was conquered, the Knights moved to Cyprus, and in 1310, to Rhodes. The Ottoman Turks forced them out in 1523, and they resettled in Malta in 1530. Their work on behalf of Christ's love for the sick and poor continued; so also did their military efforts to protect Christian settlements along the western Mediterranean. Over the centuries, the Order of Malta developed the concept of modern hospitals and was a leader in medical science. By 1834, it established its headquarters in Rome.

Great luminaries are numbered among the membership, including the late Blessed Pope John XXIII. In modern times, there are 12,500 members worldwide. Along with 80,000 permanent volunteers, 13,000 medical personnel, including doctors, nurses, auxiliaries, and paramedics, they are Our Lady's hands and heart at work around the clock, loving Jesus hidden in the least of His people, and empowering the sick and the poor to embrace Christ's healing love. The Order of Malta cares for the terminally ill, the homeless, refugees, the handicapped, children, the elderly, the wounded, and the sick on five continents, without distinction of race, nation, or religion: all are beneficiaries of the Order of Malta. Over the centuries, the Order has managed medical care and related services during numberless wars. A sovereign entity having diplomatic relations with more than a hundred states and official relations with five countries, the Order of Malta engages in humanitarian activities in a hundred twenty countries.

The white, eight-pointed Maltese Cross is recognized internationally as a symbol of godly charity toward mankind and a comfort and consolation to God's sick and poor. As direct successors of the earlier defenders of Christianity, a Knight, Dame, or Chaplain of Malta bears responsibility to maintain the inherited tradition, the obligation to defend the Christian faith, humbly and honorably live its values, and provide, as did their noble predecessors of old, aid and assistance to Jesus Christ, hidden in their "lords," the sick and the poor.

Prior to the 1990s, all officers of the Order had to be of noble birth for at least a hundred years. Membership of the Order remains by invitation only. Most of the members are laypeople, although a small number are professed religious: certain Knights of Justice take vows of poverty, chastity, and obedience, but seldom live in monastic communities. What distinguishes the Knights and Dames of Malta is their commitment to seek spiritual perfection within the Church. Their challenge, as they aspire to holiness above all else, is to grow in virtue and charity by defense of the teachings of Christ, and sacrificial service to the less fortunate.

Mary's presence in the Order of Malta is officially acknowledged the first week of May each year when members throughout the world gather at her shrine in Lourdes, France. Members come with their beloved *malades* (the sick) to the grotto of apparitions to praise God with Mary. They process with their *malades* each evening, pulling them in blue carts, as Jesus Christ in the Blessed Sacrament is held aloft for adoration and petition. They prayerfully serve God as they submerge their cherished *malades* into Mary's healing springs of miraculous water. Miracles of many kinds are bountiful at Lourdes.

Knights and Dames of the Order of Saint John of Jerusalem sometimes travel as pilgrims to the Monastery of Saint Ursula in Valetta on the Island of Malta to be near the remains of their founder,

Blessed Gerard, who died on September 3, 1120. He is a much loved Christian witness in the eyes of those who come to know of him. Faithful child of Mary, Blessed Gerard totally placed his life in the Gospel footsteps of the Lord Jesus Christ. His Epitaph at Malta reads in part: "Here lies Gerard, the humblest man in the East, the servant of the poor, and kind to strangers. His appearance was not impressive but it was a noble heart that made him conspicuous. One can see from these buildings how capable he was. He looked to the future and achieved very much. He was busy with many things in many, different places . . . Blessed Gerard was carried into heaven in the hands of angels."

Blessed Gerard, a wise student of Mary's secrets, and a prolific beneficiary of Mary's gifts, received extraordinary blessings from her that his followers continue to enjoy.

I am the Mother of all earthly sorrows.
I am the Mother of all earthly joys.
Give me your sorrows dear children.
I, alone among God's children, carry your sorrows
in my heart in peace and joy and love.
My Son, your Brother, Jesus, is the Lord of all sorrows.
His victory redeems all sorrow.
Those who give their sorrows to me
experience my peace and joy and love.
I unite their sorrows to my Son Jesus' redemptive act.
I stand at the foot of the cross to gather all the
sorrow of all mankind.
Soon your earthly journey will be over dear children of
our Father's covenant.
Persevere for the way is fraught with trials and sorrows.
It is only in Jesus that sorrow becomes joy.
It is only in Jesus that peace and love unite heaven and earth.
Those who choose to drink of His chalice taste the sweetness of
heaven on earth.
Be peace dear children. Be love. Be joy.
Be my children most faithful.

CHAPTER 3

Mother of the Church[1]

"And Mary rising up in those days went into the hill country with haste into a city of Juda, and she entered into the house of Zachery, and saluted Elizabeth. And it came to pass, that when Elizabeth heard the salutation of Mary, the infant leaped in her womb. And Elizabeth was filled with the Holy Ghost: And she cried out with a loud voice and said: Blessed art thou among women, and blessed is the fruit of thy womb. And whence is this to me that the mother of my Lord should come to me? For behold, as soon as the voice of thy salutation sounded in my ears, the infant in my womb leaped for joy. And blessed art thou that hast believed, because those things shall be accomplished that were spoken to thee by the Lord."[2]

Mary is a precious gift to each of us. The Lamb of God who takes away the sins of the world, Jesus meek and humble of heart, is Mary's son. Since the time of the Shepherds, Wise men, apostles, and disciples, and throughout the history of Christianity, people who find Mary experience God Incarnate, her son.

In difficult historical epochs, God allows strategic, extraordinary graces to flow to His people. Jesus said: *"I will not leave you orphans, I will come to you."*[3] And he does in countless, quite mysterious ways. Evil times are the breeding ground of great saints.

MOTHER OF PURE LIGHT:
SAINT DOMINIC, A.D. 1170

Consider how God blessed Saint Dominic, founder of the Dominican Order of Preachers with quite extraordinary gifts from our Blessed Mother when spiritual darkness enveloped the masses.[4] Dominic preached the miraculous effects of the Holy Rosary as he healed the sick and raised the dead in Rome. He loved Mary as his own highly venerated spiritual mother, and clearly the mother of the members of Christ's sacred body. As Mother of God, Mother of Christ, and consequently Mother of His Church, Mary brings Pure Light:

All of Paradise rejoices when so much as one sinner turns to his
Father in confidence.
The Gates of Paradise are wide.
The Blood of the Lamb has obtained entry for every redeemed
child of the Father.
Turn to your Father oh beloved children of the Lamb.
Be filled with peace. Be filled with joy.
Your tears are gone now.
By the Blood of the Lamb you are set free.
Live in hope. Live in love.
Rejoice oh beloved children.
Sing with your brothers and sisters in Paradise.
Sing to the Lamb. Praise the Lamb.
Praise the Holy Trinity,
God the Father, God the Son, God the Holy Spirit,
for the children of the Father are free.

Miracles followed Dominic wherever he went. Youth congregated around him and vocations to the Order of Preachers flourished. Great saints do spawn in clusters.

MOTHER OF THE ETERNAL WORD:
SAINT HYACINTH, A.D. 1185

One young man who watched Saint Dominic raise a prominent nobleman from the dead in Rome was Hyacinth, nephew of the Bishop of Krakow. The young man was fascinated with the charismatic, widely acclaimed Dominic. After several encounters with the great man, young Hyacinth began to seriously ponder the meaning of the Incarnation: God in human flesh in the person of Jesus Christ.

Hyacinth did not comprehend the person or power of Jesus Christ until he found Mary in the mysteries of the Holy Rosary. God, whom the Universe cannot comprehend, descended into the womb of Mary and enveloped all creation into the substance of His tiny, unborn body. And so the redemption of all creation came to life in the Redeemer, Jesus Christ. Such divine humility obviously transcends the human intellect.

Hyacinth began to model his daily life after the Scriptural path of Jesus. By continuous meditation on the life of Christ contained in the Holy Rosary, coupled with disciplined fasting and intense Scripture study, Hyacinth developed immense love for prayer. He practiced mortification of carnal desires and remained faithful to the instructions Dominic prescribed for his followers.

Gradually the young seeker awakened to the spiritual power vested by Christ in the priesthood. After years of personal and community prayer, spiritual penance and discernment, Hyacinth was spiritually, psychologically, emotionally, socially, and intellectually strong enough to respond to Christ's invitation. He was ordained a Dominican Friar. Subsequently, Hyacinth studied at Krakow, Prague, and Bologna, earning a Doctorate in Canon Law and Divinity.

Filled with passion for the salvation of souls, he founded monasteries along the roads that led to Russia. The fervent Friar preached the Gospel, healed the sick, and fed the spiritually starving with Masses and sacramental life all the way to the Great Wall of China.

The more Hyacinth struggled to live the pattern Jesus left for His followers, the more his heart was filled with secrets of the Divine. Hardship did not disturb his love for God's ways. Personal deprivation, even immense mortification could not dampen his vast love for God's people. He knew the eternal value of each immortal soul. As a true son of Mary, this missionary, with her help, traveled twelve thousand miles on foot, slept upon bare earth, and preached the gospel by deed and word every place he journeyed. Hyacinth shared Mary's concern for those souls deprived of knowledge of the Lord Jesus Christ. He believed no personal sacrifice was too great to bear for them. Hyacinth was driven by a fire of love so intense that conversions followed him like morning follows the night.

Hyacinth learned, in deep prayer with Mary, that the desire for God is engraved in the depths of each human soul. One intensely hot August afternoon, when most people were sleeping in the heat of the day, Hyacinth was kneeling before the Blessed Sacrament in the tabernacle of a side altar in an otherwise empty church. Quietly and ardently he prayed. A sudden, blinding flash of light revealed the presence of our Blessed Mother near the tabernacle, adoring Jesus in the Blessed Sacrament. Other saints and angels were there, too. The Mother of Jesus humbly turned to look Hyacinth full in the face. He was stunned at the dazzling light surrounding her. Her serenity was pure love. Her sweetness was perfect kindness. Her voice, like the sound of memories hidden in the dreams of tomorrow, echoed the safety of home and peace and contentment.

"Hyacinth, my son, rejoice; for thy prayers are pleasing to my Son, the Savior of the world; and whatsoever thou shalt ask of Him in my name, thou shalt obtain through my intercession."[5]

Those to whom much is given, much is expected. Ever after, Hyacinth turned to our Blessed Mother for her prayers and guidance in all his endeavors. A most dramatic experience in his life preserves for us what it meant to him to honor our Blessed Mother in Jesus' name.

During a terrible uprising in Russia, he was saying Mass in the

Dominican monastery at Kiev. Word reached him to flee with the Blessed Sacrament before an enemy invasion. Friar Hyacinth completed the Mass and gathered the ciborium containing the Blessed Sacrament from the tabernacle. As he did so, a modest statue of the Blessed Mother in the sanctuary suddenly become bathed in a mysterious and brilliant light.

The startled priest immediately fell to his knees and prayed: "This unworthy servant of Jesus Christ shall always guard your honor dearest Mother of God. Any symbol of your loving presence with us is sacred. I shall never abandon your image to Christ's enemies." With superhuman strength, he lifted the large alabaster statue of the Blessed Virgin Mary. To protect the statue from defilement by the invaders, he carried it alongside the Blessed Sacrament across the Dnieper River by walking on the water. Astonished followers cued behind him and crossed the waters of the deep river with him. Many onlookers could only stare in amazement, but the miracle was remembered. It is said Saint Hyacinth's footprints remained upon the water for centuries afterward and were clearly seen when the river was calm. The statue of Mary was subsequently enshrined in a church in Lemberg. Pilgrims came from great distances to see it and to meditate on the mysteries of the Holy Rosary while seeking our Blessed Mother's intercession.

Years later, while saying Mass, the elderly Hyacinth "suddenly beheld a dazzling light descend from heaven, in the midst of which appeared a long procession of angels and saints, forming an escort to their Queen. The celestial company prostrated round the altar whilst the Saint [Hyacinth] offered the Holy Sacrifice. At its conclusion he saw Our Blessed Lady crowned by her Divine Son with a crown of flowers and stars, which Mary then took from her head and showed to him saying: 'Behold! I make this crown for thee.' "[6] Shortly thereafter, on August 15, 1257, Hyacinth passed away.

The faithful attribute illustrious miracles to Saint Hyacinth's intercession. At the site of his tomb it is said that many, whose corpses were carried there, were raised from the dead. He is a most beloved saint of Europe, especially in Germany and Poland, and is the Patron Saint of Lithuania.

MOTHER OF THE AFFLICTED:
BLESSED HERMANN, A.D. 1200

In the year 1160, during the reign of German emperor Frederic Barbarossa, times were quite harsh. Many lost their lands along with any family wealth they had accumulated. The poor were the majority and starvation was common. Poverty drove entire families into hell on earth. Devils laughed and angels wept. Few knew how to access the power of the angels. The more God was lost from memory, the more misery reigned. For some, Christianity offered a bright haven of hope.

One little boy whose rich parents had lost everything was painfully familiar with the abuse of neglect, cold, and hunger. Hermann, who lived in Cologne, Germany, was blessed that his desperate parents, well aware of the dangers and temptations to which the poor are exposed, trained him to make a virtue of necessity and content himself with little. They taught him to turn to God with utmost confidence and trust for all his needs. From earliest childhood, Herman manifested a tender devotion to the Blessed Virgin Mary. His favorite prayer in times of need was: "We fly to thy patronage O Holy Mother Of God! Despise not our petitions in our necessities, but deliver us from all dangers O glorious and ever blessed Virgin."

Kindly monks invited Hermann to go to school. He was a devoted scholar and eagerly learned his lessons. When Hermann felt lonely or afraid, he crept silently into a large church next to his school and hovered close to the great statue of our Blessed Mother holding her Divine Child on her lap. He had not yet understood that Jesus is truly present, Body and Blood, Soul and Divinity in the Blessed Sacrament within the tabernacle of the churches of the world. He did know that Jesus was present in the church because the Friars had told him so.

The little boy loved to stare at the rosy cheeks of the statue of our Blessed Mother and her wonderful smile filled his heart with joy. The small boy would sometimes feel compelled to reach up and touch the tiny hand of her Baby. Occasionally he would even speak out loud. Perhaps the child prayed:

"You were hungry, too, weren't you dear Jesus? I had no break-fast this day, and no lunch either. Sometimes I am so cold that I can't breathe. You are the Son of God and You were hungry. You were cold too. Please give me a small bit of bread. You can make the least crumb nourish and strengthen me as much as the warmest, biggest meal. Please make my mind learn the lessons the good friars teach me. I am very tired and very hungry and very cold dear Lord Jesus."[7] Somehow Hermann survived extreme poverty that winter. And he managed to learn his lessons in school.

In summer, Hermann often gathered wildflowers to adorn the great statue of our Blessed Mother and her Divine Child. "I am bring-ing these to honor You dear little Jesus" he would volunteer. "They are Your flowers because You made the world and everything in it is Yours. Thank you for letting me find these beautiful flowers and for allowing me to bring them to Your Blessed Mother." Then Hermann would run off to his work.

One day a farmer gave him a beautiful pear. Hermann had never seen such a fine piece of fruit. He felt his mouth water and his in-stinct was to bite into the pear immediately. But, remembering the kindness of God, Hermann ran as fast as his small legs would carry him to the church. Realizing his excitement, he paused to catch his breath and smooth back his hair. Then he quietly and triumphantly approached the great statue of the Blessed Virgin holding the Christ Child. "For your Baby Jesus dear Blessed Mother" he whispered as he held up the pear.

Immediately it seemed that the hand of the statue reached down and took the pear. The next thing he knew, Hermann found himself in the arms of the real Blessed Virgin, sitting beside her Divine Child. In that moment of ecstasy he tasted the sweet fruit of Divin-ity as his body and soul became one with God in the mystery of Di-vine Love.

Winter came. One particularly cold and snowy day, Hermann made his usual visit to the church. As he approached the statue, he heard with the ears of his soul: "Hermann, where are your shoes? It is too cold for you to walk barefoot." Tears of shame welled in the small boy's eyes as he bravely replied: "Dear Blessed Mother, you well know that my family has no money to buy me shoes."

"My child, do you not know that anything you ask of the Father in the name of my Son Jesus He will give you if you have but the faith to ask and believe? Go to the rock," said the Blessed Mother. "There you will find all the money you need to buy a pair of shoes. Whenever you are in want of anything, you need only go to the rock. There you will find all that is necessary. You must do it with the fullest confidence."[8]

Hermann believed. One little boy of faith found God's loving providence through the kindness of the Blessed Mother. Hermann's days of hunger and deprivation were over. Yet he never approached the rock except in extreme necessity.

When he was twelve years old, Hermann entered a nearby monastery founded by Saint Norbert. As a Premonstratensian monk (as the Norbertines were then called), he lived a long and fruitful cloistered life of prayer and penance, dying in 1241. Gradually his life story became widely known: he was beatified because of the miracles that flow to multitudes invoking his intercession. Blessed Hermann of Germany loved much and received and gave much in return.

MOTHER OF THE SUFFERING: THE LONE FISHERMAN, A.D. 1218

God is with His people in mysterious ways. He is the same today, yesterday, and tomorrow. Long ago, God manifested His love for families in a special way that is remembered and honored even now. The place was La Garde, France. The year was 1218. But it could well be today, for spiritual reality never changes. In a small fishing village off the coast of Marseilles, a sudden storm shocked and frightened everyone. The wind was fierce and the waves were violent.

A small fishing boat was stranded in the storm. In it was a terrified fisherman who fully expected to perish at any moment. Just when he thought all hope of survival was gone, he spotted a celestial radiance hovering around La Garde on the granite mountain that overlooks the coast of Marseilles. Could God be summoning him to his death? he wondered. He was far from ready to meet his Maker and he knew it.

Mortal fear gripped the lone fisherman. He felt the fierce jowls of the angry sea surrounding him. Throwing his hands to the winds that howled around his ears, he desperately cried out in terror: "Holy Mother of God, please help me!" Suddenly his boat was mysteriously lifted above the raging seas and placed in the quiet inlet at the foot of the mountain.

The fisherman's family, realizing that the fierce storm would crush his small boat, was deep in prayer for him when the fisherman burst into the cottage. "The Blessed Mother saved me!" he cried. Ever after, the people of the port city began to refer to the incident as a miracle. In thanksgiving, they erected a small chapel on the summit, dedicating it to Our Lady Help of Mariners. The chapel remains to this day as a place of gratitude, praise, and worship.

MOTHER MOST GRACIOUS: BLESSED REGINALD OF ORLEANS, A.D. 1220

Amazing cures, conversions, and scientific breakthroughs flow from the minds and hands of those who become devoted to Mary through the prayers of the Holy Rosary. Our Lady herself, it is said, appeared to Saint Dominic and handed him the Holy Rosary as an instrument of light for all spiritually dark times.[9] It has always been so. Consider the life experiences of Reginald, an erudite and worldly professor of canon law at the University of Paris in the early thirteenth century. He became personally acquainted with the great preacher, Saint Dominic.

Miracles associated with the rosary were so prolific in his times that even Professor Reginald, renowned as a proud intellectual, decided to indulge himself in the devotion. He, too, began to pray the rosary but mostly as a curious experiment rather than a sincere prayer. Being a true intellectual, he also read Scriptural passages associated with each mystery of the Holy Rosary. The two pursuits, prayerful reading of Scripture and disciplined meditation on its meaning, led him unexpectedly to deep intimacy with Christ. The rosary centered him on the real Presence of Jesus in the Word, the Eucharist, and in community.

Reginald began to attend evening Mass daily at the Cathedral of Paris. Gradually, the professor found himself so immersed in the life of Christ as he meditated upon the mysteries of the Holy Rosary, and afterward, entered deeply into the holy sacrifice of the Mass, that entire nights would sometimes pass before Reginald realized he was still in the Cathedral. By praying the Holy Rosary correctly, Professor Reginald journeyed beyond his intellect, a labyrinth with many avenues of deception, to that sanctuary of pure beauty where all is one in the Heart of Christ. Through the mercy of Christ, Reginald awakened to the depths of Jesus' presence in the holy sacrifice of the Mass.

Reginald went to Saint Dominic for counsel. He realized that embracing a life of voluntary poverty was more a life of authentic freedom than deprivation. Numinous, astute Dominic recognized the spiritual giant Reginald was becoming. After a period of prayer and discernment, Dominic suggested that the professor consider vowed membership in the Dominican Order of Preachers.

Before he was able to comply with the requirements for admission to the Order of Preachers, Reginald fell mortally ill in Rome. The amelioration of Saint Dominic's disappointment rested in his immense confidence in God's mercy. He prayed fervently for the life of the intellectual aspirant to his Order.

One bright, crisp day, while Dominic was praying fervently, the Blessed Virgin Mary appeared to Reginald. Two women, Saint Catherine of Alexandria and Saint Cecilia, accompanied her. The Mother of God approached the bed where Reginald lay dying. Speaking unknown words, she ever so gently made the sign of the cross on his eyes, ears, nose, mouth, hands, and feet. Our Blessed Mother then granted Reginald a vision of a rough, white robe with the words: "Behold the habit of your Order."[10]

Reginald was filled with such strength, longing, and love that his soul instantly returned to the Empyrean heights of ecstasy. Our Blessed Mother was with him. So also were the angels and saints. Reginald was totally aware that he and the others were fully in the wonder-filled presence of God.

Of course, Reginald was cured. And he was later ordained a Dominican friar. Over the years, Reginald's vision of the scapular habit was tangible evidence to him of his apparition of the Blessed Mother.

Saint Dominic regarded Reginald's miraculous healing as evidence of God's providence for the Order of Preachers. Reginald, however, in consummate humility, prevailed upon Dominic to keep his apparitions, mystical gifts, and blessings secret. Saint Dominic did so, but, faithful son of the Mother of God that he was, the founder replaced the linen surplices of his Friars with rough, woolen scapulars similar to the one Reginald was shown by our Blessed Mother. The reason for the change in the Friar habit remained undisclosed until after Reginald's death. The Church beatified him centuries ago, calling him Blessed Reginald of the Order of Preachers.

When Joseph, John the Baptist, the Shepherds, and the Wise Men honored Mary, she gave them the delight of their hearts, Jesus Christ. Angels communicated to these men how to respond to Mary and her Son. As we honor our Blessed Mother, we also receive those gifts.[11] Mary, our Mother, the Lady of the Apocalypse, brings us Light so that we may enter into the depths of the mystery of divinity. Our Blessed Mother, if we allow her, will take us to her Son, our Brother Jesus who promises us:

> "I Am The Way, And The Truth, And The Life; No one comes to the Father but through me. Whoever has seen me has seen the Father. It is the Father who lives in me accomplishing his works. Believe me that I am in the Father and the Father is in me. He who obeys the commandments he has from me is the man who loves me. He who loves me will be loved by my Father. I too will love him and reveal myself to him. As the Father has loved me, so I have loved you. You will live in my love if you keep My commandments, even as I have kept my Father's commandments, and live in his love. This is my commandment; love one another as I have loved you."[12]

Our Blessed Mother is the safest, fastest, easiest way to the Heart of Christ.[13] Jesus, ever the faithful Son, honors His Mother's children and, always, her requests of him. The Bible is quite clear about that.[14]

To please His mother, Jesus changed water into wine at the wedding feast of Cana.[15] Mary showed us how Jesus responds to the power of faith and hope, grounded in love at that wedding feast. Faith and hope are majestic virtues that lead us to true love steeped in the enlightenment of God's Presence. Mary, the promised woman of Genesis 3:15, is the hope of the world. Her faith is enough for us. Her Son is the Savior all people seek. Jesus is Love Incarnate.

MOTHER INVIOLATE: INDIA: VAILANKANNI, A.D. 1560

God can never be outdone in generosity. Who has ever given the Savior more than His fully human Blessed Mother Mary? She knows the rewards of offering milk to the Redeemer. The ancient shrine of Vailankanni has a miraculous history that dates back to 1560, when a young shepherd was asked to fetch some milk for his master. The child did so, but it was hot and he was tired so he stopped to rest in the shade of a tree near a pond. He was awakened from his slumber by a vision of the Blessed Virgin Mary holding the Infant Jesus in her arms. She smiled at the boy and asked him to share a bit of milk with Baby Jesus. After the Christ Child drank, Mary gratefully thanked the young shepherd and the vision faded. The boy experienced such a personal taste of unconditional love that he exhilaratingly skipped back to his master. However, having shared the milk in his jug with the Christ Child, there was little left. Not surprisingly, the boy's master did not believe his story. But when the lid was taken off the milk jug, according to the official Web site of the shrine, it miraculously began to run over with milk. Ever since, the pond where the shepherd boy's vision took place has been a popular shrine. Miracles abound, we are told, in this place.

Toward the end of the sixteenth century, Mary once again visited the Shrine of Vailankanni. This time the Blessed Mother, "Health of the Sick" holding Baby Jesus in her arms, appeared to a sickly widow's crippled son who supported his mother by selling buttermilk. Mary, "Seat of Wisdom" asked the suffering boy for a cup of buttermilk for Jesus. Astonished at her contagious love for the Christ Child, he lovingly handed her the buttermilk. As the Divine Child drank, Mary, "Comfort of the Afflicted" quietly asked Baby Jesus to heal the boy. And Mary, "Mother of Our Savior" graciously thanked the cripple for his generosity. She, who is called "Cause of Our Joy," asked the boy to visit a rich nobleman in another town and request a shrine at that very place.

The boy was overcome with sorrow, for his infirmity made it impossible for him to travel such distance. Mary, "Gate of Heaven" placed the tiny palm of Baby Jesus' hand on the boy's forehead and firmly invited him to get up and walk. Only then did the cripple realize that his withered legs were amazingly strong and his entire body was muscular, powerful. The boy's physical strength was the talk of the small town for the rest of his life and the Blessed Mother and her Divine Son were much revered because of his mysterious cure. People often spoke of Christ's delight in buttermilk and one can only imagine how popular the drink must have been with aspiring athletes.

Eventually the young man remembered Our Lady's desires for a shrine, so he made the journey to the nobleman's house. There he was greeted with great joy and enthusiasm, for the nobleman was expecting him. Mysteriously, the devout man had experienced many dreams of the Holy Mother of God, so vivid that he knew exactly what Mary, "Queen of All Saints" expected of him. The nobleman, ebullient with love and devotion, had a beautiful chapel built at Vailankanni on the site where the Basilica stands today.

Yet another miracle from Our Lady, Mother of Good Health occurred at the Shrine of Vailankanni in the nineteenth century. A group of Portuguese sailors encountered fierce storms traveling from Macao, China. In desperation they beseeched Mary's help for they knew of her title "Star of the Sea." The frantic sailors vowed to build a church in her honor wherever she led them, if only Mary, "Help of God's People" would save them from the angry sea's treachery. And she did. After washing ashore near Vailankanni on Our Lady's birthday, September 8, the exhilarated men fell on their knees in thanksgiving.

A group of locals, recognizing that the sailors were Christian, directed them to Mary's shrine. True to their promise, the rescued sailors constructed a larger brick shrine in honor of Our Lady's miraculous intercessory power with God. Throughout their lives, they made several more trips to Vailankanni to enrich the shrine with treasures they acquired in China and places along the way.

Then on December 26, 2004, as the coastlines of southern Asia were being devastated by a tsunami, the village of Vailankanni was not spared. Two thousand pilgrims were attending Mass in the Basilica of the Shrine. Terrifying tsunami winds and waves overwhelmed the village, killing thousands. The tsunami, however, did not touch the Basilica. Everyone inside was spared. According to BBC reports, the shrine was the only building to escape devastation. Buildings on the same elevation further away from the shore were destroyed. Inside the Basilica, everything and everyone remained entirely dry. Shrine officials did not hesitate to call the event miraculous.

More than a thousand people perished within a one-kilometer radius of the Basilica when the tsunami, triggered by a magnitude 9 earthquake deep within the Indian Ocean, hit the coast. The miracle became even more profound over the next few days as barefoot volunteers, faces covered with surgical masks to mitigate the stench of rotting bodies, helped remove the dead from the areas surrounding the shrine.[16]

Less than four years later, on November 26, 2008, armed men attacked a Mumbai rail station and in little more than an hour, violence spread to hotels and restaurants heavily populated with foreign tourists, as well as to government buildings and hospitals, a Jewish center, and a newspaper office. For three days, the city was under siege with hostages and victims stashed away in smoking buildings. More than 180 people were killed and upward of 300 were injured. Though there were only about ten gunmen, these terrorists demonstrated that a small, highly trained gang could paralyze one of the world's major cities. The prime minister of India later accused Pakistan "of using terrorism as a policy tool and said the attackers had official Pakistani support."[17]

It is not surprising that India, a nuclear power climbing out of ancient ways and methods, is the beneficiary of Mary's protective presence now.[18] The people of India really need her. There is latent magnificence about India. Just one example is the intricate stonework and carving found throughout the Taj Mahal, built in 1631 by Shaw Jahan to honor his wife Mumtaz Mahal. The sari worn by Indian women dates back to the Indus Valley in ancient times and is customarily made of the finest cotton or silk interwoven with gold and silver thread. The gem palace in Jaipur displays tens of generations of traditional and contemporary Indian jewelry of emeralds, diamonds, rubies, 22-carat handcrafted gold reflecting the Indian philosophy that adornment must be beautiful from the front as well as the back. Blending Hindu, Islamic, and Christian styles, India is a land of natural beauty, with diverse people of hopes and dreams, whose lives are interwoven with desolation and opportunity. It is Mary's territory now. Expect great things for men, women, and children. As gender bias dissolves, harmony yields refreshing beauty.

The Blessed Mother has preemptive rights to help, guide, and protect her consecrated children. Such luminaries as the late Pope John Paul II and Mother Teresa of Calcutta are but two examples of those who freely entrusted themselves and their lives to our Blessed Mother.[19] Mary's life is filled with mystery and majesty, and she longs to share her munificence with us. The Blessed Mother loves Jesus Christ perfectly; she is His first and most distinguished disciple. Mother of the Word made flesh, Mary loves us, too, with that perfect love and is here to help us know God more intimately and love God more dearly. Our Blessed Mother's exquisite graciousness guarantees that she will never impose upon us. Even Jesus Christ, the Son of God sent His Angel Gabriel to *ask* Mary to be His mother.

We, too, have the privilege of asking Mary to be our hands-on Spiritual Mother Most Loving. She is truly "The Cause of Our Joy," for our Blessed Mother knows Jesus as no other human and she is aware of the deepest longings of our hearts. From the cross, when He entrusted His mother to John, the disciple who loved Him, Jesus had that entrustment in mind for us, too.[20] The more we draw near to Mary, this "House of God," the closer we come to Christ. He who holds the world in the palm of His hand enriches and ennobles everything that belongs to Him. His Mother's children are the apple of His eye.

MOTHER OF OUR SAVIOR: SAFE PLACES

We are learning that certain locations dedicated to our Blessed Mother Mary are special places where our prayers are answered. There will be more incidences like the tsunami. There always are. Shock and suffering, just like joy and surprise, often come when we least expect.

Jesus Christ told us that God is ever reclaiming His Kingdom on earth. God knows all things. God loves us. We have nothing to fear. But we are wise to expect the unexpected. We prosper as we allow Mary's pure mother love to nourish us into fully developed members of the heavenly kingdom all around us.

One remarkable example of Mary's guidance over a century ago that continues to enrich beneficiaries of the medical community of the twenty-first century is the eleven-hundred bed Saint Mary's Hospital, the surgery center of the Mayo Clinic Health System in Rochester, Minnesota. This eminent medical center grew out of the devastation of a natural disaster.

MARIA CATHERINE JOSEPHINE MOES AND DR. WILLIAM WORRELL MAYO

On August 21, 1883, a huge tornado left many residents of the farming village of Rochester, Minnesota, injured and homeless. One courageous woman, Maria Catherine Josephine Moes, a native of Luxembourg, garnered all her fortitude to assemble a nursing team to care for the injured. Her Methodist neighbor, Dr. William Worrell Mayo, was one of the most skilled surgeons in the region, even though he was also a steamboat officer, justice of the peace, and surveyor, and she enlisted his help. In those times, surgery was performed on kitchen tables and Dr. Mayo frequently asked his sons Will and Charlie to help him with the largely bloody pursuit. Maria, a Franciscan nun, cared for forty victims of the tornado with the assistance of teaching Sisters of her congregation.

During that time, Maria experienced the call of God to establish a healing center dedicated to our Blessed Mother in the area. Known professionally as Sister Alfred of the Franciscan Sisters of Our Lady of Lourdes, she talked of such an undertaking with Dr. Mayo. He, of course, balked. He believed the city was too small to support a hospital. He mentioned that most citizens of the town perceived hospitals as places where people go to die. But Sister Alfred knew better. A devout missionary who had come to the United States to be Mary's heart and hands in the new world for the glory of Jesus Christ, Sister Alfred believed that God's healing touch is administered through each of us to one another.

Dr. Mayo had experience with medical practices in various hospitals of the day. He understood why people considered them holding pens for the dying. The Sisters had other ideas. They extracted a promise from Dr. Mayo that he would take charge of the healing center if they would build a hospital dedicated to life, not death. He, of course, was skeptical, but resonated deeply with the concept of medicine as a key to healthy, holistic living.

The Sisters' prayers, trust in Mary's intercessory power with her Son Jesus, and hard work paid off. By 1888, construction on the healing hospital was under way. Dr. Mayo and his sons staffed the Mayo Clinic, along with Sister Alfred's congregation of nurses who believed that care of the sick is a high calling from God.

Today, the Mayo Clinic Health Center is a testimony to the highest ideals of medicine. It is a place where the patient comes first. Employees of this nonprofit, nondenominational healing center are trained to provide excellence in the art and science of medicine in a quiet, cultured environment conducive to the healing of body, mind, and spirit. Patients come from all over the world. In 1986, Mayo Clinic Medical Center was officially recognized as the largest non-profit medical organization in the United States. Its healing mission has remained intact. Mayo Clinic has "evolved from a founding group of Franciscan sisters whose dominant attributes included a focused determination, selfless commitment, compassion, advocacy for the sick and disadvantaged, understanding and respect, intolerance of waste, and the appreciation of talent and competence."[21] These characteristics shaped the Mayo Clinic's culture and influenced its perception of its mission and how to pursue it.

As we discover how to draw nearer to Mary, our Mother Most Lovable, we become aware that we are truly animated from within. All life flows from the loving hand of the Great God of Abraham who desires only the best for us. Love lightens any burden. Health and wealth and happiness and peace flow from consciousness of our souls singing in harmony with other pure beings of light, the angels and saints all around us who help us, encourage us, cheer us on. Love and gratitude and healing are interdependent and contagious. The Mighty One does great things for us through hidden Mary, Mother Most Admirable.

Mary brings blessings of love and peace and health and prosperity: her sacred secrets renew, invigorate, and inspire those who are fortunate enough to know about them. Everyone needs our Blessed Mother's sacred secrets: many are wise enough to want them, and willing to learn them and put them into practice.

Our Blessed Mother speaks clearly of eternal mysteries written upon our hearts. We do long to bask in our Spiritual Mother's heaven-sent maternal-love. Mary, Theotokas,[22] is the bearer of God's unconditional love for us, spoiling us as it were with her merited rewards and mitigating with her intercessory prayer just chastisements that await us. Our Blessed Mother brings the best to our lives, our dreams, our desires.

Few of us understand God's "unconditional" love and most of us don't truly know what heaven might be. As for chastisements, whatever they are, they are part of life. Every one of us has our share of difficulties. We truly are wise to cling to Mary, who stood with her Divine Son Jesus during His entire life on earth. Jesus Christ shared His Blessed Mother's strength; so also may we if we would be like Jesus.

Mary is here with us now to protect us and to stand with us through all the changes, good and bad that technology, international economics, innovation, artificial intelligence, and scientific advancement bring to us as a global family. Our Mother of Good Counsel reminds us:

> *You must love one another little children.*
> *You must help one another.*
> *That is God's plan for the people of the earth.*
> *I am here to help you.*
> *Please allow me to love you into holiness.*

Three children visionaries of Fatima. From left: Blessed Jacinta, Lucia, Blessed Francisco

CHAPTER 4

Mother Most Admirable

Mary, the apostles and disciples *"went up into an upper room,
where abode Peter, and John, James and Andrew, Phillip and
Thomas, Bartholomew and Matthew, James of Alpheus, and Simon
Zelotes, and Jude, the brother of James. All these were persevering in
prayer with one mind with the women, and Mary the Mother of
Jesus, and with his brethren."*[1]

Community prayer is powerful. Mary's Son prayed and taught His followers to pray together. Prayer opens our hearts and minds to the
sacred spirit world all around us. Mary, the apostles, and disciples
prayed with one mind. Mary prays for us always. We, like the apostles and disciples, are wise to pray with Mary with one mind.

Angels and saints pray together before the Throne of God. They
pray for us and with us, too.[2] These celestial beings of beauty and
light usually accompany our Blessed Mother during her appearances
on earth.

THE GUARDIAN ANGEL OF PORTUGAL

Sister Lucia (1907–2005), the last living visionary of Fatima, reached
old age in her Carmelite convent.[3] As the decades of her long life
unfolded, the visionary disclosed extensive personal knowledge and
familiarity with the Guardian Angel of Portugal. Lucia first encountered this mighty celestial being when she was ten years old. She and

her two younger cousins, eight-year-old Francisco Marto and his sister, six-year-old Jacinta, were busy at play when suddenly they observed a strange cloud formation in the sky. It fascinated the children and they watched it intently. Most suddenly, and without warning, a great, luminous angel emerged out of the cloud formation and identified himself to the children as the Guardian Angel of Portugal. "Pray! Pray much," he commanded them. With the Blessed Sacrament suspended in the air, the glorious angel prostrated himself on the ground and recited this prayer:

> O most Holy Trinity, Father, Son and Holy Spirit, I adore Thee profoundly. I offer Thee the most precious Body, Blood, Soul and Divinity of Jesus Christ, present in all the tabernacles of the world, in reparation for the outrages, sacrileges and indifference by which He is offended. By the infinite merits of the Sacred Heart of Jesus and the Immaculate Heart of Mary, I beg the conversion of poor sinners.

This celestial being appeared to Lucia many times at Fatima, and possibly for the rest of her life. Coincidentally (and we know spiritually there are no coincidences), Sister Lucia wrote the following from her cloistered convent in Coimbra, Portugal, to help us better understand who and what Angels are, and what they do for us, especially in these Marian times.

> "Yes, my dear pilgrims, the Angels in Heaven always behold the face of Eternal Light, and in it—as in an immense mirror before which everything passes—everything is present, everything remains as if carved in indelible characters: the past, the present and the future. Everything that exists and was created by God: heaven and hell, the earth, the stars, the sun, the moon, worlds known and unknown, all animate and inanimate beings, absolutely everything, receives its being and life from the wish, the power, the knowledge and the wisdom of that Infinite Light which is God, the one and only Source from which is derived all life that exists, and of which every other light and life is no more than a tiny particle, a pale reflection, one of His sparks.

Thus, the Angels in Heaven, gazing into this mirror of Light, which is God, in Him see all things, know all things, and understand all things through their complete union with God and their participation in His gifts."[4]

The Guardian Angel of Portugal continued to appear to the visionary children of Fatima. Each visit marked a time of communication between the intellects of the little shepherd children and the angel's pure intellect. The children began to experience eternal depths hidden in vast chambers within their souls, accessible only by supernatural prayer. Such prayer is not words but deep, unyielding communication with God. The angel, in union with the entire celestial court, helped the children to pray with one mind; in so doing, they entered more consciously into the omnipresence of God. Afterward, their connection to the earth became totally sacrificial.

Their families noticed that the children seemed quiet and more reserved, as if in deep concentration that none could disturb. Yet the children never disclosed their heavenly coach.[5] The great angel was preparing the little visionaries to welcome Mary, their spiritual mother, the New Eve and Eternal Mother of the Human Race. And of course, Mary would prepare the little children to receive her Divine Son, the Lord of Hosts in a most unique and intimate manner.

OUR LADY OF FATIMA

Europe was involved in a bloody war when the three Portuguese shepherd children from Aljustrel received apparitions of our Blessed Mother at Cova da Iria, near Fatima, a city 110 miles north of Lisbon. The apparitions occurred between May 13 and October 13, 1917. Portugal, having overthrown its monarchy in 1910, was in political turmoil at the time and the government disbanded religious organizations. Such anticlerical political activity was not a deterrent to Mary's apparitions in that country.

Our Lady of Fatima requested the children to return to the Cova da Iria on the thirteenth of each month for the next six months for the sake of the whole world. She especially asked them to pray and meditate on the Holy Rosary "to obtain peace for the world and the end of the war." Mary also asked the illiterate peasant children to learn to read and write, though the practice was uncommon in their village. Their joyful obedience to our Blessed Mother is a wake-up call for every child in these times. The little visionaries prayed constantly and meditated with all their hearts on the mysteries of the Holy Rosary. And they diligently learned to read and write. In that way, they were able to access the sweetness of Sacred Scripture. Our Blessed Mother requested the little children to pray and do penance for poor sinners everywhere; for the conversion of Russia (which had overthrown Czar Nicholas II that year and was soon to fall under totalitarian communist rule), and for mitigation of the horrors of World War Two. God answers the prayers of innocent little children, though we know not when or in what way.

Our Lady showed the children visions of hell where poor sinners go who have no one to pray and do penance for them.[6] The reality of hell was so terrible that the little ones embraced penances beyond their natural strength and endurance. Our Lady showed the children the earth as God's testing ground; they recognized the goodness of God and marveled at His gifts to His beloved people. They saw how God's love purifies and unites willing souls. The children learned that chastisement helps mankind shed the lava of hell. Chastisement removes graven images. Chastisement destroys golden calves. God is justice. God is pure. God is love. God is mercy.

Our Lady, Mediatrix of all Grace imparted glorious understanding of who Jesus is to the little children. The image of the invisible God,[7] Jesus took upon Himself the sins of everyone. He paid the price for all the sin in the world—past, present, and future. The little children visionaries chose to do penance in union with Jesus with love and joy so that others might come to know and love God. They learned that only those who trust God's mercy are able to repent. Those who find the courage to repent encounter Jesus through His mercy. Those who do not repent encounter Jesus through His justice. To hold on to sin is to reject God. Merciful Jesus was ridiculed, misjudged, and crucified that all of us might enjoy the rewards of Heaven. His wounds are badges of honor in the heavenly kingdom. He turns no one away who humbly comes to Him with a contrite heart.

With such knowledge, the children visionaries' love for poor sinners grew stronger than the powers of hell. Our Lady showed them that God's mercy is the garment that shields everyone from the blood of hell. Supernaturally obedient, the little visionaries responded heroically to our Blessed Mother's invitation to pray and do penance for poor sinners. Our Lady's call from Fatima to everyone on earth has not changed.

Francisco received a special spiritual gift during his apparitions of the Blessed Mother. Ever after, he spent untold hours hidden in his little village church communing with Jesus, truly present in the Blessed Sacrament. He and Jacinta, unbeknown to their parents, mystically united themselves to Jesus on the cross. They embraced penance and fasted so strenuously that their immune systems became compromised. As Our Lady had warned him, Francisco died of influenza in his family home less than two years later. He was buried in the parish cemetery and then later in 1952, reburied in the Fatima basilica. Jacinta, too, died of influenza soon after in Lisbon, mystically uniting all the pain of her final suffering with Jesus on the cross. (She endured lung surgery without the benefit of anesthesia.) Jacinta accepted heroic penance with astonishing fervor; the child had sagacious awareness of the spiritual value of human suffering mystically united to the sufferings of Christ on the cross for the salvation of souls. Her body was later found to be incorrupt, beautiful, and grown to about fifteen years of age.

Their cousin Lucia became a Carmelite nun and was still living when Jacinta and Francisco were beatified in 2000. She was a close confidant of popes, bishops, and cardinals, and most especially Pope John Paul II. Sister Lucia died in February 2005 at the age of ninety-seven. On February 13, 2008, the third anniversary of Lucia's death, Pope Benedict XVI officially placed the last Visionary of Fatima, known in religious circles as Sister Mary of the Immaculate Heart on the "fast track" to sainthood, and rightfully so.[8]

FATIMA SECRETS

The shrine of Our Lady of Fatima is visited by tens of millions of people. People throughout the world have patiently awaited the

Vatican's promulgation of Mary's Fatima secrets. In 1960, Pope John XXIII read the Third Secret and made a geopolitically astute decision not to reveal its contents. A product of the Vatican Diplomatic Corps, he had vast knowledge of global terror flowing from Cold War issues that affect nations, races, and ethnic groups. The contents of the Third Secret of Fatima were so uniquely provocative that he put it once again under Papal Seal. Although he was of advanced years, Pope John XXIII responded to the treacherous times by convening the great and highly controversial Vatican Council II. The contents of the Third Secret were subsequently shared with all his successors to the Chair of Saint Peter: they, too, chose to keep its contents under Papal Seal.

Some of the contents of the Third Secret of Fatima occasionally leaked. Twenty years later, in 1980, Pope John Paul II confided to a German audience:

"Because of the seriousness of its contents, in order not to encourage the world wide power of Communism to carry out certain coups, my Predecessors in the Chair of Peter have diplomatically preferred to withhold its publication. On the other hand, it should be sufficient for all Christians to know this much: if there is a message in which it is said that the oceans will flood entire sections of the earth; that, from one moment to the other, millions of people will perish . . . there is no longer any point in really wanting to publish this secret message. Many want to know merely out of curiosity, or because of their taste for sensationalism, but they forget that 'to know' implies for them a responsibility. It is dangerous to want to satisfy one's curiosity only, if one is convinced that we can do nothing against a catastrophe that has been predicted."

Pope John Paul II then held up his rosary and said:

"Here is the remedy against the evil! Pray, pray and ask for nothing else. Put everything in the hands of the Mother of God! . . . We must be prepared to undergo great trials in the not-too-distant future; trials that will require us to be ready to give up

even our lives, and a total gift of self to Christ and for Christ. . . .
Through your prayers and mine, it is possible to alleviate this
tribulation, but it is no longer possible to avert it, because it is
only in this way that the Church can be effectively renewed.
How many times, indeed, has the renewal of the Church been
effected in blood? This time, again, it will not be otherwise. . . .
We must be strong, we must prepare ourselves, we must entrust
ourselves to Christ and to His holy Mother, and we must be attentive, very attentive, to the prayer of the Rosary."[9]

Prayers and meditations of the Holy Rosary help us to know Jesus in
spirit and truth. If we do not know Jesus in that way, we will be unable to choose Him and His ways in our daily lives. Jesus brings re-
lief in conflict for those who trust His ways. The longings of mankind
are often fickle. For those who are rooted in Christ's Heart there is
only peace. Our Lady wants us to know His ways and trust His
power in all circumstances.

In June 2000, Pope John Paul II finally released what was called
the Third Secret of Fatima. Though brief, it warned of tribulation
for the world and persecution of believers, including a Papal assassination. Pope John Paul II actually had survived an assassin's bullets
on May 13, 1982. He personally believed that Our Lady of Fatima,
whose feast day it was, saved his life. Pope John Paul II spent the rest
of his Pontificate spreading Mary's messages of peace through trust
in Christ's ways around the world. He proclaimed to all nations that
global peace is a divine gift possible only through strong faith in
God's love, fervent prayer, generous penance, and sincere fasting:
these spiritual tools lead to reconciliation between God and man;
then reconciliation between man and man is possible.

Some believe that the Third Secret of Fatima has yet to be fully
revealed or fulfilled, while others continue to believe that the full
details of the Third Secret may have actually been disclosed.[10] There
is little doubt that the Vatican is committed to disclosure of the secrets of Fatima and high-ranking curia encourage people to live up
to the commitments asked by Our Lady.[11]

Mary comes to us, in all her apparitions, at God's bidding to help us avoid filling our bodies and souls with the refuse of the earth. Gifts that flow to earth from Mary's apparitions throughout the ages, and particularly at Fatima in 1917, do bear sweet fruit throughout the world. Our Blessed Mother's sacred secrets carry gifts for all creation. In this Third Millennium, Mary, Mother of God brings anew to this explosive time the light and healing power of God's unconditional love for the whole world.

MEDJUGORJE

A vibrant, handsome, and deeply loved grandfather had a sudden stroke that left him paralyzed. His family was devastated. It was painful, wrenching to see the man everyone so admired drooling and helpless in his bed. His bewildered grandchildren looked on, their parents stifled sobs and the pitiful man could not respond at all. Though he seemed to know nothing, the elderly man clung to the gold medal of Our Lady of Fatima that his grieving wife kept securely pinned upon his hospital gown. His middle daughter, Deborah (not her real name), was more stalwart than the others and she vowed to find a miracle for her father. The doctors whom she consulted patiently explained that her father's condition was hopeless. Not to be deterred, Deborah went on line searching for miracles.

Medjugorje in Bosnia-Herzegovina (the former Yugoslavia) seemed the logical place to go to find miracles. Never before in recorded Marian history has it ever been reported all over the world that Our Lady appears daily for so long a period of time to so many chosen seers with such a profound impact worldwide as she is allegedly doing in Medjugorje. For nearly thirty years, it is said the "Gospa" (Croatian word for Blessed Mother) appears daily in the quiet, rural village of Medjugorje, Bosnia-Herzegovina. This unprecedented series of apparitions to six youths (two boys and four girls), and later by inner locution to two more young girls, began in June of 1981. Our Lady, it is reported, continues to appear to three of the Medjugorje visionaries every day with one overriding objective: to bring the world back to God. The messages are poignant and urgent as our Blessed Mother allegedly reveals that these are her final ap-

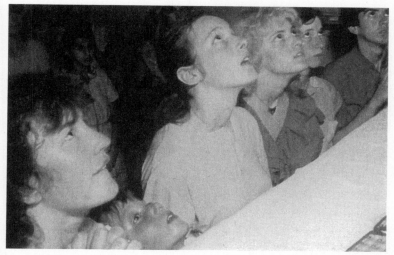

The six visionaries of Medjugorje in 1981, during an apparition of the Blessed Virgin Mary as Queen of Peace. From left: Vicka (16), Jacov (9), Ivanka (16), Mirjana (15), Marija (15), and Ivan (15). This apparition allegedly continues daily to three of the visionaries: Marija, Ivan, and Vicka. Mirjana, Ivanka and Jacov continue to see the Blessed Mother at least annually.

paritions on earth in this way.[12] The visionaries say Mary pleads with everyone to return to God immediately for after certain secrets unfold, those who are still alive will have little time to do so.[13] All that is not seen will be seen throughout the world as the first secret of Medjugorje begins commencement.

The Resurrection of Mary's son Jesus Christ blazes through the pages of human history bringing meaning to bloodstained events that shatter men's dreams and goals. Suffering can be valuable. Resurrection is inevitable. Medjugorje is living proof. Medjugorje pilgrims, not all of course, but many often see the sun spin; the metal of their rosary beads mysteriously turns gold and they see rainbows (though there is no rain) fill the sky. Many are healed of physical, psychological, and spiritual maladies. Those of goodwill receive the gift of peace.

But Medjugorje is far away from Pittsburgh and Deborah was well aware that the apparition site was located in the center of a war zone. Deborah was both fascinated and concerned that the Mother of Jesus would be appearing in a war zone. Though Deborah had little if any faith (that she was aware of), her heartache about her sick father overrode her disbelief. And so she continued to search for miracles. As her father's condition became more pathetic, Deborah prayed more and more. Not real prayers, she would later say. Just cries from her anguished heart that "Someone up there" would help her dad. Finally Deborah decided to take the risk and go to Medjugorje for her father and ask Mary for a miracle for him.

SHRINE OF THE IMMACULATE CONCEPTION

Deborah began to vigorously research the Blessed Virgin Mary online. And she found "Mary's Shrine": The Basilica of the National Shrine of the Immaculate Conception in Washington, D.C. Something happened to Deborah as she looked at the images of Mary in the Shrine. A quiet longing to be with her spiritual mother became almost an obsession. So Deborah got in her car and drove five hours from Pittsburgh to the great Marian basilica in Washington, D.C. Little did she know then that more miracles are wrought in that shrine than at any other place on earth.

In 1857, when Thomas J. Shahan was born, his family did not suspect that he would grow up to become a founder of the great American National Shrine of the Immaculate Conception. First he was ordained a Catholic priest. Then he became a bishop. Through the years, his heart burned with desire to honor the Mother of Jesus Christ in a most special way. He prayed for guidance to create a national shrine to honor our Blessed Mother comparable to her great sanctuaries of Europe. This became his life's dream. He was so on fire with zeal that he journeyed to Rome in 1913 to present his vision to Pope Pius X. The Pope not only gave his enthusiastic support, but also a personal contribution to begin the project. Americans of every background joined the project.

It is widely accepted that miracles and cures are prolific and bountiful at the National Shrine of the Immaculate Conception in Washington, D.C.[14] Mary did not appear and ask for the shrine: her faithful children from all over the world came together in great love and sacrifice to build their Blessed Mother a magnificent basilica in the capital of the United States. Jesus, of course, is aware of that love and sacrifice to honor His Holy Mother. God cannot be outdone in generosity. Mary's intercession on our behalf is most effective in that sacred place of worship.

Deborah found consolation she never believed possible in the Shrine of the Immaculate Conception in Washington, D.C. She prayed in the vast shrine for several hours, totally certain she was in God's House. And she received an amazing phone call from her mother, who informed her that her father had shocked the doctors and staff, and become well again. "Dad is well?" she heard herself gasp into her cell phone. "Yes, Mom, I believe!" was all she could tearfully mutter as she ever so silently approached the Blessed Sacrament Chapel in the National Shrine. It was time to say thank you.

We are truly safe in Mary's maternal care. Though we are sinners, broken by life's uncertainties, Mary clothes us in her knowledge; Mary dresses us in her virtues; Mary feeds us choice morsels of wisdom from the Heavenly Banquet where she is seated at her Divine Son's right hand; Mary mends our broken hearts with great graces from the Heart of Christ; Mary cradles us in her arms and sings us gentle songs; Mary teaches us to play; Mary gives us joys of such immense beauty that our hearts spontaneously sing before the Trinity, merging as clear bells calling all lost children to the Throne of God our Father for the last time. Mary prays with us; Mary praises with us; Mary loves with us; Mary lives with us; Mary dies with us. She is our perfect Mother who feels all our pains, assuages all our fears, comforts all our aches, enlightens our entire intellect, and protects our blessed dreams and holy desires. Mary our Mother soothes our tortured souls with sacred secrets from the mind of God.

THE GUARDIAN ANGEL OF
INTERNATIONAL BUSINESS

Mary's presence in our lives is humble and easily ignored. Yet the smallest prayer or thought of her opens vast storehouses of treasures within our souls that heal and restore our minds and bodies. Often, as the three visionaries of Fatima discovered, angels prepare us to serve God with the help of the Mother of Jesus Christ.

The second atomic bomb ever used in warfare was dropped on Nagasaki, Japan, in 1945. Hundreds of thousands died and the war with Japan ended. Coincidentally, but there are no coincidences, three and a half centuries before, twenty-six Christians, including doctors, simple artisans and servants, priests, brothers and laymen, Franciscans, Jesuits and members of the Secular Franciscan Order, catechists, old men and innocent children were brutally killed on a hill, now known as the Holy Mountain, overlooking Nagasaki. These martyrs were united in faith and love for Jesus and his Blessed Mother. As so often happens, their blood fell upon others as a fruitful rain.[15] In the 1860s, when missionaries returned to Japan, at first they found no trace of Christianity. Gradually they discovered that thousands of Christians had secretly preserved the faith and lived around Nagasaki. Many died with their Japanese brothers and sisters when the atom bomb hit in 1945.

By 1980, Japan was a highly industrialized nation that was approximately one percent Christian. Women worked side by side with men and traditional family life was in desperate transition. The old ways seemed impossible to implement when women were doing the work of men and children were an interruption to economic development. Yet people still fell in love. Old people still clung to their children. And children were being born.

In northwestern Japan, in the city of Akita, not too distant from Nagasaki, a most amazing and inexplicable series of heavenly visitations occurred from 1981 to 1984 that influenced in-the-know decision makers all over the world. Japan and much of the world was touched with Divine Grace in a special way, thanks to our Blessed Mother Mary's unique apparitions, with the miraculous help of certain angels, in Akita.

The secular mayor, high-ranking Buddhist dignitaries, Protestant officials, and the Roman Catholic Bishop of Akita officially acknowledged Mary's supernatural apparitions in their city from 1981 to 1984. This phenomenon happened fifty-six years after Mary's prophetic apparitions at Fatima, Portugal, in 1917 and simultaneously with Mary's apparitions in Medjugorje, which also began in 1981.

Our Lady of Akita was the first "Marian apparition" officially approved by the Catholic Church since Fatima.

In the 1980s, few Japanese knew about the 1917 apparitions of Our Lady of Fatima, even though Mary showed the three young children visions of the heights and depths of God's love for all His people of the earth. Mary spoke prophetically at Fatima about unnecessary suffering World Wars I and II would bring if her messages were unheeded.[16] The Blessed Mother's more recent apparitions in Japan are strikingly similar. One can hope that times are better now. Global communications are far more advanced. The twenty-first century offers mankind opportunities to respond to our Blessed Mother Mary as never before.

The visionary at Akita is not a child. Agnes Katsuko Sasagawa is middle-aged, single, and handicapped. She is a fully professed member of a Roman Catholic Religious Order, the Servants of the Eucharist. Her convent at Yuzawadai is in a village within a two-hour drive of the Akita airport. Agnes' Guardian Angel was and remains an active participant in the Blessed Mother's ongoing apparitions to Agnes Sasagawa. And so also is a most remarkable being, the Guardian Angel of International Business.

Sometimes, celestial angels take the form of living, helping persons: they appear as human beings to human eyes.[17]

In 1991, the presiding Catholic Bishop of Akita, Most Reverend John S. Ito, D.D., invited an American couple visiting in the Far East to his diocese and to the convent where Mary appeared at Yuzawadai.[18] He stressed the deep global component of Mary's messages, and asked the American couple to do all they could to help disseminate information about Mary's apparitions at Akita. Without angelic help, the following eyewitness account would not be available for us today.

"Though we had no prior intentions of stopping in Akita, Japan, on our way home from a trip to Asia in July of 1991, the Bishop of Akita insisted that we accept his invitation to investigate and disseminate information about Marian apparitions and messages in his diocese at Akita. He said he was certain that when people realize the significance for the entire world of Mary's apparitions in his diocese, they will do everything possible to spread the messages of Our Lady at Akita. Even though his beliefs were strong, we could not imagine the extraordinary manifestations that awaited us in Akita.

"Our Asian hosts graciously arranged to have our return tickets rerouted through Tokyo, with a one-day stopover that allowed us to travel to Akita. Our 747 plane was filled to capacity as we took off from Manila, en route to Tokyo. As we neared our destination, my spouse realized that a time change would occur, making our connections from Tokyo to Akita nearly impossible.

"We were scheduled to land at Narita-Tokyo International Airport at the height of rush hour. It would then be necessary to travel across town, a journey of seventy-five miles to Haneda—the domestic airport. From there we would board the last departing flight of the day to Akita in northwestern Japan.

"We asked the senior flight attendant to advise us. She studied our tickets carefully and sighed as she informed us that our connection was humanly impossible. We both should have detected a hint of God's mystery when we heard her say that our plane connections to Akita were 'humanly' impossible. But our practical training was in command. We asked about other alternatives to get to Akita that evening. The stewardess informed us that the distance from Narita-Tokyo International Airport to Akita was so great that airline connections, available only at the domestic airport, Haneda, would work for us on our tightly scheduled international stopover in Japan.

" 'Is it possible that we could land early?' we asked. 'It rarely happens' she responded. Perhaps the stewardess felt sorry for such ill-advised Americans. She kindly promised to allow us to depart the huge plane first. Then she told us if we were 'lucky' enough to have our luggage exit the plane first, and obtain seats on the helicopter from Narita-Tokyo International Airport to the Haneda domestic airport, we *might* make our connection to Akita. My incredulous spouse inhaled slowly before saying: 'What chance do you *really* think we have of getting our luggage off this 747 first?'

"I did what I usually do when situations look humanly impossible: pray and remind our Blessed Mother that we are consecrated to her. After all, we did not seek to come to Akita. Rather, the Roman

Catholic bishop requested our presence there in service to the church. I knew many stories of God's intervention in the affairs of the world when He had a point to make. I mentioned this to my spouse, as a way of calming him, but he quickly replied: 'What makes you think the Lord is even aware that we are in such a dilemma?' Before I could stop the words, I heard myself say: 'We are traveling on *His* business as servants of *His* Mother. If Almighty God wants us at Akita to-night, nothing will stop us.' My spouse was rightly troubled, but he did smile at my comment. Prom a human point of view, there was no way we could get to Akita that night. The time change made a very tight connection essentially impossible.

"We gathered our personal belongings as our jumbo jet approached Narita-Tokyo International Airport and proceeded to the front of the 747. We were the first to depart. My spouse suggested that I go to the helicopter desk and arrange for seats to the domestic airport while he procured our luggage. Then, of course, we would need to clear customs with our luggage. The lines were quite long. I quickly discovered there was no helicopter flight across town at that time. So I hurried to the baggage claim area. There stood my spouse, as astonished as I had ever seen him. Our luggage was the first off the ramp!

"A line opened and we sped through customs. Then we rushed to find a taxi. Though our cabdriver spoke no English, he understood our pressing need to get across town, more than seventy-five miles to the domestic airport. I prayed. My spouse nervously 'studied' his wristwatch. Perhaps he was praying, too. Mysteriously, we encountered no red lights or traffic jams along the way, though we were in the height of rush-hour traffic. We crossed town, from northeast Tokyo to southwest Tokyo—at best an hour and three-quarters journey, in less than fifty minutes.

"Arriving at Haneda, the domestic airport, a young Japanese woman wearing a smart uniform including a pink golf shirt, gray skirt, and black shoes was holding a pink flag as she opened our cab door and ushered us out of the car. We never communicated with her, for we do not speak Japanese. She, however, seemed to know all about us; she assigned our luggage to someone I did not see and hurriedly escorted us through the domestic airport. We did not go through airport security, we did not hand our tickets to anyone. The young woman led us to the disembarkation ramp of an All Nippon Airways jet. The door, though it had already closed for take-off, slid open. As we entered the plane, the door quickly closed behind us, the plane immediately taxied down the runway and ascended into the sky before we could reach our seats. I wondered where the luggage might be. My spouse was totally amazed. He inquired if the plane was actually en route to Akita. It was. Shortly after we fastened our seat belts, we were served a lovely meal. (That fortuity should have been a clue of coming events.) When we landed in Akita, we realized that our plane was the last one to land that day and the airport was closing. There was no one there to meet us.

"We could find no one in the airport who spoke English. All the signs were in Japanese. We followed other fellow passengers to the baggage claim area. There, in full view was our luggage. While my spouse assembled our bags, I tried to telephone the convent of the apparitions, but complex directions for using the public telephone were in Japanese. There was no cell phone service at all. My spouse then made an effort to engage a taxi to take us to the convent, but our instructions were written in English and the cabdriver could not understand where to take us.

"My weary spouse was becoming visibly upset. 'I suppose we will sleep on the sidewalk with our luggage tonight and wait for the airport to open in the morning' he ventured as guards were locking doors. Only then did I experience a moment of concern. 'Never mind,' I told him. 'We'll rent a car!' I found the Hertz counter and handed the agent my credit card. But I received only a blank stare from the agent. 'Do you speak English?' I inquired. 'May I rent a car?' There was no response. My heart began to pound and I rather desperately shouted: 'Does anyone here speak English?'

"Immediately a highly refined Japanese man stepped forward and said: 'May I be of assistance to you, Madam?'

"'Oh yes!' I exclaimed. 'Will you help me fill out the forms to rent a car?'

"'Where are you going?' he inquired. I showed him the piece of paper I was carrying with the telephone number and address of the convent at Yuzawadai.

" 'Ah yes,' he said as he bowed. 'It will not be necessary for you to rent a car. It would be my great honor to take you to this place.'

"Just then, my spouse approached the rental car counter where I was standing. The gracious Japanese gentleman by now was insisting that he personally take us to the convent. He put my spouse at ease immediately. That was highly unusual. I looked at the man again. 'This is no ordinary human being,' I realized. His blue suit was of the finest fabric, perfectly fitted. His starched white shirt and dark tie were the best. His shoes were shiny black leather. It is difficult to remember his features though he had extraordinarily kind eyes filled with compassion and a smile that warmed our hearts.

"The gentleman seemed to know that I recognized him. He turned and placed his arm around my exhausted spouse's shoulder as we walked out of the airport to his car. I was praying: 'Dear Lord, if this truly is an angel, please give me a sign. Let him have a white car.'

"I was not surprised when we approached the white car he pointed out, though to this day I do not know how our luggage got into the car. By now, I was somewhat convinced the caring man who was driving us to the convent of Akita was in fact a celestial being sent to help us. But I quickly disregarded that thought as foolishness.

"I listened carefully from the backseat as the man and my spouse spoke about many things, including global business and finance. The man's diction, vocabulary, and choice of phrases were inspiringly beautiful. His wisdom was immense. I commented on the brilliancy of his language and asked the man where he had acquired such exquisite linguistic skills. Chuckling agreeably, he did not respond.

"My unsuspecting spouse asked the man many questions. It was amazing to hear his eloquent responses. One particular conversation was logically enigmatic. He said: 'I travel much in my work.' My husband asked: 'Are you a golfer?' The gentleman replied: 'I know well the golf courses of the world. Some are truly magnificent.' When my husband asked where the most challenges might be, the man spoke of some extraordinary challenges in the Middle East. Though my spouse rightfully thought the man was speaking of golf, I believe he was speaking of global politics. My spouse asked about the difficulty (of such golf courses). The man (angel?) spoke of problems that flow from not concentrating at all times on the right thing to do. This double entendre–infused conversation continued for quite a while. The more I listened, the more impossible it was becoming to believe the man was *not* an angel. Though I tried to get my spouse's attention to alert him to the probability of a celestial companion, he had no ears to hear anything but the wisdom emanating from the man's conversation.

"Gradually I began to realize the angel was speaking to both of us about different things we each were meant to hear. My sorrow now is that I did not take notes or record the conversation, for it was filled with information about the coming of God's kingdom on earth. The man truly sounded like an angel as he ever so graciously assured us the population of the world will be Judeo-Christian. Incredulous, we asked how that could come to pass. 'It is the only international business language that makes sense,' he firmly responded. Then he looked at me in the backseat and said: 'Unless the world becomes Christianized, there will be no more family life. Without family life, there will be no purpose to life on earth at all.' We asked him if he was aware of the multitude of religions on earth, most of which have no knowledge of Christ as the Word Incarnate. He said: 'When Christians realize who Christ is, all will come to know.'

"The drive was just under two hours in duration. As we passed through the last village before arriving at the convent at Yuzawadai, I asked the gentleman to stop at the local florist so that I might purchase some flowers to bring to the sisters. He turned and looked directly at me as he authoritatively commanded: 'That will not be necessary.' I was stunned. Any lingering doubts about his identity took flight.

"We pulled into the driveway of the convent. The narrow, one-way entrance road wound up a small hill, passed the large house (convent) to a parking space for one vehicle. My spouse jumped out of the car and walked back to the convent. In the meantime, I spoke briefly to the man about a book I had with me, *Queen of the Cosmos: Interviews with the Visionaries of Medjugorje*. The man said: 'Oh yes, I know all about that book.' I was surprised, in spite of myself. 'Would you like one?' I asked, presenting a copy to him. 'Mary's messages in *Queen of the Cosmos* are for everyone, especially the lost,' he responded as he returned the book to me.

"At that moment my spouse returned to the car and amazingly stated: 'You won't believe this! A young Japanese journalist who speaks excellent English opened the convent door holding *Queen of the Cosmos* in his hand. He is reading (translating) the book to the sisters and their guests at the dinner table right now. They did not even know we were coming. Apparently the Bishop forgot to tell them.'

"I got out of the car and walked the few steps with my spouse to the door of the convent. There I met the English-speaking journalist from Tokyo. Before I could explain to my spouse that our mysterious driver might be an angel, we noticed our luggage beside us on the front porch of the convent.

"At that moment, my spouse's startled voice shocked me: 'The car is gone! There is no way that man could have driven out of here on this one-way road! How did he and the car vanish?'

"'We're here on God's business.' I sighed, realizing there is far more global significance to the apparitions of the Blessed Mother in Akita than heretofore recognized. We were learning that when God sends our Blessed Mother on a mission to the earth, His angels are overjoyed to assist her.

"Mary, Queen of All Saints is our Mother in the order of grace. During the evening meal, pilgrims at the convent were invited to stand and speak of their reasons for being there. Approximately twenty pilgrims from five continents did so. Only afterward did we realize that no one else in the group spoke English. Yet we understood one another perfectly. It was Mother Superior who told us that such experiences are normal for pilgrims of Our Lady of Akita at the convent of the Servants of the Eucharist."[19]

I am your Mother Most Faithful.
I do not disappoint.
Come and sit at my knee little ones.

I have much to disclose to you as the years go forward.
Pray little children.
Pray. Pray. Pray
Labor peacefully and courageously in the land of exile.
God's grace is sufficient for you as it was and is for me.
We are God's family.

Wooden statue of Our Lady of All Nations at the Convent of the Servants of the Eucharist at Yuzawadai, near Akita, Japan. This statue bled and wept human tears 101 times between January 4, 1975 and September 5, 1981. The Vatican's Sacred Congregation for the Preservation of the Doctrine of the Faith in Rome, Italy, headed by Joseph Cardinal Ratzinger (now Pope Benedict XVI) approved the phenomena surrounding the statue as supernatural and worthy of belief.

PART II

Queen of Prophets

SUPERNATURAL HOPE

*"When Jesus therefore had seen his Mother and the disciple
standing whom he loved, he saith to his mother, 'Woman behold
thy son.' After that, he saith to the disciple: 'Behold thy mother.'
And from that hour, the disciple took her to his own."*[1]

rinceton Scripture specialist Beverly Gaventa found that appearances of Mary in the Gospel are "longer and more strategically placed than those of any other character in the Gospels except Jesus."[2] *Time* magazine noted: "[A] growing number . . . Who are neither Catholic nor Orthodox (another branch of the faith to which Mary is central) have concluded that their various traditions have shortchanged [Mary] in the very arena in which Protestantism most prides itself: the careful and full reading of Scripture."[3]

Jesus' friends, like Saint John, the disciple whom He loved, take Mary into their hearts, culture, art, literature, architecture, music, and history. As Mary is venerated, the integrity of men, women, and children is amplified. Sacred Scripture recounts story after story of the immense kindness, steeped in unconditional love, that Jesus lavished upon men, women, and children of every background during His public life. He who is omniscient wants us to know that love lightens any burden. Of course, Mary, Queen Mother of Jesus' Sacred Heart dwells eternally in the supernatural love of her Divine Son. Our Blessed Mother longs to carry all of us into the Sacred Heart of Jesus so that we, too, may experience Divine Eternal Love.

Christ's Blessed Mother is a vital segment of God's plan for the human race: in Christ she knows the past and the future; she truly knows what is best for each one of us. Mary is forever Queen of Prophets. Prophesy shows us what can be if we do the right things; prophesy is not what *must* happen. In the final analysis, our future is always up to us. We personally choose life or death, goodness or evil, blessings or curses. Our every thought, word, and deed has consequences we must bear.

In this section, you will find more wondrous vignettes centered in our Blessed Mother's apparitions and generous intervention in difficult situations and circumstances. Those who have sought her intercession in trying times have received much solace and light. Mary never disappoints.

Because we all need to feel the loving arms of God wrapped around us, God came to us as Mary's child to embrace us and deeply bond us to His Sacred Heart. Without His blessing, life is one torture after another. Even with His blessing, life can be quite a challenge. Jesus is the best child. His Mother wants for nothing. She, who is Queen of the Heart of God by divine edict, is Queen of all Creation through, with, and in Jesus. We are blessed to have Mary as our own dear Mother most faithful, most loving; mother of our eternal life. Jesus speaks to every heart that loves. Listen and you shall hear, for the Prince of Peace is near.

> *Please allow my Mother Most Humble to bring you to Me*
> *little children of My Heart.*
> *Come to Me anew My little ones.*
> *Come to Me with humble and contrite hearts.*
> *Bring Me your woes and sorrows.*
> *I AM WHO AM.*
> *All the joys of creation are Mine to give as I choose.*
> *I reward. I punish. I give and give and give.*
> *Hear Me in the wind that calls to your hearts.*
> *See Me in the depth of the sky.*
> *Bless Me in the light of day.*
> *Rest in Me in the darkness of night.*
> *Cling to Me for I am meek and humble of heart.*
> *I am your Savior.*
> *I am your ransom.*
> *I AM WHO AM.*
> *Bless Me little ones as I bless you.*
> *Bear with one another.*
> *I see all things.*
> *I know all things.*
> *I bless and bless and bless.*

Find your peace in behavior that mirrors My love for you.
Pray and fast and bless all that happens to you during your
life on earth.
I reward. I chastise. I bind up. I renew.
I replace all that you hold dear with newness, brightness,
freshness, completeness.
Pray little ones. Pray much. Pray always.
Trust Me.
My love is your garment now and throughout all eternity.
Come to Me in the arms of My Mother Most Faithful.

Mary, Mother Most Loving

CHAPTER 5

Queen of All Saints

"And a great sign appeared in heaven: A woman clothed with the sun, and the moon under her feet, and on her head a crown of twelve stars."[1]

SECRETS AT AKITA

Mary's secrets at Akita came from Heaven in the following way. Sister Agnes, who now bears the stigmata (wounds of Christ in her hands, feet, and side), resides full-time in the convent at Akita. She told the author that in 1981, while kneeling before the Blessed Sacrament in her convent chapel in deep prayer, she heard a clear voice she had never before heard and which certainly could not have come from this world, as prayerful as gentle wind, sweet and mysterious as flowing water, distant as eternity and close as her heart. She recognized the voice of the Blessed Mother of Jesus Christ.

"I seek souls to console the great God of Abraham. . . . My Son asks me to seek souls who will offer their suffering and renunciation with His in atonement for human ingratitude. My Son and I unite with us generous souls as a gift to our Heavenly Father.

"Creation is subject to Divine Justice. Creatures reap what they sow. Rebellion against God's ways spawns evil consequences. Profane souls who are ungrateful and outrageous against God's goodness bring chastisement upon the entire human race. Consequently, a great tribulation shall befall all humanity. My Son unites His sufferings, along with mine and those souls who entrust their sufferings to us, as a love offering to Divine Justice.

"Prayer and courageous sacrifice mitigate the consequences of evil behavior. . . .

"Dear children of the world, seek holiness above all else. Offer yourselves entirely to the Lord.

"Souls are being gathered together all over the world who are willing to pray and sacrifice for others out of love for God. This remnant will become more evident as the [twentieth] Century closes. In the coming [twenty-first] century, those who love and obey God will live on in peace and abundance. The others will perish in their own evil. Be faithful and fervent in your prayers. Console the Heart of God.

"Pray with awareness of its meaning. Offer prayers for those who do not pray, who offend the kindness of God. Ask everyone throughout the world, according to their understanding, to pray as a sin offering."

MITIGATE CHASTISEMENTS

On October 13, 1983, coincidentally (and there are no coincidences), the sixty-sixth anniversary of the great cosmic miracle of the spinning sun at Fatima,[2] Sister Agnes was in the Chapel praying before the Tabernacle that housed the Blessed Sacrament. She once again heard a clear voice, prayerful as gentle wind, sweet and mysterious as flowing water, distant as eternity and close as her heart:

"Listen carefully to what I say to you . . . If the people of the earth do not improve, a terrible punishment shall afflict all humanity. It will be a punishment greater than the flood in Noah's time, such as humanity never has seen before. Fire will fall from the sky and wipe out a great part of the human race, the good as well as the evil. Neither the holy nor the faithful will be spared. Survivors will experience such misery that they will envy the dead. The only consolations that will remain for you will be the Holy Rosary and the Great Sign left by my Son. In the meantime, less onerous precursors of the dreaded event will occur all over the world as warnings and calls to repentance. Many souls are being lost in these last times. Pray the Holy Rosary every day. Pray for all people in the world. In all faiths, those who revere me are scorned and opposed. Places and objects of worship are being desecrated. Christianity is full of those who accept compromises and the demons press many consecrated souls to leave the service of the Lord. Demons are especially implacable against souls consecrated to God. The loss of so many souls deepens the grievous sorrow in my heart. As wickedness grows and immoral behavior becomes more accepted, people do not seek pardon for egregious offenses against God's love and kindness. Pray very much the prayers of the Holy Rosary. Those who place their confidence in me will be saved. My Son honors His Mother's children.[3]

AKITA VALIDATING MIRACLES

On January 4, 1975, a hand-carved, wooden statue of Our Lady of All Nations located in the convent began to weep and bleed. Between January 4, 1975, and September 15, 1981, the statue wept 101 times. Much speculation surrounded the origin of such tears. After extensive scientific investigation, experts concluded that the tears shed by the wooden statue were in fact human tears and the blood was human blood. All agreed there is no known human explanation. By 1984, the local bishop, in concert with other secular officials, declared that the events in the convent of Akita, including mystical experiences of Sister Agnes and the mysterious tears and bleeding of the statue, were of supernatural origin and worthy of belief.

The twentieth century lumbered to a close and the world prepared for a technological breakdown that has not yet happened. A Wall Street lawyer who worked at the World Trade Center grew up with love for Our Lady of Fatima. In the early 1990s, he became aware of the messages of Our Lady of Akita. The attorney had enough experience to know the harsh reality of life's uncertainty, and so he took up his rosary, long ago abandoned for more exciting uses of his time, and began to pray fervently for his own soul, and for his family.

When the planes hit his building on September 11, 2001, he ran out of the bombed World Trade Center through the smoking rubble clinging to his rosary. Body parts fell upon him; he tripped over metal debris from the fallen planes; his eyes, scorched from the burning fuel, were nearly blind, his breath came in coughs filled with blood. He experienced fire falling from the sky and knew that it was wiping out a great number of his friends and coworkers. Would he be next, he wondered. Remembering Our Lady's warning at Akita that the good as well as the evil would die together, he didn't know of which category he was a member. He prayed as never before, not knowing how long he could survive as he stumbled through the wreckage, bearing more and more injuries. His horror increased as he personally experienced our Blessed Mother's Akita warning: "Survivors will experience such misery that they will envy the dead."

Summoning his last vestige of strength before he blacked out, he prayed: "Mary my Mother, please take care of my family." He awoke in a hospital. His eyesight was amazingly restored over time and his lung damage left no permanent infirmity. His scars are reminders of his miraculous gift, and he believes September 11, 2001, is a harbinger of things to come. He thanks God often for Mary's prophetic presence in the world.

Our Blessed Mother among us is a wonderful sign that God has high hopes for us and is not yet finished with the human race, though obviously there are some grave corrections in store for this generation. Akita reaffirms Mary's promise at Fatima: "In the end, my Immaculate Heart will triumph. . . . [A] period of peace will be granted to the world.[4]

The Blessed Mother's meetings with humble, hidden people such as Agnes Katsuko Sasagawa, or to famous spiritual leaders like Mother Teresa of Calcutta, are God's wonderful, amazing, inexplicable gifts to us. Holy prophets speak of Mary. Great saints revere her. Angels serve God's people with her. The humble and the lowly flee to her side. Kings and presidents and world leaders invoke her aid.

Christ's Blessed Mother, in apparitions all over the world, is a sign that God's ways, expressed in Sacred Scripture, taught in monolithic religions, the laws of nature, and the hearts of all humans, bring the Kingdom of Heaven to earth for those who hear and respond. The Lord of the Heavens is also Lord of the Cosmos and Lord of the Earth. All treasures of creation flow from God's Heart of Pure Love. Christ's Blessed Mother is integral to God's human benevolence. She is the pearl of great price among the human race. Those who seek their Blessed Mother find her when they least expect. To heed her loving voice and follow her secret ways is to enter into the glories of God's Kingdom.

THE FAITHFULNESS OF GOD

Throughout the centuries, our Blessed Mother has continuously assured us that God is love. God responds to His children's cries. God is the Faithful One. God blesses those who bless. Mary asks all of us to bless and help one another. She comes to us in many ways to show us how to make our hearts living centers of peace where God may dwell in fullness. The Blessed Mother urgently calls everyone in the world to return to God's ways:

> "Hurry and come back to God. Do not wait for God's Great Sign. For unbelievers, it will then be too late. For you who have faith, this time is a graced opportunity for you to respond to God, to deepen your faith. Before God's Great Sign comes, several warnings will be given to the world. Pray. Fast. Do penance. Sacrifice yourselves for the conversion of the world. It will be too late when the Great Sign comes."

THE GREAT SIGN

Little is known about the promised Great Sign.[5] Many believe it is intended for this generation. According to certain prophetic voices, those who do not yet know God's love will perish of fright when the Great Sign appears. For those who do know God's love, however, the Great Sign will provide an opportunity to practice all the virtues.

With the proliferation of Marian apparitions all over the world, the Marian messages remain consistent: our Blessed Mother asks us to embrace God's ways with all our hearts as we know them, and to disseminate her requests to the entire world for repentance, prayer, spiritual penance, and fasting. In this way, we become more aware of God's divine presence all around us. Of course, such awareness necessarily mitigates chastisements—and illumines heaven on earth. Truth is that we are each held accountable for our efforts or our indifference. Our job is to try to pray always and to set a good example.

Blessed Mother Mary's contemporary apparitions give everyone a renewed opportunity to prepare for their own personal "end times," for each of us will face our own personal apocalypse at the moment our body and soul part company. We do not know the day or the hour, but each of us *will* have a rendezvous with death. Mary reminds us:

"No pain, no suffering is too great for me in order to reach you. I pray to my Son not to allow the evil of the world to harm you. I beseech you, voluntarily turn away from evil and seek holiness above all else! You can neither imagine what is going to occur, nor what the Eternal Father will send to the earth. For your own sake, immediately turn away from wickedness and do much good. Renounce everything that distracts you. Sacrifice everything that takes your mind and time away from God's ways. I bring all your efforts to my Son. I thank you who pray, fast, and sacrifice yourselves for others. Know your gifts have immense eternal value.[6]

Our Blessed Mother asks us to pray for faith stronger than death, hope more powerful than mere earthly life, and love that lasts forever. She reassures us:

*Thank you, dear little children of my Immaculate Heart, for caring so much about my Son's presence in your hearts.
Do not fear His displeasure.
Please accept the gracious love He bears for you.*

You have nothing to fear little ones.
Please spend more time alone with me.
Allow me to nurture Jesus' presence within and about you.
Allow His love to fill your hearts with joy.
In that way you will have no fear.
Be my voice and my heart and my hands in these times of my
Son's manifestations throughout the world.
Be living peace.

Those who sincerely encounter our Blessed Mother find Jesus in deepest intimacy. His ways, long hidden in Sacred Scripture, echo in the winds for those who have ears to hear. We do not need to search for Jesus. He is with us.[7] He asks us to be *in* the world, but not *of* the world.

THE MYSTERY OF HELL

The Blessed Mother tells visionaries of the mystery of iniquity: new kinds of evil unleashed upon the earth. In an ever so humble way, our Blessed Mother speaks of the "One True God of Love and Mercy." Yet she continues to warn us of the ubiquitous presence of evil. Mary explains how desperately we need one another. Our Spiritual Mother desires to unite us, all of us of every race, gender, religion, and nationality. We are a family—God's family. Where the Spirit of God dwells, there is unity. Evil, to the contrary, brings division, degradation, desolation, despair, and death.

No thinking person would dispute that evil entities have power on earth now as never before. The Blessed Mother warns us they enter every home, seeking to destroy all vestiges of love. The good news is that they are being unmasked as never before. God has blessed this generation with the ability to recognize immorality for what it is. Explaining the problem of evil, Pope Benedict XVI says sin is the illness that truly disfigures the person and society, and only God can heal this infirmity. Remembering the ten lepers whom Jesus healed, the Holy Father said:

"This Gospel passage invites us to a double reflection. Above all, it makes us think of two levels of healing: one that is more superficial, affecting the body; another, more profound, reaching the depths of a person, that which the Bible calls the 'heart,' and from there, irradiating to all of existence. . . . In reality, the leprosy that truly disfigures the person and society is sin; pride and egotism give birth in the spirit to indifference, hate, and violence. Only God, who is Love, can cure this leprosy of the spirit, which disfigures the face of humanity. Upon opening the heart to God, the converted person is healed interiorly of evil."

The Pope, recalling the apparitions in Fatima prays to our Blessed Mother for all of us:

"We ask the Blessed Virgin for the gift of conversion for all so that they may announce and give a faithful and coherent witness to the perennial evangelical message, which indicates to humanity the path to an authentic peace."[8]

Mary keeps reminding us that God loves us unconditionally and His ways protect us. When we stray from the safety of God's ways, we fall into sin, encounter severe pain, and harm others. While we are on the earth, we have the capacity to overcome malfeasance.

Hell in the life to come, however, is eternal; there is no escape. That place and state of being has been described as constant, unrelenting desolation; hopeless, unceasing screaming; fiery rage, despicable denigration, ignominious insults, detestable, derisive degradation, macabre, scornful shame, violent mocking, wretched misery, deceitful treachery, damning despair; sordid terror all heaped together and constantly hurled at a soul; unending assignments of darkest evil beyond imagining loaded upon a soul that are impossible to accomplish, yet are punishable for failure—cruelty, too horrible to fathom. It is a type of torture that assails all the senses and a human body is not necessary for the infliction of such abominations.

As long as we are on the earth, as we open ourselves to repentance, pray and fast, in whatever way we can, we do receive light and power to return to the safety of God's loving providence. With God and in God, we are able to dwell in His blessings that fill our hearts with all delight.

THE MAGNIFICENCE OF HEAVEN

Our Blessed Mother often speaks of the brevity and uncertainty of life on earth. One hundred years is longer than most people hope to live. Mary knows without doubt that if we truly knew the magnificence of Heaven, we would be sitting on the edges of our seats waiting to be called Home. Unfortunately for most of us, our faith is weak. Perhaps that is why God allows Mary to visit us. Our Holy Mother counsels us that we never know when we will be called into eternity. She wants to help us be prepared always for that moment with this promise:

> "If you abandon yourselves to me and allow me to nurture you into God's love, you will not even feel the passage from this life to the next life. You will begin to live the life of heaven on earth."[9]

Prayer, spiritual penance, and fasting are personal tools for achieving spiritual victory. When times grow difficult, prayer, penance (even something as simple as doing without just one cup of coffee, or some sort of treat each day as a love offering to God), and fasting (perhaps something as small as avoiding chocolate on Fridays with a simple prayer—God, I love You more than this chocolate) help us to cast out whatever darkness might well up within us. Of course, as we practice our spiritual penances and fasting, we gradually are able to do more. God loves a cheerful giver: a sorrowful giver reveals his or her own greed. As we learn to rely on God's strength, love, patience, providence, kindness, mercy, goodness, forgiveness, and justice, we come to rest upon the Heart of Jesus our Savior in true happiness.

Blessed Mother Mary has come to these times with powerful graces of light and love for all of us. She tells visionaries throughout the world that she has no preferential love. We are all her children.

Our Blessed Mother has more than enough graces and gifts for all of us. We need merely to grow in awareness of our Blessed Mother's majestic love for us. As we commit ourselves to God and His ways as best we can, our lives do begin to overflow with joy and hope. We are one family, the triumphant in Heaven and the faithful on earth. Nothing in life or death can separate us from God's love and from one another except our unintelligent choices. As long as there is life in us, we can always turn to God with confidence. Such is the quality of His Divine Mercy.

BLESSED POPE JOHN XXIII (ANGELO RONCALLI)

Pope John XXIII became pope on October 28, 1958. He is best remembered as the "Good Pope" who opened the Third Secret of Fatima in 1960 and made a pontifical decision not to reveal its contents to the waiting world. Instead, when he opened the floodgates of Catholicism by convening Vatican Counsel II on October 11, 1962, he forever changed the face of religion in the world. Pope John used the great council as an instrument of mercy and understanding, presenting to the world the riches the Church has received from Jesus Christ.

Blessed Pope John XXIII was named after the holy angels as an infant, Angelo Giuseppe Roncalli. He was a sharecropper's son and the fourth born of fourteen children. He was deeply spiritual and dedicated his life to Our Lady while still a young child. History has revealed what a special "Blessed Mother protégé" Angelo Roncalli truly was, but he had hints of his destiny along the way. Angelo wrote of the morning of his ordination to the priesthood, August 10, 1904, in the Church of Santa Maria in Rome:

> "When all was over and I raised my eyes [being prostrate upon the floor for ordination], having sworn the oath of eternal fidelity to my superior, the Bishop, I saw the blessed image of Our Lady to which I confess I had not paid any attention before. She seemed to smile at me from the altar and her look gave me a feeling of sweet peace in my soul and a generous and confident spirit."[10]

Almost immediately after his ordination, Roncalli entered the Vatican diplomatic corps. His first assignment was secretary to Bishop Tedeschi of Bergamo.

As a young scholar and seminary professor, Father Roncalli taught history, patrology (study of the insights of the Patristic Fathers of the first five centuries of Christianity), and apologetics. People found him to be warm, caring, and, in his own way, quite elegant. All who approached him, or heard him preach were touched by his contagious joy and sensitive, subtle humility. He proved to be a master diplomat. During World War One, Father Angelo served as a sergeant in the Italian medical corps and was chaplain to wounded soldiers. In 1921, he was sent to Rome to serve as Italian president of the Society for the Propagation of the Faith. Then, in 1925, the Pope promoted him to Bishop of the titular Diocese of Aeropolis, and appointed him Apostolic Visitator of Bulgaria.

The assignment could have been quite a challenge for a less loving man. Roncalli was a Roman Catholic representative in a thoroughly Orthodox region. His love for Our Lady was deeply shared by his Orthodox brethren. He made many friends and learned much. But the people in the Vatican had apparently forgotten him. Angelo remained in Bulgaria for ten years. During that time, he forged relationships of respect and cordiality among Orthodox, Muslim, and Roman Catholic people that broke down a thousand years of mistrust.

He remembered well and often spoke of a pilgrimage he had made to the Holy Land in 1906 that forever changed his perceptions of God's fatherhood of all people and our underdeveloped ability to comprehend the vastness of His Divine, unconditional love for each of us. The confusion and disorder of people, objects, languages, rites, and beliefs that he found in the Church of the Holy Sepulcher in Jerusalem caused him pained astonishment. He prayed there as a very young priest, and every day afterward, and most especially when he became Pope, for the miracle of reunification of God's spiritually separated people of the world.[11]

Angelo Roncalli's diplomatic service in the Balkans introduced the kindly Roman priest to a vast world of diversity such that he could find goodness in God's plan for humanity everywhere. He saw ecclesial unity *"with* Peter, not *under* him."[12] He said of his service to Orthodox Christians:

> "I think that I have been well understood by them. The respect I've always tried to have for everyone, both in public and private; my unbroken and non-judgmental silence; the fact that I never stopped to pick up the stones that were cast at me from this or that side of the street—all this leaves me with the clear certainty that I have shown everyone that I love them in the Lord with that fraternal, heart-felt and sincere charity that is taught in the Gospels. . . . The way of love is the way of truth."[13]

By 1935, Bishop Angelo was appointed Apostolic Delegate to Turkey and Greece. He blended peacefully into the worlds of Islam and Orthodoxy by means of kindness, respect, and sincere dialogue. When Roncalli left Sophia for Constantinople, he found it to be the "finest city in the world."[14] He said he was "on the threshold of the mysterious world of Islam in which there are new stirrings whose direction is in the hands of God."[15] He was the Vatican representative in "an Islamic country that was busy rejecting Islam and all religion as retrograde."[16]

When the Second World War broke out, Roncalli was in Greece. Because of his diplomatic position, he was able to help vast numbers of persecuted Jews. His thinking was simple enough: "Above all I wish to render good for evil and in all things try to prefer the Gospel truth to the cunning of human politics."[17] Throughout the debauchery of World War II, stalwart Angelo Roncalli served quietly, effectively, and prayerfully as people everywhere suffered the horror inherent in the unprincipled nature of dictatorships and the irresolute weakness of democracies at war with one another.

Warsaw fell on September 28, 1939. Papal Diplomat Roncalli's agenda would now be the corporal works of mercy.[18] Though the Vatican remained neutral during the entire world war, Roncalli spoke little and prayed and worked tirelessly behind the scenes. He advertised his services quite subtly, refurbishing the door to his office with the text *Ad Jesum per Mariam* (to Jesus through Mary) boldly imprinted over the top. As Bishop of Istanbul, he remained cheerful, smiling, a man of warmth and kindness to everyone. Turkey was not at war. He walked daily, publicly praying his rosary as he strolled amid the archaeological ruins. As to the warring countries of the world, Roncalli wrote: "I read in the Old Testament that Jacob also had sons who disagreed among themselves. But he, the father, pondered the matter in silence."[19]

Nuncio Roncalli saw his papal ministry as service, not power. He said of the Church that it is new because it is ancient, youthful because it is old. He believed that all legitimate authority is set in the context of charity. Consequently, by 1943, Roncalli became adept at tracing prisoners of war. He helped 24,000 Jews, providing them with clothes, money, and documents.[20] He said of the hideous persecution Jews were undergoing: "We are dealing with one of the great mysteries in the history of humanity. Poor children of Israel: daily I hear their groans around me. They are relatives and fellow-countrymen of Jesus. May the Divine Savior come to their aid."[21] Somehow, he knew, possibly by interior illumination, the Third Secret of Fatima concerning the Shoah, and Bishop Roncalli was in a position to help.

By the aegis of divine providence, neutral Turkey was the last escape route out of Nazi-occupied Europe through the Balkans via Istanbul. It was the road that led to Palestine. Roncalli used his skills and office to help find places of refuge that would receive suffering people who had escaped the concentration camps. The Grand Rabbi of Jerusalem Isaac Herzog met with Angelo Roncalli on January 22, 1944, and twice more in February. The Grand Rabbi wrote to Roncalli:

> "I want to express my deepest gratitude for the energetic steps that you have taken and will undertake to save our unfortunate people, innocent victims of unheard of horrors from a cruel power which totally ignores the principles of religion that are the basis of humanity. . . . The people of Israel will never forget the help brought to its unfortunate brothers and sisters by the Holy See and its highest representatives at this saddest moment of our history."[22]

Though Angelo Roncalli was Pope for only five years, and is best remembered for calling to life Vatican Council II, his gift to the world is his global humanitarian vision perhaps best summed up in his own words:

"[I]n the light of the Gospel and the Catholic principle, this logic of division [Catholic, Orthodox, Protestant, Jew, Moslem, believers or nonbelievers] does not hold. Jesus came to break down all these barriers: he died to proclaim universal brotherhood; the central point of his teaching is charity, which is the love which binds all men to him as the elder brother, and binds us all with him to the Father."[23]

Blessed Pope John XXIII is much beloved. Those who knew him well remember him mostly for the inward peace he carried and shared. His commitment to Jesus through Mary was complete. He knew much about Our Lady's secrets and her gifts. He left us this wisdom:

"Choose always to have less rather than more. Seek always the lowest place and to be beneath everyone. Seek always and pray that the will of God may be wholly fulfilled in you. Behold, such a man enters within the borders of peace and rest."[24]

WOMAN OF THE APOCALYPSE

Pope John XXIII, aware of Mary's Fatima secrets, was a peacemaker in the purest sense of the word. Even Nikita Khrushchev, who in mid-October 1962 dared to place Soviet missiles in Cuba, ninety miles off the coast of the United States, said of Pope John XXIII: "What the Pope has done for peace will go down in history."[25] After tense negotiations both nations found avenues to save face and avert nuclear war. Pope John XXIII said at the time:

"I beg heads of state not to remain insensitive to the cry of humanity, peace, peace. Let them do all that is their power to save peace; in this way they will avoid the horrors of war, the appalling consequences of which no one could predict. Let them continue to negotiate. History will see this loyal and open attitude as a witness to conscience. To promote, encourage, and accept negotiations, always and on every level, is a rule of wisdom that draws down both heavenly and earthly blessings."

Khrushchev listened. He closed the Cuban missile bases and ordered the Soviet warships to return to Russia. Pope John XXIII believed that the Church exists to serve the world. Knowing some of Our Lady's secrets, he observed:

"The Russian people are a wonderful people. We must not condemn them because we do not like their political system. They have a deep spiritual inheritance which they have not lost. We can talk with them. We must always try to speak to the goodness that is in people. Nothing is lost in the attempt. Everything may be lost if men do not find a way to work together to save peace."[26]

Pope John XXIII was deeply concerned about the spiritual conversion of atheist Russia. He knew the consequences to the world if such conversion should fail. On December 26, 1962, the aged Pope knelt on the floor of his bedroom before a crucifix and reconsecrated his life and the final sacrifice of his whole being as his spiritual contribution in the great pursuit; the conversion of Russia to harmony with the Christian world. He knew that only with such accord would the world taste peace.[27]

Suffering is part of every life on earth. We all suffer, some more than others. The cross of Christ is God's promise not only that He understands our suffering, but that He brings resurrection out of even the most difficult, deathly events. Christ drew all human suffering unto Himself. When we personally unite ourselves to God, in whatever way we can, our suffering sanctifies. The cross of Christ is God's sign of eternal, unconditional love for all of us. We, too, like

Jesus, need our Spiritual Mother Mary to stand beside us during trying times.

Christ raised His Blessed Mother to the heights and His Church crowned her Queen of Heaven and earth. Muslim tradition proposes Mary as a model to the faithful of Islam.[28] Jewish tradition sees Mary, descendant of Abraham and Sara, as the mother who helps us seek holiness above all else. Half a million people, most of whom were Muslims, saw the Blessed Mother in Egypt in 1968.[29] On some evenings, she appeared with the Infant Jesus and Joseph her husband. During her appearances, Mary did not speak. Her presence was the message to Muslim, Jew, and Christian alike. A revered rabbi in Jerusalem, highly skilled in the Kabala, said that he believes the coming of the Messiah and the Second Coming of Christ are the same occurrence. He said contemporary apparitions of Mary are a great portent signaling the eminence of the event.[30] In 2006, the Israeli ambassador to the United States was quoted on CNN evening news saying that if it is revealed to them that the Messiah is in fact Jesus Christ, the Jews will follow Him wherever He leads.

VISIONARIES FOR ENTIRE REGIONS

Not only do groups see the Blessed Mother in these new times, but certain individuals are visionaries for entire regions. During the 1990s, hundreds of thousands of pilgrims gathered to welcome and honor the Blessed Mother as she reportedly appeared or spoke to visionaries in Birmingham, Alabama; Conyers, Georgia; Lubbock, Texas; Phoenix, Arizona; Ambridge, Pennsylvania; Denver, Colorado; Betania, Venezuela; Rwanda, Africa; Akita, Japan; and other places too numerous to mention here. Great blessings flow from authentic visitations of Mary. Millions travel annually to pilgrim sites of antiquity: Lourdes in France; the Basilica of the Virgin of Guadalupe in Mexico City; the Marian Shrine at Fatima, Portugal; the Marian Shrine of Walsingham in England; the Black Madonna Shrine in Poland; Our Lady of Kazan in Saint Petersburg, Russia; the Basilica of the Immaculate Conception in Washington, D.C.; and countless others. There are thousands of places throughout the world where pilgrims gather to drink the pure spiritual milk Blessed Mother Mary brings from heaven. Many people today claim to have witnessed the "miracle of the sun" in such places and experience other supernatural phenomenon never before reported on such a massive scale.[31]

Blessed Mother Mary is guiding the multitudes of this generation, just as she helped the apostles and disciples in the days of the early formation of the Church.[32] Some people today hear her actual words. Others experience their Mother of Good Counsel communicating directly to their intellects.[33] Many experience a quiet understanding that is not conducive to mere words. Billions see our Blessed Mother with eyes of faith. They know her and commune with her through prayer with their hearts.

Mary, Mother Most Faithful, is the "Woman" God promised us in Genesis (3:15). She is the "Woman of the Apocalypse" described in Revelation (12:1), clothed with God's Son, with the moon under her feet, and on her head a crown of twelve stars. Our Spiritual Mother Mary is our Eternal Mother, our joy, our hope, and our delight—God's promise fulfilled. When we finally understand, not through human means, that Mary's biological Son is God Incarnate, we know for sure that all of us are her spiritual children because He made it so.

Please draw ever closer to my Immaculate Heart dear little
children of God's love.
Praise Jesus dear little ones.
Adore Jesus, love Jesus, and obey Jesus.
Be like Jesus in your thoughts, your words and your actions.
Love, only love little children.
Thank you for consoling my Son.
Those who console His Sorrowful Heart bring joy to
my sorrowful heart.
I am the Mother of the Word.
I am the Mother of all God's children.
I am the spouse of the Consoler.
Pray to the Holy Spirit dear children.
Pray that you might experience the gift of Wisdom.

Pray for the gift of Knowledge.
Pray that you might always cherish God's will
little children of my sorrowful heart.
God's will is realized through obedience to God's commandments.
Only those who pray much are capable of such love.
It is love that frees God's children.
Love is the elixir of eternal life.

The Two Hearts—Sacred Heart of Jesus and Immaculate Heart of Mary

CHAPTER 6

Queen of Heaven and Earth

*"And the Lord God said to the serpent . . . I will put enmity be-
tween you and the woman, and thy seed and her seed: she shall crush
thy head, and thou shall lie in wait for her heel . . ."*[1]

Scripture unfolds in the signs of the times. The Internet, television, and
the news media show footage of actual beheadings of people. Humans still live in degradation and ignorance beyond telling much as
they did two thousand years ago.[2] Mysteriously, the death of John
the Baptist continues to reveal the way, truth and life. And his ancient enemies still stalk the living.

AVERTING CATASTROPHE

Fear can easily become endemic throughout the world. Certain nations
claim they possess the means to wreak nuclear holocaust. It is no secret
that some have nuclear weapons. Experts say Washington, New York,
and the California coastal regions are targets because terrorists want
to traumatize the United States and kill as many people as possible.

One thing, however, is certain: when our Blessed Mother is here, the
Prince of Peace is near. In the midst of horrible nuclear possibilities
and constant terrorist activities, believers cling to the hope that the

God of love and mercy and unfathomable kindness is still in charge of all reality. A great sign of His providential protection is Mary as she miraculously appears on Saint Juan Diego's *tilma* [poncho]: the Lady of the Apocalypse clothed with God's Son, Jesus Christ, with the moon under her feet and on her head a crown of twelve stars.[4] Our Blessed Mother, for reasons of which we mortals are not privy, serves as an intermediary between forces in the material and spiritual worlds.

When the earth's people stand upon a precipice, there must be hope for global cooperation and peace. It has always been so. Our only decision is when and how much it will cost us to embrace the yoke of God's love. Realistic people find ways to solve problems before they explode into self-generating violence. Historic precedent clearly demonstrates that where our Blessed Mother's apparitions are welcomed with gratitude and love, God rewards with solutions to any problems, no matter how grave. Cynics, however, scoffing at God's decision to send Christ's Mother to help His people, may create a self-fulfilling holocaust. If we are successful in obliterating the supernatural gift of Mary's apparitions that God offers this generation, a whole civilization will fall upon the sword of disbelief.

PROSPERITY AND PEACE

You and I do have a wonder-filled opportunity now. The secrets of Mary contain seeds of new life and goodness and prosperity and peace for everyone. Scripture gives hints for all of us:

> *"When the Son of Man shall come in His majesty, and all the angels with him, then shall he sit upon the seat of his majesty . . . and all nations shall be gathered together before him. . . ."*[5]

RUSSIA AND FATIMA

The fate of the Russian people was a significant element of Mary's messages at Fatima in 1917. During seven apparitions to Fatima visionaries Lucia, Francisco, and Jacinta, Mary warned that world war would continue to plague the earth's people if they did not engage in both prayer and sacrifice.[6] An East-West, bipolar balance of terror, the Cold War enveloped much of the twentieth century until Russian president Mikhail Gorbachov and U.S. president Ronald Reagan found peaceful ways to communicate.[7] The messages of the Mother of God are better known now. Hopefully they are better believed. And surely more people of *all* faiths are responding to Mary's messages of peace.

According to worldwide press reports, more than 75,000 people witnessed the "miracle of the sun on October 13, 1917."[8] The miracle authenticated the actual presence of Our Lady and affirmed her warnings to the world, some of which include the outbreak of World War II, persecution of the faithful, Russia's promulgation of errors and terrors throughout the world, and annihilation of various nations. Our Lady's promise confirmed by the great Fatima "miracle of the sun" in 1917 is: "In the end, my Immaculate Heart will triumph. Russia will be converted and a period of peace will be given to the world."

Humans are dependent upon familial love and are coming to realize the mutual interdependence of all living things. That truth hopefully will lead people everywhere to peaceful, fruitful means of dispute resolution. All over the world, men, women, and children in these times report personally seeing the "miracle of the sun." No one really knows why this is occurring. Everyone on earth is a beneficiary of the warmth of the sun. Without warmth and light, things die. Conversely, those who venture too close to the sun die a fiery annihilation. The heavenly warning of the "miracle of the sun" does serve to remind all of us that there is always a fragile balance between life and death.

Our Lady says the gift of peace in our hearts, homes, cities, towns, and countries comes only from the loving mercy of God. She counsels us that prayer, penance, and fasting for spiritual reasons bring the blessings of God that stop wars in families, cities, regions, and countries. Countless numbers of innocent, unsuspecting, uninformed people have endured horrendous suffering since 1917, simply because they did not know about Mary's Fatima messages. Such horror need not be repeated if every thinking person responds generously to her wisdom. We all have the power to choose blessings or curses.

Our Blessed Mother, clothed with God's Son, greatly desires that we avert further human tragedy by means of prayer, sacrificial penance, and disciplined fasting. These are concrete means by which to mitigate catastrophic horrors. The Law of Attraction reveals that we draw to ourselves what we most deeply desire. Prideful people think they have little need of authentic prayer and so they never see or hear the humble Blessed Mother. Prudent people seek her guidance. Wise ones respond to her requests.

Wars, concentration camps, ethnic cleansing, lethal disease, bombed cities, and economic crises are grotesque reminders of urgent, unheeded warnings from Heaven. We may be slow learners, but we now have hindsight to help us. If we are wiser people in the twenty-first century, suffering has made it so. God has dominion over every reality. Christ's Mother has much to reveal to us.

Be at peace dear children of my Immaculate Heart.
I am the lowly one.
I am the Mother of the Only-begotten of the Father.
His will is done dear children in lowliness.
His will is done in absolute obedience.
Obedience to the will of God is meekness.
Be meek as I am meek my children.
Seek lowliness.
Seek silence for in silence the will of
our Father is discovered.
The ways of the world bring greed, violence, and war.
The ways of God bring abundance, peace, and generous love.
Dear children, our Father rewards a thousandfold.
The evil one detests the generosity of Our Father.
Live in truth dear little children of my heart.
Practice obedience.
I wish to speak to you. Please come to me now.

Soon I will leave my children's side in this way.
Help me in Russia dear little children.
Come and serve my Son in Russia.
Bring my Immaculate Heart to Russia.
Help my families in Russia who know not how to love.

THE FATEFUL RUSSIAN ICON

Since Mary's final apparition in Fatima with her Divine Son Jesus and her husband Joseph on October 13, 1917, untold millions of believers have prayed billions of individual prayers and offered sacrifices that they hope have ascended as incense before the Throne of God on behalf of the people of Russia, and the entire world. God hears all prayer. God is faithful. We have much hope for peace.

The Icon of the Mother of God of Kazan, a sacred mother-child work of art with a mystical history, was mysteriously removed from a cathedral in Moscow at the time of the Bolshevik Revolution in 1917. Later in the century, the icon was discovered in a castle in England. Some believe the sacred icon is linked to the fate of the Russian people and the world.

During the more than eighty years that the Kazan Icon was absent from Russian soil, millions of Russian citizens suffered mercilessly. World War II undermined family life and depleted valuable resources. The nine-hundred-day siege of Leningrad was like a never-to-be-forgotten black plague of death. The long Cold War ravaged the Russian people even deeper.

With the collapse of the Iron Curtain (although the entrepreneurial class has acquired wealth), many Russians have fallen even deeper into poverty, oppression, ignorance and suffering. Over half the population is crowded into one- and two-room apartments in the towns and cities. There is a chronic shortage of food: fresh vegetables and fruit are particularly scarce and quite costly in the cities. Lawlessness allows the black market to thrive. Russian mothers do the same work as men and have little time to spend with their families. Children's souls are formed in state-run day-care centers.

Russia, climbing out of a century of atheism, is spiritually needy. History assures us that prayer, the penance of pilgrimages, and fasting for spiritual purposes stop war.[9] Prayer, penance, and fasting also change the natural law.[10] Public prayer and fasting are once again visible in Russia. Prayerful Russians hope to bring God's bountiful blessing to their families, their nation, and the world.

The Iron Curtain collapsed silently on Christmas day, 1991, when the red flag was lowered for the last time from the highest peak of the Kremlin. Coincidentally, and there are no coincidences, ten years earlier, unprecedented apparitions of Mary were reported in Medjugorje, a village of Roman Catholics, Orthodox, and Muslims in Eastern Europe. Millions of people from all parts of the earth made pilgrimages there. Mary allegedly identified herself at Medjugorje as the Queen of Peace.[11] The Blessed Mother also appeared in Akita, Japan, during the 1980s with messages for the world that were strangely reminiscent of her Fatima requests. Mary specifically asked for prayer and fasting for Russia.

Marian apparitions and celebrations continue to draw tens of thousands of praying, fasting people from every nation to small villages, major cities, towns, and hamlets. Because of reported apparitions of the Blessed Mother throughout the world, pilgrims responding to Mary's call are once again embracing prayer, spiritual penance, and fasting as if their lives depend upon it.[12]

Technological advances, the Internet, television, and telecommunications intertwine our lives ever more closely. The pain, absurdity of terrorism, and war sicken wise people throughout the world. We have an opportunity now as never before to recognize one another's needs and gifts. In the springtime of the twenty-first century, the significance of grace the Blessed Mother brings to earth from Heaven becomes clearer. Global interest flourishes anew in effective means of peaceful, fruitful, mutually beneficial conflict resolution.

The Blessed Mother asks that we sacrifice our lives for the conversion of the world. Troops in war-torn regions understand the call as do aid workers across the world. Those who add a prayer or two, do without a treat for a higher purpose, or help another even when it is inconvenient are also responding to Mary's requests.

In Russia, reconstruction of the great church at Red Square in Moscow that once housed the miraculous and sacred Icon of the Mother of God of Kazan, the Patroness and Protector of all Russia, is under way. Similar projects, large and small, throughout the world are instruments of peace and light. Those who work to restore beauty and bring dignity to God's people and earth are true peacemakers. They bring hope and life and light for all to enjoy.[13]

Seventy-five years after the great "miracle of the sun" at Fatima, His Holiness, the late Aleksey II, Patriarch of Moscow and of all Russia, received a delegation of foreign pilgrims that included Catholic, Protestant, Orthodox, Jewish, Hindu, and Muslim worshippers from the United States, Europe, Asia, Africa, and Australia. They gathered in Moscow Cathedral at Red Square to praise God as one people of faith. Obviously deeply touched, the Patriarch announced:

> "We know of the message of Fatima. During the dark years that message was our hope. We know that the original Icon of the Mother of God of Kazan was housed in a beautiful, Byzantine-style Shrine constructed especially for its exile at Fatima. We look forward to its return to Russia. Perhaps then, we the people of Russia shall know peace and abundance once again. Those who have kept the faith should not be proud. We are all sinners. Now, together, we have a great task to accomplish."[14]

The icon, providentially removed from Russian soil in 1917, was kept safe. And it hung over Pope John Paul II's Vatican desk when, in October of 2001, spurning Vatican protocol, he invited ecumenical leaders of every faith to gather at Assisi, Italy, to discuss ways for peace and reconciliation. It was during that unprecedented convocation of global spiritual leaders that the Holy Father publicly offered to return to Russian soil the sacred and revered icon of the Mother of God of Kazan, patriotically known as the Patroness and Protector of the Russian People. His affection and dedication to the icon was evident. He himself had become the personal custodian of the powerful icon, removing it to his private apartment for veneration and safe-keeping. His offer was welcomed with ecstatic joy by Russian Orthodox believers.

Under the leadership of the late Patriarch Alexy II, the Russian Orthodox Church began a long-sought renaissance. During more than eighty years of harsh atheistic rule, the Church had become a subversive arm of the totalitarian Soviet regime. Hundreds of "onion-domed churches once used as Soviet animal pens and garages" are in the process of restoration to spiritual places of worship.[15]

MYSTICAL CONTACT WITH JESUS AND MARY

Mary's apparitions at Fatima are filled with lovely cameos of God's plan for His people not only in Europe but everywhere. Certainly not every encounter with Mary is authenticated in such a grand, world-wide manner as her Fatima apparitions. Visionary Lucia was only ten years old when she and her cousins Francisco and Jacinta Marto first saw Mary on May 13, 1917, in the Cova de Iria. In a pastoral letter dated October 13, 1930, the bishop of Leiria-Fatima, José Alves Correia da Silva, declared the apparitions of Fatima worthy of faith and allowed public devotion. He in effect authenticated the divine pattern Fatima cut. Since then, the shrine has become a center of spirituality and pilgrimage for nobility as well as ordinary people of all faiths.

Visionary Lucia lived under a strict vow of obedience in a convent for much of her life. Her mystical gifts were carefully observed and monitored by Roman Catholic ecclesial hierarchy. The Roman Catholic Church effectively established through Lucia a safe global methodology for mystical contact with Jesus and Mary. The official Vatican explanation of Lucia's life is the following:

"Born in Aljustrel in 1907, Lucia moved to Oporto in 1921, and at 14 was admitted as a boarder in the School of the Sisters of St. Dorothy in Vilar, on the city's outskirts. On Oct. 24, 1925, she entered the Institute of the Sisters of St. Dorothy and at the same time was admitted as a postulant in the congregation's convent in Tuy, Spain, near the Portuguese border. She made her first vows on Oct. 3, 1928, and her perpetual vows on Oct. 3, 1934, receiving the name Sister Mary of the Sorrowful Mother.

"She returned to Portugal in 1946 and two years later entered the Carmelite convent of St. Teresa in Coimbra, where she made her profession as a Discalced Carmelite on May 31, 1949, taking the name Sister Maria Lucia of Jesus and the Immaculate Heart.

"She wrote two volumes, one entitled 'Memories' and the other 'Appeals of the Fatima Message.' In her writings, she recounts how the Virgin Mary and Child Jesus appeared to her on other occasions, years after the initial apparitions.

"The mortal remains of the Carmelite were moved in 2006 to the Shrine of Fatima. The body of the nun, who died at age 97, is buried next to Jacinta. Francisco is buried in the same basilica."[16]

POWER TO CHANGE HISTORY

Lucia's visionary witness has consistently been not only of spiritual matters, but also has a distinct geopolitical nature. Our Lady of Fatima said to Lucia:

"God wishes to establish in the world devotion to my Immaculate Heart. If what I say to you is done, many souls will be saved and there will be peace. The war [World War I] is going to end: but if people do not cease offending God, a worse one will break out during the Pontificate of Pius XI. When you see a night illumined by an unknown light, know that this is the great sign given you by God that He is about to punish the world for its crimes, by means of war, famine, and persecution of the Church and the Holy Father. To prevent this, I shall come to ask for the consecration of Russia to my Immaculate Heart and the communion of reparation on First Saturdays. If my requests are heeded, Russia will be converted, and there will be peace; if not, she will spread her errors throughout the world, causing wars and persecution of the Church. The good will be martyred; the Holy Father will have much to suffer; various nations will be annihilated. In the end, my Immaculate Heart will triumph. The Holy Father will consecrate Russia to me, and she will be converted, and a period of peace will be granted to the world."[17]

Visionary Lucia would suffer much during the rest of her life bearing prescient knowledge of how dangerous world events could become if people disregarded Mary's calls. Lucia prayed and fasted as best she could that all would come to know Mary's requests so that people everywhere could enjoy a period of peace.

Less than two years after Mary's apparitions in Fatima, the Treaty of Versailles (June 28, 1919), which ended World War I, created an enormous reservoir of blind anger among groups who perceived it to be fundamentally unjust. Under the Treaty's Articles 231–248, Germany was required to accept responsibility for causing World War I, totally disarm, forfeit territory, and pay financial reparations in gold to the victorious allies (calculated at approximately 11.3 billion pounds sterling, but later reduced to 4.99 billion pounds sterling). Anger poisons life. Few could foresee that this slush fund of anger would be hurled onto a Jewish scapegoat in World War II that would morph into the Shoah with all the horrors of the Holocaust.

On the night of January 25–26, 1938, spectacular light illumined the skies of Europe. Though astronomers identified the lights as the aurora borealis, Lucia believed differently. She recognized the lights as the heavenly sign referred to in the secret she received at Fatima on July 13, 1917. Lucia wrote in her Memoirs that God made use of the lights to reveal to guilty nations that they were about to be punished. Lucia, to the best of her ability, began to plead for the Communion of Reparations on the First Saturdays and for consecration of Russia to Mary's Immaculate Heart.[18]

Throughout her long life, Lucia continued to see and hear our Blessed Mother. Her contact with Mary was a source of wisdom and grace for Lucia. From her convent, Sister Lucia wrote to the popes of the day concerning Our Lady's secrets. In her final years, she had three personal meetings with Pope John Paul II. Lucia knew that the Church teaches us to "trust in the love and care of an all-loving God, whose punishments are indeed manifestations of his love, but who nonetheless does not work by means of dire, vague predictions that tend to stifle all initiative and planning for the future."[19] Lucia also knew that God always warns His people.[20]

Pope Benedict XVI is familiar with Lucia's messages from Mary. As Cardinal Ratzinger, he said: "Prophesy gives us a glimpse of the baleful consequences of certain individual or collective actions or behaviors. It gives us a glimpse of them—but this doesn't mean that they are necessarily bound to occur. On the contrary, prophesy is an urgent invitation to conversion, penance, and prayer and the point is that these things have the power to change history."[21]

Lucia feared that World War II would be even worse than the First World War "in the sense that it would be an atheistic war attempting to exterminate Judaism, which gave the world Jesus Christ, Our Lady, the Apostles who transmitted the Word of God and the gift of faith, hope and charity. The Jews are God's elect people whom he chose from the beginning. 'Salvation is from the Jews.' "[22]

THE SHOAH

It is little wonder that the small children visionaries of Fatima who saw the horrors of the Shoah (extermination of the Jews) during World War II engaged in such heroic penances to help these valiant martyrs. Francisco and Jacinta truly sacrificed their lives for the mitigation of the atrocities of World War II. So, too, did the troops who helped eradicate the evils of that war.

On December 10, 1925, Mary and the Child Jesus appeared to Lucia at her convent in Ponte Vedra, Spain. Our Lady rested her hand on Lucia's shoulder, revealing her heart encircled by thorns. The Child Jesus said: "Have compassion on the heart of your most holy Mother, covered with thorns with which ungrateful men pierce it at every moment, and there is no one to make an act of reparation. . . ."

One particularly heart-wrenching meeting with the Savior and His holy Mother happened to Sister Lucia on February 15, 1926, at her convent at Ponte Vedra. Returning from the garden after doing her chores, Sister Lucia saw the Child Jesus, who asked her, "Have you showed the world what the Mother of Heaven has asked?" Lucia acknowledged that no, she had not.

In March of 1939, as Hitler was scheming to conquer the world, the Lord Jesus spoke again to Sister Lucia:

"The time is coming when various nations will undergo the sway of Divine justice. Some of them will be annihilated." Portuguese Catholic bishops were aware of Sister Lucia's mystical visits with Jesus and Mary. They entrusted Portugal to Jesus Christ through the Immaculate Heart of Mary before World War II began. Bishops and clergy of no other European nation emulated the Portuguese bishops' consecration. Some argue that it is by mere coincidence that Portugal was spared any involvement in World War II.

CELESTIAL PHENOMENA

Pope Pius XII had the experience of seeing the Fatima "miracle of the sun" on three successive days at four p.m.—October 30, 1950; October 31, 1950; and November 1, 1950—while praying the Holy Rosary in the Vatican Gardens. This phenomenon certainly influenced him. A year later, on October 13, 1951, he ordered a huge celebration at the Shrine of Fatima. More than one million people assembled there to hear Cardinal Tedeschini solemnly disclose to the massive crowds that the Blessed Virgin had visited the Holy Father.

"Pope Pius XII was able to witness the life of the sun (a burning sphere 866,000 in diameter) under the hand of Mary. The sun was agitated, all convulsed, transformed into a picture of life . . . in a spectacle of celestial movement . . . in transmission of silent but eloquent messages to the Vicar of Christ."[23]

This announcement at Fatima marked the first time in the history of the Roman Catholic Church that a papal vision was announced during the pontiff's lifetime.

Pope Pius XII had previously consecrated the entire Church and the world to Jesus Christ through the Immaculate Heart of Mary on October 31, 1942, during the height of the Second World War. He did this without concurrent consecration by the world's bishops, clergy, and leaders.

Later, in 1964, at the Second Vatican Council in Rome, Pope Paul VI renewed the consecration of the world to Jesus Christ through the Immaculate Heart of Mary. He again publicly made the consecration at the Fatima shrine in 1967, during a pilgrimage celebrating the fiftieth anniversary of the apparitions of the Mother of God to the three children. In October 1984, Pope John Paul II acted in concert with the Catholic bishops of the entire world in celebrating a solemn consecration of the world to Jesus Christ through the Immaculate Heart of Mary. Most recently, Pope John Paul II repeated the global consecration in May 2001.

Such consecrations and devotions are spiritually important because of the revulsion the Lord Jesus expressed about those who are spiritually lukewarm of heart.[24] Consecrations and devotions enflame the human heart and lift the veil that separates the human eye from the Divine Gaze. Without them, the human heart becomes as barren as the fig tree Jesus cursed.[25]

Perhaps a global consecration to Jesus Christ through the Immaculate Heart of Mary will flow from the hearts of world leaders and citizens alike, not just Catholic hierarchy. Such an act of humility may usher in Mary's promised reign of peace. God does not scorn humble and contrite hearts. Only the humble draw toward Mary. Yet her role in human affairs has never before been so globally apparent. Lucia of Fatima summed up God's message to our times as a heavenly call to keep the Law of God.[26]

Lucia, a messenger of the Lord Jesus and His Blessed Mother Mary believed her heaven sent information is not just for Christians but for everyone. Because she lived in a cloistered convent hidden in the hills of Portugal, few knew of her celestial encounters. Pope John Paul II traveled personally to Portugal three times to meet privately with her. He became a devoted servant of Our Lady of Fatima and used his pontificate to spread Mary's requests throughout the world.[27] Only toward the end of his life would he begin to disclose some of Mary's secrets.

Christ and His Mother have included all of us in Mary's apparitions to Sister Lucia. Mary reveals that prayer, sacrificial penance, spiritual fasting, and personal entrustment of ourselves and all we hold dear to God is the means to avert war and catastrophy. Spiritual indifference seems to be the most dangerous human pursuit.

Lucia enjoyed the protection of several popes, her Roman Catholic bishops and Carmelite religious superiors. Her secrets and messages from Jesus and Mary continue to carry the authenticity of the Vatican,[28] the Russian Orthodox faith,[29] and much of the praying world.[30] History continues to authenticate Lucia's messages from Our Lady of Fatima: prayer, consecrated penance, and spiritual fasting have eternal significance in Heaven and on earth.[31]

On the eve of Sister Lucia's death (February 12, 2005), Pope John Paul II sent a fax to her in which he expressed his closeness and assured her of his prayers so that she would be able "to live this moment of pain, suffering and offering with the spirit of Easter, of the passing." Sister Lucia's death brought both joy and sorrow to millions around the world. Her funeral resembled a state occasion:

> "There was a guard of honor around the coffin: 35 bishops from Portugal, the 17 nuns of Sister Lucia's community, her family members, and the Portuguese people. There were political representatives who, as a sign of mourning, suspended their electoral campaign. The faithful waited in long queues from the early hours of Tuesday morning to bid Sister Lucia farewell. For them, she was 'the person who was touched by an extraordinary experience, but who was able to incarnate it in ordinary life,' as Cardinal José da Cruz Policarpo, patriarch of Lisbon, said in his brief homily.[32]

On Valentine's Day, February 14, 2005, Pope John Paul II sent the following message to be read by the Bishop of Coimbra, Portugal, at the funeral of Sister Lucia. Cardinal Tarcisio Bertone, special papal envoy, presided at the funeral Mass in the cathedral of Coimbra.[33]

> "With profound emotion I learned that Sister Maria Lucia of Jesus and the Immaculate Heart, at the age of 97 years, was called by the heavenly Father to the eternal dwelling of heaven. She has thus reached the end to which she always aspired in prayer and in the silence of the convent. The liturgy has reminded us in these days that death is the common heritage of

the children of Adam, but at the same time it has assured us that Jesus, with the sacrifice of the cross, has opened to us the gates of immortal life. We recall these certainties of the faith at the moment we give our last farewell to this humble and devout Carmelite, who consecrated her life to Christ, Savior of the world. The visit of the Virgin Mary, which little Lucia received in Fatima together with her cousins Francisco and Jacinta in 1917, was for her the beginning of a singular mission to which she remained faithful until the end of her days. Sister Lucia leaves us an example of great fidelity to the Lord and of joyful adherence to His divine will. I remember with emotion the various meetings I had with her and the bonds of spiritual friendship that, with the passing of time, were intensified. I have always felt supported by the daily gift of her prayer, especially in the harsh moments of trial and suffering. May the Lord reward her amply for the great and hidden service she has done to the Church.

"I love to think that the one who has received Sister Lucia in the passing from earth to heaven has been precisely She whom she saw in Fatima so many years ago. May the Holy Virgin accompany the soul of this devoted daughter of hers to the happy encounter with the divine Spouse."[34]

A year later, a Vatican website, Zenit.org, carried the following:

FATIMA, Portugal, FEB. 20, 2006. The mortal remains of Sister Lucia, witness of the 1917 apparitions of the Blessed Virgin, have left the Carmelite Convent of Coimbra, to rest in the Shrine of Fatima. The body of the nun, who died a year ago at age 97, was taken Sunday to the Basilica of Our Lady of the Rosary. According to the Portuguese Catholic news agency Ecclesia, some 250,000 people accompanying the arrival waved white scarves, a custom in the farewell procession in large pilgrimages to the shrine. The history of the apparitions was recounted during the brief ceremony, beginning with the first, on May 13, 1917. Sister Lucia is buried next to Blessed Jacinta Marto (1910–1920), another of the Fatima visionaries. Blessed

Francisco Marto (1908–1919), the other witness of the apparitions, is buried in the same basilica. A stone to be placed on Sister Lucia's tomb reads: 'Sister Maria Lucia of Jesus and of the Immaculate Heart, to whom Our Lady appeared. March 22, 1907–February 13, 2005. Translated to this basilica on February 19, 2006.' On the stones of the other two little shepherds there is, in addition, an inscription that states: 'Beatified on May 13, 2000.' "[35]

No one suspected that Pope John Paul II would follow Lucia of Fatima to the eternal Kingdom so quickly. Less than seven weeks after her death, he, too, passed away. Hundreds of thousands who crowded the Plaza of Saint Peter for his funeral cried out in sorrowful longing "Sainthood Now!" His successor, Pope Benedict XVI was quick to begin the process on the ensuing feast of Our Lady of Fatima.[36]

There are untold millions of ordinary people throughout the world who desire the speedy canonization of Pope John Paul II. There are also tens of millions of individuals who believe that Sister Lucia of Fatima also deserves to be canonized, along with her already beatified cousins, Francisco and Jacinta.

In the meantime, Mary's people all over the world are finding special ways to ascend to celestial realms through the intercession of the Blessed Virgin Mary. The feast of the Immaculate Heart of Mary is a widespread and cherished devotion of Christian people. Beginning in the summer of 2005, thousands of members of Marian movements and associations set a wonderful precedent for peace-seeking prayer warriors by gathering in Rome to celebrate the feast of the Immaculate Heart of Mary in Saint Peter's Basilica.[37] The annual celebration begins with the arrival of the venerated image of the pilgrim Virgin of Fatima. The sacred statue is received by faithful people from many places with prayer and sincere, filial devotion. An archbishop leads a meditated rosary, followed by Mass presided over by a cardinal.

The faithful see in the Virgin Mary's "heart" the highest model of obedience to the will of God. Everyone longs to experience her maternal concern. After all, each of us was entrusted to her by the Savior dying on the cross. The feast of Mary's Immaculate Heart has a long tradition that was given strong impulse with the events of Fatima (1917). During those apparitions of the Blessed Virgin, the three little visionaries heard words that later went all over the world: "Jesus desires to establish in the world devotion to my Immaculate Heart" (June 13); "I shall come to ask for consecration to my Immaculate Heart," "At last my Immaculate Heart will triumph" (July 13). The Blessed Virgin introduced herself as Our Lady of the Rosary at Fatima and called to believers and nonbelievers, urging all to return to the path of goodness.

GRACED OPPORTUNITIES

Our Blessed Mother suggests some graced opportunities for us to facilitate personal peace, joy, love, holiness, happiness, health, contentment, prosperity, sobriety, proximity of family and friends, mutual love and respect. To experience harmony and enrich our cultures, communities, and quality of life, we are urged to do the following:

1. Meditate daily, especially on the life of Christ in the Holy Rosary. This discipline is efficacious for everyone and leads to deep enlightenment.
2. Personally entrust ourselves and all we cherish to our Savior Jesus through His Blessed Mother Mary. After all, Jesus Christ entrusted Himself to Mary. John the Baptist leapt for joy in His Savior's presence at the sound of her voice. Following the advice of Visionary Lucia of Fatima, we may choose to share the blessings of the brown scapular of Our Lady of Mount Carmel.[38]
3. Become comfortable with consecrated penance in union with Christ's sacrifice on the cross through sanctification of our daily duties. This means to peacefully accept the inconveniences and difficulties that are part of life.[39] Embrace spiritual fasting[40] of some sort as a way of life.
4. Endeavor carefully to avoid things, places, and people who drive us away from God's Kingdom. It takes wisdom to know how to do this. Pray for wisdom.
5. Enter into the global spiritual renewal occurring all over the world.[41]

6. Unite ourselves with the Hearts of Jesus and Mary in a special way, ideally on the First Friday and Saturday of each month, and if possible, make Communions of Reparation.[42]

The sacramental mother-infant relationship protected by the abiding strength of fatherly love most deeply depicts our actual relationship with God. Christ's Mother is here to help us.

I am your Mother.
My love for you is beyond measure.
Trust me more.
Be certain of my love for you in all things.
My love for you is eternal.
It has no bounds.

The Pilgrim Statue of Our Lady of Fatima—Our Lady of the Holy Rosary

CHAPTER 7

Queen of the Holy Rosary

"Thus says the Lord: I know their works and their thoughts, and I come to gather the nations of every language; they shall come and see my glory."[1]

For those who have difficulty understanding why the prayers and meditations of the Holy Rosary[2] are of such global importance in these times, it may be of some help to consider the following Scripture: *"For my thoughts are not your thoughts: nor your ways my ways, saith the Lord. For as the heavens are exalted above the earth, so are my ways exalted above your ways, and my thoughts above your thoughts."*[3]

Prayer accesses the rewards of God's glory in the world and it has always been so. Miracles of every kind occur all over the world. God is sustaining the world on the nourishment of prayer.[4] People everywhere are finding solace and light in prayer groups. God alone knows who benefits from each human prayer and in what way. God answers all prayers.

INGRID BETANCOURT

Few people could have withstood the humiliations that Colombian-French hostage Ingrid Betancourt experienced during her six-year captivity in the jungles of Colombia. She was born on December 25, 1961, served as a senator in Colombia, and was nominated for a Nobel Peace prize before her capture by the Revolutionary Armed

Forces of Colombia (FARC) on February 23, 2002. Upon her release in the summer of 2008, she publicly thanked God and the Blessed Virgin Mary for her freedom. The former Colombian presidential candidate described her release in a bloodless military operation by the Colombian army as a "miracle of the Virgin Mary." She said her faith was the source of her strength during captivity, which included brutal torture and every human indignity. Ingrid described the torture she endured at the hands of her "diabolical" captors as "monstrous" acts that must have disgusted even themselves. Ingrid emerged from captivity holding a rosary she made for herself out of rocks and twigs she found in the jungle. Day and night, she said she found strength and consolation in constant repetition of the sacred rosary prayers and meditations. After government debriefing, Ms. Betancourt's first visit as a free citizen was to the sacred French Shrine of the Immaculate Conception at Lourdes to say thank you to Our Lady.

IMACULEE ILIBAGIZA

Imaculee Ilibagiza, born in Rwanda in 1972, studied electronic and mechanical engineering at the National University of Rwanda. During the Rwandan genocide in 1994, her entire family was slaughtered. Imaculee escaped the killers because a Protestant minister hid the twenty-two-year-old and seven other women in a bathroom of his parsonage for ninety-one days. During that life-saving time of silent hiding, Imaculee prayed the rosary constantly. It was only as she focused upon the sorrowful mysteries of the rosary, meditating on the passion and death of Jesus that she was able to consider forgiving those who had so mercilessly obliterated her family. Her personal story is contained in her book, *Left to Tell*.[5] Imaculee knew of the apparitions of Our Lady during the 1980s. Unfortunately, few heeded the messages and rivers of human corpses flowed there as Mary had warned.[6] Imaculee's life is a living witness that God does bring good out of all things, even those as hideous as genocide. The rosary prayed faithfully in good times and in bad is truly a chain that binds generations living, deceased, and yet to be born to eternal life.

LIFE AFTER DEATH

The fact that Mary is appearing all over the world now, pleading with visionaries to ask everyone to pray, pray, pray, points to a wonderful benevolence from on high. This is not unprecedented. The spirituality of all times includes some level of understanding of the world of spirits and eternal life after death. Ancient history includes belief, as new as today, that happiness in this life and in the afterworld is rooted in accountability for time spent on earth. Even the Neanderthals of 32,000 years ago believed in accountability both in life and after death. And Neanderthals, hoping to better their afterlife, buried their dead with ritualistic codes they believed were significant to the spirit world. The earliest traces of spirituality in history point to our Blessed Mother of life, peace, and wholeness. Mary's very real presence in spiritual history reveals God at work in creation making all things new, bright, fresh, and complete.

All creation in some way reveals hints of God's unfathomable glory to us. Mary's messages of love and peace are sparkling gems that heal us of our base tendencies to fill our souls with transitory things. Love is the most expensive of all the virtues. Suffering is the price of progress. Little wonder our Blessed Mother warns us of looming, self-inflicted chastisements. How tired and lonely the world can become. But Mary joyfully reminds us of God's merciful rewards. Our loving God bears no cruelty. As we appropriate more holy ways of being, we progress through earth's vestibule to His luminous Kingdom of Love. God is living kindness. And so He sends our Blessed Mother to us to take us by the hand and ever so gently lead us out of the darkness into His Kingdom of eternal love.[7]

How do we find our Blessed Mother, so full of grace and blessings for us? Our ability to discern Mary's presence among us is no longer an isolated, rare spiritual occurrence for the privileged few. Mary is visible through the eyes of faith to untold multitudes of people of every background and belief.[8] The ubiquitous presence of our Blessed Mother is itself the divine message of eternal life that God sends to us at this time in the world's history to remind us of the wonders He has prepared for those who remain faithful to His ways.

Mary's presence among us is of course rooted in the dogma of the Assumption: our Blessed Mother enjoys a singular participation in her Son's Resurrection by which God took her up body and soul into heavenly glory when her earthly life was over.[9] Our Blessed Mother's human body is spiritualized. She is more than two thousand years old by earth calculations, yet forever is eternally young and perfectly beautiful in the fullness of God's glorious, loving majesty. Our human bodies also will be spiritualized at the end of our life on earth if we remain faithful to God's Plan for us. The resurrection of our body is a mercy of God whereby His children's corporeal substance is restored to its intended splendor.[10]

REWARDS

Mary of history, a Jewish Mother who lived in Palestine two thousand years ago, comes from Heaven into today's world robed in the majesty of the risen Christ with her arms open wide to everyone. Those who see and hear Mary, and who rest in her motherly embrace, know her as their very own dear Spiritual Mother. To encounter Mary is to fully discover how deeply loved and cherished we are.

Who among us, other than Mary, has ever been invited to consult with God about how to run the world?[11] No one. Wise people know that all joys of creation are God's to give as He chooses. God rewards. God punishes. God gives and gives and gives. God alone is the source of all that is good and wonderful and beautiful and permanent in this world. Today, God's gift to us is Mary. However, proud people do not desire to see or hear her. This Maiden Most Pure[12] is our Mother Most Humble.[13]

Mary reminds us to seek God and we shall find Him.[14] We are capable of hearing God in the wind that calls to our hearts,[15] seeing God in the depths of the sky,[16] blessing God in the light of day,[17] resting in God in the darkness of night,[18] clinging to God who is meek and humble of heart,[19] praising God in the fullness of His creation,[20] bearing with one another for a time will come when each of us shall cringe.[21] God sees all things. God knows all things. God blesses and blesses and blesses because He loves us. God is busy at work re-creating, reordering, and refashioning a never-ending symphony of love. We mortals are each a vital segment of that eternal beauty. Such rewards are ours to keep or lose.

Today, the Blessed Mother's worldwide apparitions, locutions, and visions bring sweet, loving guidance; urgent, sometimes tearful pleading; a global call to deep, heartfelt prayer and exquisite heavenly consolations.[22] Our Blessed Mother assures this generation that God's unique Plan, for each of us is hidden in the depths of personal prayer. Mary our Mother is here to escort her Son's flock into the Kingdom of the Good Shepherd.

It is impossible to love our Blessed Mother too much.[23] Jesus reveals His Mother to disciples He loves.[24] Mary is the delight of Christ's heart. It is by His decision that she is also the delight of our hearts. We can never love our Blessed Mother enough.[25] She clearly has the Lord's blessing.[26] Mary never squanders her time on earth with useless pursuits. We are wise to emulate her. Like Mary, we, too, need to busy ourselves with the work of God's Kingdom: love and serve and sing and praise with total trust in His governance of all life. Mary told the Archangel Gabriel: *"Behold the handmaid of the Lord."*[27] Our Blessed Mother, at the Lord's bidding, is now quietly helping us—people of every race, nation, faith, and educational background. Perhaps you are among this group. If not, please be quite confident that you are most certainly invited to pursue the secrets of Mary and seek her most wonderful gifts.

Pope John Paul II long espoused Mary's virtues, but most of all her immense power to lovingly intercede before the Heavenly Throne for all of us. On the eve of the U.S. invasion of Iraq in March 2003, he sent his personal emissary (the late) Cardinal Pio Laghi to Baghdad to consecrate the nation of Iraq, along with its twenty-five million inhabitants, to our Blessed Mother's Immaculate Heart. The global jury is still out regarding the fate of Iraq.

This generation is blessed with Mary's ubiquitous presence. Perhaps technological innovations—cell phones, television, and the

Internet—connecting the world allow more of us to know about this amazing spiritual truth as never before. Roman, Anglican, and Eastern Rite Catholics have traditionally maintained steadfast devotion to our Blessed Mother. Protestants, Jews, Mormons, Muslims, Hindus, Buddhists, New Agers, all faiths, and even professed unbelievers have claimed the blessing of discovering Mary in their lives. Some privileged persons have convincingly shared their personal encounters with our Blessed Mother. Others, on the other hand, feel called to keep their spiritual experiences with Mary quite private. Life changes dramatically for people who encounter Mary. One of the telltale signs of an authentic experience of the Blessed Mother is the aftereffects of such a blessing.[28] We become what we observe.

Christ, because of who He truly is, necessarily made His Mother so exalted in holiness that she is the "New Eve." Mother of the redeemed, Mary uniquely qualifies to intercede for us and with us. Those who know the Blessed Mother, Mediatrix of All Grace,[29] receive special knowledge—a "preview" as it were—of Paradise. They speak of our Blessed Mother as "the most loving of all human beings." If that is *not* their recollection, they have *not* encountered the Mother of Jesus Christ and do not deserve to be taken seriously as children of Mary.

There are, unfortunately, false visionaries who, among other things, seek to draw attention by claiming apparitions of the Blessed Mother. And of course, there are those who are mentally unbalanced who also claim miraculous experiences. All encounters with spiritual entities require immense spiritual discernment and guidance by experienced, highly trained experts.[30]

Jesus' life, death, and resurrection, which Mary shared with the Redeemer, endowed His Mother with the ability to love each of us as we most deeply need to be nurtured with pure mother love.[31] Christ has made it so. True apparitions of our Blessed Mother, always rooted in the mercy of God, are dazzling gifts that bring light and the burning desire for loving intimacy with God. Visionaries claim that to experience the boundless love of our Blessed Mother is to leap for joy as did John the Baptist from his mother's womb at the sound of Mary's voice.[32] Because of a most special grace, this generation is privileged progeny of the Mother of Jesus Christ. Proclaiming the greatness of the Lord, Mary personally invites all of us to enjoy her special protection and guidance. Joyful are those who hear her voice. Blessed are those who respond to her calls. Holy are those who persevere to the end.

THE SHELTERING BLESSED MOTHER

Every culture since the beginning of time clings to the shelter of the Blessed Mother. Her sacred mysteries hidden in antiquity unfold in the beliefs and legends of every tribe, group, and nation. She is present in humanity's dreams and longings. Mary is the perfect feminine archetype. Her titles[33] and gifts are as unique as human creativity at its finest. Her globally reported apparitions draw millions who search for healing, transformation, and global peace. All over the world seekers reap what they sow.

Huge crowds gather for Mary's apparitions and such celebrations generate receptivity to new, creative ideas steeped in harmony and mutual respect among people. The Blessed Mother silently inaugurates great new historical trends. In Cuapa, Nicaragua, in October 1980, she told visionary Bernardo Martinez:

> *"I am with you though you do not see me.*
> *I am your mother, the mother of all sinners.*
> *Love one another. Pardon one another. . . .*
> *Fulfill your duties.*
> *Put the word of God into practice.*
> *Try to be pleasing to God.*
> *Help your neighbor.*
> *In that way you will be pleasing to God."[34]*

Authentic apparitions of the Blessed Mother deeply inspire people with awareness of their own personal sacredness. Mary sometimes appears in times of darkness and grave danger. When the Blessed Mother's appearances are dishonored, desecration, desolation, despair, and death mock the cynical and the faithful alike. Woe mysteriously follows those who miss the time of their Blessed

Mother's visitation. Genocide in Rwanda and Bosnia speak for such spiritual error.

GIFTS

Many ponder reasons for the great proliferation of Marian apparitions. Some respond with joyful, grateful appreciation. The gloom-and-doom crowd worry about global devastation. Many think Mary's presence augurs the Second Coming of Christ. Experts claim no authentic visionaries have a complete picture of the future that they are willing to share. Urgent warnings and calls for global awakening to God's goodness are a common thread among all of Mary's messages.

Some people speculate about a massive strike by an asteroid that would wipe out most inhabitants of the earth and send humanity back to the Stone Age. There is evidence that this has happened before. The Chicxulab Crater in Mexico (about 190 miles west of Cancun), a depression measuring about 120 miles in diameter, came from an asteroid that may have wiped out the dinosaurs sixty-five million years ago. The comet or asteroid hit simultaneously with the mass extinction of species.[35]

Mary is not the classic "fairy godmother" of the Cinderella story. Yet that fable offers insight into the actual effects of our Blessed Mother's apparitions. Mary shows those who welcome her how to lift the drudgery of life's more unpleasant twists, chores, and responsibilities into the light of earth's divine purpose and beauty. After all, Mary is the Mother of the Omnipotent Prince of everyone's dreams. Her Son Jesus Christ, the Son of God, searches the highways and byways for those who cry for real meaning. The Savior sends His gentle Blessed Mother to tend to His little ones, to comfort us, feed us, dress us in her beautiful virtues, teach us her spiritual refinement, and make us comfortable to dine at the Table of the King of Kings in the House of the Great God of Abraham. Most humble of all God's creatures, and most blessed among women, Christ's ever Virgin Mother Mary, filled with grace, gently awakens her Son's beloved flock to the Voice of our Eternal Father deep in our being as He calls us to higher realms of life.

There are infinite mysteries about God's Kingdom on earth. We have not yet scratched the surface of the truths about life, death, and resurrection. Mary knows those sacred secrets. Sometimes the Blessed Mother, Our Lady of Cana uses miraculous methods to help ordinary people acquire peace, health, prosperity, and eternal life. More often than not, Mary, most humble of all God's creatures because she knows God best, helps us in hidden, unrecognized ways. Famous as Mother of the Poor, our Blessed Mother does not abandon the rich. Rather, she brings eternal value to wealth. Mary has wonderful power to heal and enrich dysfunctional family life. Known as Help of the Sick, the Blessed Mother cares for her ailing children with love beyond telling. We are only beginning to comprehend our Blessed Mother's prophetic secrets and gifts for these last days.

HIDDEN MIRACLES

A man required open heart surgery. He had great love for the Blessed Mother and asked her to pray for a miraculous healing of his heart. He prayed much and trusted God's mercy. His heart, however, did not heal spontaneously. Finally, as his health deteriorated, he had no choice but to undergo dangerous and complicated surgery. Many die from the operation and yet the surgery went far better than expected. He amazed the medical team with his faith, good humor, and quick recovery. He healed quickly and experienced no negative aftereffects of the surgery. God did not spare him the operation. Instead, He blessed the work of the medical providers, mitigated the pain, eliminated the cardiac disability, and restored the man to full strength. Those gifts could be supernatural. Perhaps they are not. The man did not hear humble Mary's voice. He did not see his Blessed Mother. His faith assured him she and her Divine Son were with him. He received an extraordinary answer to his prayers in an ordinary way, and that is actually how most miracles happen.

It is not unusual to experience the unexpected from our Blessed Mother. She helps us to do the right thing but frequently in ways we least expect. She is kind to us. The more we respond to Mary, the more we become aware of the intensity of her love for us, especially when we need her most. Our souls know Mary. As you intuit our Blessed Mother's reality, listen quietly. Our souls hear spiritual sounds. Our hearts are able to recognize our God-given Spiritual Mother.

God allows our Blessed Mother to speak to us to spur us on to holiness.[36] As you become skilled at discerning Mary's ways, entrust your heart, your family, your yesterdays and tomorrows to her. Mary is the best spiritual banker for she loses nothing we entrust to her. Rather, she augments everything with her own love and grace. Our Blessed Mother takes all that you and I entrust to her, swaddled in her perfect virtue, to the Throne of God where glistening stars reflect each of our treasures forever. Mary's willingness to take our meager gifts to the Throne of God is a hope of immense consolation and a source of great joy. Though we may have little, if any merit, with which to approach the Throne of God, Mary, our Blessed Mother has a special place in God's Heart to share with us. Our Blessed Mother likes to nurture our souls with the sweetness of her love. Her Divine Son is exquisitely kind to her children. Our Blessed Mother wants to show us God's Kingdom all around us. She joyfully praises God for each one of us.

Our imagination can be God's tool. This is a wonderful time to begin thinking about perfect motherhood. Consider the beauty and mystery of Mary holding us in her arms as she presents us to God our Creator. She shares the Lord's joy in us. She has eyes to see God's gifts planted deep in our souls. Her presence among us reminds us of the reality of the saints, life everlasting and the fulfillment of God's promises to us in Christ.

When we seek the "pot of gold" at the end of a rainbow, we discover that it belongs to our Redeemer, Mary's Son. His mercy is the gold necessary for our eternal life. Just as Jesus clung to Mary, we deeply need to cling to our Blessed Mother as we travel somewhere over the rainbow to eternal life. We do this by way of supernatural faith grounded in supernatural hope. We allow Mary to enter into our lives through the portal of faith. Hope gives meaning to our faith. There are other ways, of course, but if you choose to believe, you will be able to believe.

LOVE IS EXPENSIVE

The Bible, regulating human morals and directing us to wisdom and virtue, informs us that fear of the Lord is the beginning of wisdom. We have the power to separate ourselves from divine love. Our choices are dangerous if they lack wisdom. Cowards die many deaths. Wise ones live forever. Mary, Seat of Wisdom reminds us that God created us to love and be loved in return. Yet as life unfolds on earth, those who love most suffer most, for love is the most expensive of all the virtues. It is not easy to love in the face of sickness, sorrow, poverty, and violence, though it is the height of wisdom to do so. When we are faithful to the call to love, we truly are wise. Our Blessed Mother encourages us to be wise, to bond perfectly with her Son's commands to love one another, and do unto one another as we would have done to us.

When we deviate from what we most deeply are, we destroy ourselves. Love that is less than sacrificial love is only sentimentality. Or worse, it is selfishness disguised. Wisdom teaches us that sickness, sorrow, poverty, and violence are opportunities to embrace true love. True love connects us to our own personal reality. We belong in the Heart of the God of Love. A leader who did not fear God ordered the slaughter of the Holy Innocence in Bethlehem as a welcome gift to Jesus Christ at his birth.[37] True love is tough love. Joseph and Mary, responding to an angelic warning, courageously sacrificed familiar, loved people, places, and things and fled under the cover of night to Egypt to protect their sacred infant. If we are wise, we, too, must recognize evil and learn to escape its claws.

Evil has many faces. A refined, beautiful, highly educated woman managing a multibillion-dollar budget at an international organization in Washington, D.C., came home from work exhausted and sorrowful. She was embroiled in a highly abusive marriage. Her husband, a childhood sweetheart from her native village in central Africa, was not at home. The woman fell on her knees half praying and half sobbing, when she heard sweet sounds of a lullaby from long ago. Looking up, the woman saw Mary standing in the doorway. That was the first of several meetings with Mary. During those celestial visitations, the woman learned lessons of holy wisdom from the Mother of the Savior. She found the courage to end her abusive relationship, and discovered professional ways to increase the effectiveness of her work for the poor, sick, and suffering in Africa. Mary, Seat of Wisdom is the finest confidante and always our Mother Most Faithful.

We share memories of yesterday and dreams about tomorrow. Prayer, spiritual fasting and wise self-sacrifice are godly disciplines that strengthen us to recognize evil, avoid hell, and with Christ conquer death. As we continue to believe and sacrifice, pray and fast, all we touch will prosper in the way of God's plan. Our Blessed Mother would like each of us to strive valiantly to become more virtuous. She encourages us to pray more and make extra sacrifices for one another because she knows that doing so will make us happy. Mary is not asking us to do anything she herself has not already done for the love of God and us.

We are all poor sinners. We are all needy in some way. Our Blessed Mother asks us to love one another as Jesus loves us. What would Jesus do now? We need to pray and study sacred scripture to know. He showed us that no one has greater love and greater happiness than the person who wisely heals, blesses, serves, nurtures, educates, and lays down his or her life for the good of another. Life not lived for a higher purpose than mere self is no life at all. God honors wise generosity but never foolishness.

Each soul must pass through the valley of suffering to return to God's waiting arms. No one really knows why this must be as none of us likes to suffer. When we become unsure of our way, God's love leads us to His Blessed Mother. She is His most faithful daughter who, through God's compassion, guides, comforts, and consoles His suffering children of the earth. She who mothered the afflicted Son of God from the cold cave of Bethlehem to the bitter cross on Calvary brings perfect mother love to God's sorely afflicted people.

PRAYER AND FASTING STOP WAR

Our Blessed Mother's wisdom brings hope in these times and all times. She leads by example as a fierce spiritual battle for souls rages on every continent. People are suffering everywhere and stress is high throughout the world.[38] Though nations rise against nations, the call to peace has never been more valuable or more elusive. Mary calls us all to wisdom's table. Wisdom has many faces.

At Medjugorje, Mary said: "Dear children, have you forgotten that prayer and fasting stop war? Prayer and fasting change the natural law." September 13, 2001, was a National Day of Prayer in the United States. Worshippers in Washington, D.C., filled the National Cathedral to capacity. Throughout the land, Americans flocked to houses of worship to publicly honor God and seek His blessing. God promises that those who seek Him will find Him. Mary's calls to the world for peace were reflected in the hopes of congregations that day from sea to shining sea.

A notable artwork, the beautiful statue of Mary, *Notre Dame de la Visitation,* was formally blessed and crowned during noon Mass at the Pentagon in Washington, D.C., on Monday, May 13, 2002, the feast day of Our Lady of Fatima. This was probably the first ever May crowning in the heart of the Pentagon. The presence of this image of the Sheltering Blessed Mother brings calm and hope. As we discover how to welcome our Blessed Mother among us, even if only in a symbolic way, we all advance in our relationship with Christ, the Price of Peace. Peace is His to give.

Mary continuously pleads with us to pray for peace. She tells us that without our prayers, she can do nothing. She reminds us of her Son who is Wisdom Incarnate. Jesus assured us that strong faith will move mountains. In these times, as always, the world experiences terrible wars, sickness, and poverty. Loving prayer and spiritual fasting cover the troops, medical personnel, and aid workers wherever they are. Loving sacrifice and prayer allow God's joy to fall anew upon the earth. Prayer, penance, and fasting save nations, cities, families, and individuals.

THE BATTLE OF MONS

During the early days of World War I, thousands of British troops were slaughtered. The British army, with no available escape, was trapped at Mons. The German army was well postured to annihilate the stranded British troops. At the onset of battle, a huge angel appeared between the two armies, surrounded by thousands of other angels clearly visible to both sides. The charging German cavalry were horrified to find their horses fleeing in terror from the front. Nothing would convince them to proceed against the angelic host. The British retreated to safety under angelic protection. Later, Portuguese and Americans joined the Allies and they went on to victory.

British intelligence officers later questioned captured German officers of the Battle of Mons. They wondered why, when the British were so few in number, such a large force of Germans had fled. The German officers admitted that not only were they unable to control their horses, but that they observed the British with legions of supporting troops. Obviously, to the German army, the angels appeared as a large cavalry about to charge them.[39]

DUNKIRK

The miracle of Dunkirk is well known. World War II began in 1939. Britain poured men and supplies into France in support of French and Belgium armies. As much of the armament and supplies were leftovers from World War I, the British were ill prepared to meet a modern fighting force. Consequently, the Germans soon overran the Allies. The British army abandoned equipment and retreated to Dunkirk, the only available port of escape. Though Dunkirk was only a small port with long, sandy beaches and shallow water, the lives of nearly half a million men stranded on the beaches at Dunkirk were at risk.

In the face of such horror, King George VI of England appealed on the radio for a National Day of Prayer and Sacrifice for the troops. People responded wholeheartedly and filled places of worship to overflowing. Within three days, eight hundred boats, including those of the Royal Navy, private launches, canoes, rowboats, fishing boats, yachts, and a paddle steamer assembled along the South Coast of England. Under the cover of night, the boats continuously lifted wounded and stranded soldiers from the beaches at Dunkirk. Three hundred thirty-nine thousand men were rescued in this way over the three consecutive nights—obviously a miracle. Nautical experts calculated that, given the sizes and variety of boats used for the evacuation, such a rescue was not mathematically possible, but it happened none the less. Prayer was the cover weapon at Dunkirk.[40]

CHAIN THAT BIND GENERATIONS TO ETERNAL LIFE

During World War II, Jack's young American bride and his mother were distraught when he was drafted into the U.S. Army. He was quickly trained and immediately sent into combat in Europe. Every day, without fail, Jack's wife and mother went together to daily Mass in their small town in the midwest. The church was a long walk, and the weather was often cruel, but Jack's wife and mother believed in the power of prayer. They prayed fervently for Jack, said many rosaries for his safety each day, and they fasted for him. Every Friday afternoon, they spent time in adoration before the Blessed Sacrament. Jack escaped injury and death during his deployment, but he saw carnage all around him. He received a battlefield promotion to second lieutenant and returned home to his wife and mother free of post-traumatic stress syndrome. His mother continued her Friday eucharistic adoration for the rest of her life in thanksgiving. She ever after called the Holy Rosary the chain that binds generations to eternal life, love, peace, and abundance.

Prayer, spiritual fasting, and wise personal sacrifice have always been the way of believers. They are tools of peace and sentinels of wisdom. At the end of our life, our biggest regret may be the things we could have done to help ourselves and others but did not.

VIETNAM

During the Vietnam war, a young college freshman, whose older brother was a navy officer serving in Da Nang, was drafted into the U.S. Army. His parents were sorrowful as he left for war and his mother and sisters, even his two-year-old niece, promised to pray and fast for his safety. His dad was speechless; all he could do at that moment of sorrow was hand his son his well-worn rosary. Joe understood: he didn't know if he would ever see his folks again, so he tried his best to be cheerful. Things didn't go well for him. He was sent into combat near Saigon. One fiery night as he slept in his tent, he distinctly heard his mom call to him: "Joe, Joe, get up! Come here immediately!" Half dreaming, he leaped from his cot and raced out into the darkness. A bomb blast burned his ears and shrapnel scorched his left side. All his battalion died in the attack. Joe suffered multiple minor injuries and severe post-traumatic stress syndrome for the rest of his life. He never understood why he alone was spared. So every day Joe prays the rosary for his fallen comrades and helps others as best he can. He figures that is the least he can do. Joe doesn't know whether his dad's rosary that he keeps in his hands at night saved his life. He simply accepts that his "duty" is to pray the rosary daily for his fallen brothers and visit the Vietnam Memorial in Washington, D.C., annually to say a prayer for the fallen troops.

IRAQ

During the war in Iraq, a Pentagon employee shared the following eyewitness account.

"I am sure that all of you heard about the sandstorm in Iraq Tuesday and Wednesday [March 18 and 19, 2003, the worst in a hundred years some say] and the drenching rain that followed the next day. Our troops were bogged down and couldn't move effectively. The media was already wondering if the troops were in a 'quagmire' and dire predictions of gloom and doom came yesterday. After the weather had cleared, the Marine group that was mired the worst looked out at the plain they were just about to cross. What did they see? Hundreds if not thousands of anti-tank and anti-personnel mines had been uncovered by the wind and then washed off by the rain. If they had proceeded as planned, many lives would have undoubtedly been lost. As it was, the troops simply drove around them and let the demolition teams destroy them. Thank you, God, for protecting our young men and women! One person once asked George Washington if he thought God was on his side. His reply is reported to be, 'It is not that God should be on our side, but that we be on His.' P.S. In God we trust!"[41]

SPIRITUAL WINDS

Discipline does not come easily for most people and nations. Today, there is opportunity for prosperity for those who have highly defined, market-friendly skills. However, much of the world's population is illiterate, poor, and sick. Because we are one family in God, when one of us is sick, we are all sick. When some of us starve, we all starve in some way whether we are aware of it or not. Spiritual winds are bringing opportunities to overcome these difficulties.

Our Blessed Mother is with us to help us help one another, to become God's messengers, His angels, who gather the elect from the four winds. Mary asks us to give her our cares, concerns, hearts, dreams, hands, eyes, ears, so that we may serve her Son with all our strength. She invites us to allow her to be our Mother Most Faithful. As we trust her to change the direction of our lives, we begin to notice how much closer to her Son she brings us with each change.

THE VAGRANT IN GEORGETOWN

A famous media anchor whose husband was a prominent Washington power broker went to Medjugorje in 1990. She saw the "miracle of the sun" there along with several thousand other pilgrims. The woman decided to take her Catholic faith more seriously and become more spiritual. So each day she walked from her Georgetown home to Dahlgren Chapel of the Sacred Heart on the campus of Georgetown University for noon Mass. Along the way, she prayed the rosary.

On the third day of her noon journey, the woman came upon a beggar seated in front of a McDonald's fast-food restaurant on Wisconsin Avenue. He looked quite dirty and smelled terribly. The woman was appalled and wondered what was happening to her upscale neighborhood. The next day, the same vagrant was seated in front of McDonald's. The woman was even more appalled at his presence. That afternoon after Mass, she decided to pray in front of the Blessed Sacrament, something she had not done since early childhood. The next day, the woman came upon the homeless man once again. Her disdain was intense. She prayed for him after Mass in front of the Blessed Sacrament: not prayers of love or kindness. Rather, her prayer was a plea to rid her neighborhood of undesirables.

On her way home, the woman again saw the vagrant. Much disturbed by his unsightly appearance and dreadful smell, she spoke to him. "Don't you have somewhere to go? Why are you littering our beautiful neighborhood?" The man said nothing. Irritated, the woman hurried into the fast-food restaurant and ordered a large black coffee and a cheeseburger to go. She stomped back out of the restaurant, and tossing the food at the man said, "Here! I suppose you are drunk. Maybe this will induce you to leave!"

Suddenly, time stopped. The "man" began to glow like the noonday sun. Beauty and love and glory surrounded Him as He said, "Thank you, My beloved daughter." Ever so slowly, the light faded. There was no one there: only the sweet scent of lilies and myrrh. An unopened bag containing a large black coffee and cheeseburger lay on the sidewalk. The woman was awestruck. Was it the Lord? The event was life-changing for her and for her colleagues with whom she shared the experience. A friend told her, "You have finally experienced real love. Saint Augustine says love has hands to help others, feet to hasten to the poor and needy, eyes to see misery and want, ears to hear the sighs and sorrows of others."

We know not the day or the hour or the way of our own visitations. The Mighty One does great things for us. Holy is His Name.

My name is Beauty.
I make all things new. Do not cling to the past.
Recognize with vigor and pleasure that the time of your
visitation is at hand.
Embrace My Plan in your lives with joy and peace.
Do not allow apprehension to color your obedience to My will.

Grotto at Lourdes where the Blessed Virgin Mary appeared to Saint Bernadette in 1854.

CHAPTER 8

Queen of Peace

Jesus said to his Disciples: "Let not your heart be troubled. You believe in God, believe also in me. In my Father's house there are many mansions. If not, I would have told you; because I go to prepare a place for you. And if I shall go, and prepare a place for you, I will come again, and I will take you to myself that where I am, you also may be."[1]

Our Blessed Mother knows the safest, easiest, and fastest way into the Heart of Christ.[2] Her biological son Jesus is one person who combines both a human and a divine nature.[3] The person of Christ is God and Mary is Mother of God.[4] Great minds have always attempted to explain Jesus Christ and His Mother. Mary is fully human and highly favored by God. Visions of Jesus' Blessed Mother involve prophesy and give a preview of future events.[5] Her apparitions leave no doubt that the Communion of Saints is real and the promised resurrection of our bodies in an afterlife will happen. Openness to the loving presence of our Blessed Mother is a great grace and a wondrous heavenly gift that can make our present lives happier and more valuable.

As the trees, birds, sky, sea, and wind all work together in harmony to bring peace to people who love and remain faithful to God, so also the Blessed Mother ever so graciously is among us to guide and help those who welcome her. Mary's presence with us cannot be compared to God's presence in us by sanctifying grace, by which we are made partakers of Divine Life. Mary is not omnipresent. Rather, as Mother of God, Mary is morally present to us and we to her as she cooperates with the Holy Spirit in forming Jesus in our souls. Saint Louis de Montfort explains: "Mary is present in our souls as the sun is present in a room by its light and warmth, even though it is not there itself."

Wherever the sun rises on earth, diverse people see our Blessed Mother, hear her, or find ways to the Throne of God in her arms. Technology and ease of travel are great blessings that allow Mary's visitations to become globally known. One who prays can almost sense Mary's delight in bringing her protégés into the Sacred Heart of her Son where all the joys of paradise await them.

OUR LADY OF AMERICA

In 1954, exactly one hundred years after the official proclamation of the dogma of the Immaculate Conception, a cloistered Sister in a religious community in Ohio was having personal visits, not only with the Archangels Michael and Gabriel, but also with the Lord Jesus and our Blessed Mother under the title Our Lady of America, the Immaculate Virgin. Sister Mary Ephrem, née Millie Neuzil, died on January 10, 2000, in Fostoria, Ohio. Shortly thereafter, the Catholic Church, by means of the appropriate bishops involved in supervising and investigating the apparitions,[6] authenticated the messages of the Lord and Our Lady to Millie. These are the first and only Marian apparitions formally approved in the United States by the Roman Catholic Church. Some excerpted messages from Our Lady of America are:

> "I am pleased with the love and honor my children in America give to me, especially through my glorious and unique privilege of the Immaculate Conception. I promise to reward their love by working through the power of my Son's Heart and my Immaculate Heart miracles of grace among them. I do not promise miracles of the body but of the soul. It is mainly through these miracles of grace that the Holy Trinity is glorified among men and nations. Let America continue and grow in its love for

me, and I in return, in union with the Heart of my Son, promise to work wonders in her.

"I am Our Lady of America. I desire that my children honor me, especially by the purity of their lives. I wish [America] to be the country dedicated to my purity. I desire Americans to have faith and firmly believe in my love for them. I desire that they be the children of my Pure Heart. I desire through my children of America to further the cause of faith and purity among peoples and nations. Let them come to me with confidence and simplicity."

Our Lady of America was overjoyed at the love and devotions of her American children. She appeared with an image of the world in her hands and tears flowing from her eyes as though to cleanse the earth from guilt. She said:

"Assuage the sorrow of my Heart over the ingratitude of sinful men by the love and chasteness of your lives. I come to you O children of Americas as a last resort. I plead with you to listen to my voice. Cleanse your souls in the Precious Blood of my Son. Live in His Heart, and take me in that I may teach you to live in great purity of heart which is so pleasing to God. Be my army of chaste soldiers, ready to fight to the death to preserve the purity of your souls. I am the Immaculate One, Patroness of your land.[7] Be my faithful children as I have been your faithful mother. I desire to make the whole of America my shrine by making every heart accessible to the love of my Son."

Our Lady of America appeared on October 13, 1956, smiling with heaven's beauty. She held with both hands a small replica of the Basilica of the Shrine of the Immaculate Conception in Washington, D.C. Our Lady joyfully announced:

"This is my Shrine. I am very pleased with it. Tell my children I thank them. Let them finish it quickly and make it a place of pilgrimage. It will be a place of wonders. I promise this. I will bless all those who, by prayers, labor or material aid, help to erect, maintain and visit this shrine."

Our Lady requested that a statue be made according to the likeness of her apparitions to Sister Mary Ephrem. She specifically asked that this statue be carried in solemn procession to the Shrine of the Immaculate Conception in Washington, D.C. Our Blessed Mother asked to be honored there in a special way as Our Lady of America, the Immaculate Virgin. The great statue of Our Lady of America is venerated in the Pope John Paul II Cultural Center in Washington, D.C. It is only a short journey from there to the Basilica. One can hope that Mary's request of her American children will be answered quickly.

Our Lady of America said:

"The hour grows late. Suffering and anguish, such as never before experienced, is about to overtake mankind. It is the darkest hour. But if people will come to me, my Immaculate Heart will make it bright again with the mercy which my Son will rain down through my hands. Help save those who will not save themselves. Help bring once again the sunshine of God's peace upon the world. Will my children in America listen to my pleadings and console my Immaculate Heart? Will my loyal sons and daughters carry out my desires and thus help bring the peace of Christ once again to mankind? Pray and do penance that this may come to pass. Trust me and love me. Do not disregard the voice of your Mother. It is the voice of love trying to save you from eternal ruin. My Immaculate Heart desires to see the Kingdom of Jesus my Son established in all hearts. You must pray with greater fervor and offer yourselves with greater love to the Heart of my Son. My Immaculate Heart is the channel through which the graces of the Sacred Heart are given to humanity.

"My children of America, unless you do penance by mortification and self-denial and thus reform your lives, God will visit you with punishments hitherto unknown to you. There will be peace as has been promised, but not until my children are purified and cleansed from defilement, and clothed thus with the white garment of grace, and are made ready to receive this peace, so long promised and so long held back because of the sins of mankind. My dear children, either you will do as I desire and reform your lives, or God Himself will need to cleanse you in the fires of untold punishment. You must be prepared to receive His great gift of peace. If you do not prepare yourselves, God will Himself be forced to do so in His justice and mercy.

"Making the rosary a family prayer is very pleasing to me. I ask that all families strive to do so. But be careful to say it with great devotion, meditating on each mystery and striving to imitate in your daily lives the virtues depicted therein. Live the mysteries of the rosary as I lived them, and it will become a chain binding you to me forever. They who are found in the circle of my rosary will never be lost. I myself will lead them to the throne of my Son, to be eternally united to Him."[8]

Our Blessed Mother, Immaculate Tabernacle of the Indwelling God, wants us to be unafraid. She asks us to pray for great faith, immense trust, and abiding love. Mary promises that our families will have much healing because we have come to her. She has great graces in store for us, our children and grandchildren. Our Blessed Mother gives us many to serve, and she sends her people to serve us as we do her Son's work on earth. Mary promises that days ahead shall fill our hearts with God's choicest blessings. Our Blessed Mother hears her children's cries. She wants to rearrange our lives so that we never again must taste the bitter grapes of wrath that come from the jowls of the evil one.

Though we do not know when or in what way, these last days are the time of the return to the earth in glory of our Blessed Mother's Son. The multitudes await His return. Our Blessed Mother asks us to protect our children carefully, free them from the influences of envy, greed, and lust that destroy their innocence; free them from arms that grasp but do not love. Jesus is among us. Our Blessed Mother asks us to pray that all may hear His voice and respond to

His call. Mary asks us to pray in the silence of our longings. Pray always. Pray lest we miss the time of our own visitation.

No one is born alone, no one walks the earth alone, and no one dies alone. We draw to ourselves what we most deeply desire. Undoubtedly many see Mary, our Spiritual Mother, but do not yet recognize who she is. Research and study lend powerful credence to Mary's presence among us, along with other celestial beings, angels, saints, and prophets who guide and help us in our ordinary, everyday life on earth. We are constantly surrounded by loving, caring, and helping spirits of pure love who desire to encourage and help us as we learn to love. Some have more capacity than others to recognize them. We need the gift of discernment of spirits now more than ever.

In God and through God's love we receive grace to avail ourselves of the presence and power of His celestial court all around us. Mary, the most humble of all God's creatures, Queen of the Heavenly Court, is queen of each heart that loves and honors God. She brings her children into His Heart that they may taste His love. Soon all God's people shall recognize their Spiritual Mother. When we know our own Spiritual Mother, we shall have our identity.

Our Blessed Mother, Star of the Sea, Comfort of the Afflicted helps us to be aware that gratitude pleases God. God is the Generous Heart. Those who would be godly are generous. God our Father rewards a generous heart but never a foolish heart. Our Blessed Mother promises that we can never outdo God in generosity.

OUR LADY IN SOUTH AMERICA

The following is just one widely reported example of how Mary helps her children:[9]

> "The Colombian daily 'El Tiempo' revealed on Holy Saturday that a crisis that could have ended in an open conflict between Colombia, Ecuador and Venezuela was averted by Colombian President Alvaro Uribe confiding the situation to the intercession of Mary under the three different titles by which she is the country's patroness.

"The crisis between Colombia and its southern (Ecuador) and northeastern (Venezuela) neighbors started On March 1, when Uribe ordered a military raid into Ecuador's, territory against a rebel camp used by Marxist guerrillas to launch terrorist strikes. The raid targeted and killed the No. 2 FARC rebel leader, Raul Reyes.

"In response, Ecuador's President Rafael Correa cut all diplomatic relationships with Colombia. Venezuela's Hugo Chavez, Correa's political ally, ordered a massive military surge to the Colombian border as well.

"Quoting Fr. Julio Solórzano, Chaplain of Colombia's Presidential Palace, 'El Tiempo' revealed that on March 5, when the rhetoric and blames between the presidents was increasing tensions, President Uribe called for a Rosary to pray for the end of tensions.

"The Rosary, prayed at the Presidential Palace's chapel, was dedicated, upon Uribe's request, to Our Lady of Chiquinquira, Our Lady of Coromoto and Our Lady of Mercy, respectively the patronesses of Colombia, Venezuela and Ecuador.

"Uribe invited all officials at the Presidential Palace to the Rosary, as well as the minister of Defense and the Interior.

" 'For believers'—'El Tiempo' wrote—'the prayer was more than effective, since only two days after, the presidents of the three countries shook hands during the Group of Rio summit, and for many the crisis was over.'

"In fact, on April 7, at the Dominican Republic summit, the three presidents vented their differences, but agreed to stand down after Colombia apologized for the raid."[10]

SPIRITUAL VISIBILITY

Facing dangers of war, global economic crisis, nuclear holocaust, and political unrest, it is not surprising that God grants many people the ability to see, hear, and respond to our Blessed Mother. In all times, but especially in difficult times, Mary and the angels and saints who travel with her necessarily become exquisitely visible to searching hearts of longing souls who love and serve with honor.

When everything around us crumbles in the sands of illusion, our Blessed Mother is most powerful for she knows Truth as no other human.[11] We, like little starlings, are not yet "big enough" to approach "I AM WHO AM"[12] without fear and trembling. Infinitely humble God allows our Blessed Mother to be His hands and arms in the world of the twenty-first century. Through Mary, the great God of Abraham stoops low to pick up His little ones and hold us in the palm of His Hand. Eternally gracious God sends our Blessed Mother now in a special way never before granted, because we need her.

All over the world, "I AM WHO AM" allows His own to taste the sweetness of His Presence and peace through Mary. We are each hidden in Mary's sacred secrets. She is our gift and we are her gift. Our Blessed Mother takes God's little ones by the hand and brings us to rest serene upon the Heart of Jesus, even if we do not yet know Him by name. Mary's Son, the Good Shepherd is leading His flock ever closer to the Presence of God in us, around us, always with us.

You and I stand at a threshold we must cross. Before us are two doors. One leads to life—awareness of the sacredness of all creation; the other door opens to death—quicksand fields of illusion fraught with unrequited longings. Our choice is eternally irrevocable. Mary is here to help us choose wisely.

World leaders are becoming aware of the need to widen and deepen geostrategic cooperation among nations.[13] In a world of complex interdependence, we all share the risks of climate change and nuclear proliferation. Through the mercy of God, our shared Spiritual Mother is with us to guide us into a harmonious world of mutual cooperation and personal empowerment.[14]

Resistance to change is the greatest peril of our times. Just one example is the tragedy in Kibeho, Rwanda. Mary appeared there to six young people from 1981 to 1983 with urgent warnings. Jesus appeared there to a young pagan boy, Segatasha, and instructed him in the faith. Unfortunately, though heavenly visitations occurred and warnings were given, a bloodbath of genocide brought forth rivers of human corpses in Rwanda.[15] Sadly, many people throughout the world still cling to ways of ancient bondage.

Our Blessed Mother gently mentors us in the process of letting go of ideals and practices steeped in cobwebs of the past. She helps us climb the mountain of asceticism, discarding customs and possessions that weigh us down. Our Blessed Mother, if we allow her, shows us how to live in simplicity amid the splendor of God's presence, to hear His loving Voice, ever so quiet, in the depths of our longings.

All generations call Mary blessed for He who is mighty has done great things for her. Wise people watch and wait. This is the time of our visitation. Events laden with terror and even annihilation are displayed daily on television and the Internet. We all share the air, water, skies, and soil of the planet. Nuclear war and global economic collapse spare no one, but have no fear. The world is awakening to our Blessed Mother's urgent, most loving guidance from Heaven. We all have a part to play in the unfolding drama of spiritualizing the earth and the cosmos.

Our loving Creator made us to seek holiness above all else yet most of us would admit that even the definition of holiness is difficult to grasp. We all need to increase our spiritual visibility. Supernatural light is the means. Mary knows much about holiness. Her Son is the Savior of the world. God offers Mary to each of us. She is our Spiritual Mother who loves us, nurtures us, protects us, inspires us, and gives us supernatural light for life's great quests.

There are no coincidences; it is not by accident that you and I have the opportunity to learn about God from our Spiritual Mother. With the help of God's angels and saints, our Blessed Mother brings us wonderful spiritual illumination of all life. Prayer keeps us open to such light, and being open, we must be willing to receive Mary's sacred secrets in the way our Blessed Mother chooses. Mary is Queen of Angels.[16] Angelic guidance is a great, yet largely unused gift available to all of us. Our Blessed Mother and her angel coterie bring fullness of life to faithful people who seek peace and contentment.

THE COST OF SPIRITUAL NEGLIGENCE

History shows us that if we negligently disregard our Blessed Mother's assistance and spurn her advice, we allow ourselves to be cruelly swallowed by misfortune. Consider the people of France when their country was at the height of its power under the reign of King Louis XIV. The monarch was so insulated in his grandeur that he did not receive, and consequently did not act upon, messages from heaven that were given to Saint Margaret Mary.[17] His grandson, King Louis XVI was deposed and condemned to death during the bloody French Revolution that changed life for everyone in the country. While imprisoned in the Bastille awaiting death by guillotine, Louis XVI heard about heavenly messages requesting the French king to consecrate his kingdom to the Sacred Heart of Jesus. Desperate, King Louis immediately obeyed. But legend says the Lord's voice reverberated throughout the prison: "It's too late." In 1799, the French Revolution unleashed its fury upon all citizens of France.[18] Humble, wise leadership, open to the ways of God is imperative for peaceful coexistence of the world's population. We all need to pray for one another for those graces.

There is a delightful way to live in the loving providence of God and a difficult path spread with atrocities. We suffer too much unnecessarily. Woe comes to those and their offspring who miss the time of their visitation. Blessed are those who respond in a timely manner to heaven's calls.

Mary joyfully illumines God's bountiful presence on earth. Our Blessed Mother knows God's marvelous plan for us. Her sacred secrets contain our life, our sweetness, and our hope.[19] Mary is forever our hands-on mother who has authority over collective evil.[20] The only safe harbor in the world is God's will. His love heals all things.

In the United States, Marian prayer groups abound.[21] Notice the unveiling of darkness in places consecrated to Mary. Evil cannot abide for long in her territory. Since the inauguration of global Marian prayer groups in the 1990s, largely in response to Our Lady's purported requests at Medjugorje, dark, long-hidden practices are coming to light. Marian societies, charities, and conferences throughout the world seek healing, prosperity, and peace through faith, prayer, fasting, conversion, and reconciliation.

Our Blessed Mother humbly emerges from the pages of Sacred Scripture to bring this generation to her Son who is the conqueror of evil. Mary asks us all to study Sacred Scripture. The Bible reminds us that Satan is strong. He is aware his time is short. If any generation has doubted the reality of evil, its face is manifest now as never before through electronic media. Earth is a testing ground for souls destined for eternal happiness.

SEEKING THE HOLY GRAIL

We all seek the Holy Grail in one way or another. We have choices to make about virtues that we need to be happy now and in our afterlife. Anyone can abandon the spiritual journey and cowards usually do. When times become difficult, it helps to remember that virtue untested is no virtue at all. There is a noble way to acquire virtue. Our Blessed Mother knows sacred secrets that illumine the valiant way.

Love is the supreme virtue we all must master if we hope to live happily ever after. Those who love most suffer most for love is the most expensive of all the virtues. A person freed from the chains of guilt and oppression is capable of great love. As we welcome our Blessed Mother into our lives, she is able to loosen shackles we may not even know we wear. When difficulties loom, Mary can bring unfathomable graces to those who invite her into their lives. Has anyone ever calculated how much wine Jesus miraculously produced at the wedding feast of Cana in response to His Mother's request?[22] Those wine vats (or ones of similar size and content) still exist at the shrine at Cana in the Holy Land. There was not a village population in Galilee large enough to consume the quantities of wine Christ made that day. It is little wonder so many people followed Him everywhere. Love always triumphs. God's love is the elixir of freedom.

FULTON J. SHEEN

There are those who believe Servant of God Archbishop Fulton J. Sheen was "perhaps the most popular and socially influential American Catholic of the twentieth century."[23] His seventy-three books, videos, television shows (from 1951 to 1957 with a viewing audience of thirty million) and radio programs (from 1930 to 1952 with a listening audience of four million) are known around the world by people of all ages and background. Rumor has it that Pope John Paul II studied Fulton J. Sheen's programs. The great archbishop was the voice of American Catholicism at a time when the Great Depression sent claws of fear and fangs of anger to the throats of ordinary citizens seeking home, family, and security. Few really knew the Gospel of Christ's glory that Fulton Sheen so eloquently brought to his Catholic Hour radio programs from 1930 to 1952. In 1952, Reverend Sheen began his television show, *Life Is Worth Living*, and it was said: "Bishop Sheen can't sing, can't dance and can't act. All he is . . . is sensational."[24]

When Fulton Sheen, Auxiliary Bishop of the Archdiocese of New York (1951–1965) preached in Saint Patrick's Cathedral in New York, as many as six thousand people crowded into the pews to hear the man of God tell them the Good News of Jesus' promises. He brought America to fullness when he effectively promulgated the quintessential American principle: "It is the home which decides the nation. What happens in the family will happen later in Congress, the White House and the Supreme Court. Every country gets the kind of government it deserves. As we live in the home, so shall the nation live."[25]

Fulton Sheen understood well what it means to be called to the vocation of priesthood. Successors of the apostles are, after all, ordinary men whose work Christ makes extraordinary. Sheen wrote that a vocation to the priesthood begins when one is confronted with a presence, not as dramatic as Paul when he encountered the risen Lord, but with a sense of the unworldly, the holy, and the transcendent. The second stage of understanding this great mystery of the priesthood is the individual's profound sense of unworthiness. God is holy: the aspirant is not. But God calls men, not angels. Archbishop Sheen said, "God can do something with those who see what they really are and who know they need cleansing, but can do nothing with the man who feels himself worthy."[26] Purgation, he reminded people, begins in seminary and "continues through life in the form of physical suffering, mental anguish, betrayals, scandals, false accusations—all of which summon the one called to become more worthy of the treasure."[27]

Archbishop Fulton Sheen was completely dedicated to our Blessed Mother. As the nineteenth century was the "Age of Mary" and the monumental apparitions of Our Lady to Saint Bernadette at Lourdes in 1858 became known throughout the world, so children of the twentieth century inherited the fervor and dedication that children of Mary cherish.[28] In 1917, the year Fulton Sheen entered seminary, Our Lady began appearing to the visionaries at Fatima. How the Fatima "miracle of the sun" impacted ordinary people who read eyewitness accounts of the divine phenomenon in the *New York Times* is known only by the fruits of their lives. Huge miracles do make the journey of faith easier. Fulton Sheen consecrated his life to our Blessed Mother. He spoke and wrote and lived as Mary's priest, and identified totally with her powerful role in the Church and in the world.

The America of Father Fulton Sheen was quite different from twenty-first-century America. Young Fulton Sheen numbered among 21,000 priests to serve 18 million U.S. Catholics. With more than 16,000 churches and 5,000 parish schools, there was ample work and respect for committed priests and nuns. "Many if not most Catholics were convinced that they were the future in America and already the superior guide in theology and morals."[29]

Reverend Sheen was a man of asceticism. He ate little, slept little, worked harder than most, and prayed constantly. One mystical experience young seminarian Sheen wrote about is the following that occurred about 5:30 p.m. during a retreat:

"My mind seemed to be suffused with light . . . there came to me an illumination of soul, a light that suffused my intellect, bringing with it an overwhelming conviction of the certitude of Faith. . . . I was momentarily possessed of the absolute and irrefutable character of Faith. . . . My faith centered not just in the Creed, but in the Church, and it became personalized in the Pope as the Head of the Church and the Vicar of Christ."[30]

His mystical illumination was so profound that afterward, Fulton Sheen began his lifelong practice of spending a continuous hour every day in the presence of the Lord Jesus in the Most Blessed Sacrament. Using the forum of radio, television, books, pamphlets, preaching, and evangelizing, Archbishop Sheen urged everyone, of every faith and background, to make a Holy Hour every day with Jesus in the Blessed Sacrament. He wrote that such practice is to "aid souls in securing an inner peace by meditating one continuous hour a day on God and our immortal destiny."[31]

Fulton Sheen's television program was so popular that, in 1952, he won an Emmy Award. As he accepted his Emmy, he smiled and said that he desired to pay tribute to his four writers: Evangelists Matthew, Mark, Luke, and John. Thunderous applause followed.

Archbishop Sheen had consuming dedication to the mercy of God. In late February 1953, he foretold the death of Soviet dictator Josef Stalin on his television program. Stalin, son of an abusive alcoholic father and pious mother, moved nine times before he turned ten years old. His mother enrolled him in the Gori Church School when he turned ten. Josef sang in the choir, wrote poetry, and was first in his class. The town where he lived was a violent and lawless place. His addict father, a cobbler, abandoned his wife and son, leaving them to fend for themselves. At sixteen, Stalin received a scholarship to the Georgian Orthodox Seminary of Tiflis and became an atheist within the first year. Stalin went on to become the head of the Union of Soviet Socialist Republics. It is conservatively estimated that under his reign, more than ten million Soviet citizens died because of famine and repression.[32]

Fulton Sheen, ever the man of God, knew the Scriptures. He had high hopes for the spiritualization of all people throughout the world, and he trusted the mercy of God. Consequently, on his television program, he predicted the eminent death of the Soviet dictator when he said: "Stalin must one day meet his judgment." Within days, Stalin unexpectedly suffered a stroke and was dead within the week, on March 5, 1953. One can hope that somehow Josef Stalin had become aware of Archbishop Sheen's warning and consequently had prepared himself to meet his Maker.

Fulton Sheen's path to holiness was quite simple: on the day of his ordination he vowed to keep the daily Holy Hour and to offer a Mass every Saturday in honor of our Blessed Mother to "solicit her protection on my priesthood."[33] He writes of his reliance on Mary's benevolence:

"When I was ordained, I took a resolution to offer the Holy Sacrifice of the Eucharist every Saturday to the Blessed Mother, renewing my feeble love of her and invoking her intercession. All this makes me very certain that when I go before the Judgment Seat of Christ, He will say to me in His Mercy: 'I heard My Mother speak of you.'

"During my life I have made about thirty pilgrimages to the shrine of Our Lady of Lourdes and about ten to her shrine in Fatima. One of the first pilgrimages to Lourdes was while I was a university student at Louvain. I had just enough money to go to Lourdes but not enough to live on once I arrived. I asked my brother Tom if he had any money, but he was a typical university student too—no money. I said to him: 'Well, if I have faith enough to go to Lourdes to celebrate the fifth anniversary of my Ordination, it is up to the Blessed Mother to get me out.'

"I arrived in Lourdes 'broke.' I went to one of the good hotels—though by no means would any hotel in Lourdes ever be considered in the luxury class. I decided that if the Blessed Mother was going to pay my hotel bill, she could just as well pay a big one as a little one. I made a novena—nine days of prayer—but on the ninth morning nothing happened, the ninth afternoon nothing happened, the ninth evening nothing happened. Then it was serious. I had visions of gendarmes. . . .

"I decided to give the Blessed Mother another chance. I went to the grotto about ten o'clock at night. A portly American gentleman tapped me on the shoulder: "Are you an American priest?" "Yes." "Do you speak French?" "Yes." "Will you come to Paris with my wife and daughter tomorrow, and speak French for us?" He walked me back to the hotel; then he asked me perhaps the most interesting question I have ever heard in my life: "Have you paid your hotel bill yet?" I out-fumbled him for the bill. The next day we went to Paris and for twenty years or more after that, when I would go to New York on weekends to instruct converts, I would enjoy the hospitality of Mr. and Mrs. Thomas Farrell, who had become the agents of the Blessed Mother to save me from my creditors.

"When I finished my university studies, I made another pilgrimage to Lourdes. I was deeply concerned that perhaps I would not be permitted to return to Mary's Shrine again, for I knew not to what task the Bishop would assign me. I asked the Blessed Mother to give me some sign that despite the odds of returning to Lourdes, she would do what seemed impossible. The sign I asked for was this: that after I offered the Holy Sacrifice of the Mass and before I would reach the outer gate of the shrine, a little girl age about twelve, dressed in white, would give me a white rose. About twenty feet from the gate I could see no one. I remember, saying: "You had better hurry, there is not much time left." As I arrived at the gate a little girl age twelve, dressed in white, gave me the white rose."[34]

Mary delivered more than mere protection, payment of a hotel bill, and a white rose to her archbishop. Nearly a hundred years later, his zeal continues to circumnavigate the globe with choicest morsels from the Heavenly Banquet for every sincere truth-seeker.

On the Feast Day of the Guardian Angels, October 2, 1979, Pope John Paul II spoke to Fulton Sheen during his visit to Saint Patrick's Cathedral in New York. Embracing the frail archbishop, the Pope said publicly: "You have written and spoken well of the Lord Jesus Christ. You are a loyal son of the Church." Two months later, Archbishop Sheen was laid to rest in the crypt of Saint Patrick's Cathedral.

In 2002, Sheen's Cause for Canonization was officially opened and he is now referred to as a Servant of God.

HUMAN TABERNACLES

Twentieth-century atheism emanating out of Soviet Russia spread abroad in numerous forms, becoming a quasi-fashionable belief system. Simultaneously, witnesses all over the world began seeing weeping icons and bleeding statues, a spinning sun in many places and metal segments of rosary beads inexplicably turning gold. Such phenomena are considered visual effects of the invisible world of spiritual reality, which atheism denies.

True freedom is spiritual, precious, and the pearl of great price we seek, either actively or subconsciously. By deciding to participate in the fullness of life through faith-filled harmony with God's loving presence, we may achieve true freedom. When God's presence is unrecognized, unprotected, and unappreciated, our true freedom degenerates into slavery.

The earth, the cosmos, and the heavens follow immutable laws of nature. So also must we if we would be happy. God eternally loves and blesses what He creates. It is most unwise to give valuable time to negativity. Our job is to accept divine peace, live divine peace, spread divine peace, and maintain divine peace. Too many of us continue to fight truth. Often we are not even aware that we are engaged in such a battle. Whole regions of the earth are torture chambers for misguided men, women, and children who do not yet taste God's love.

We are all cherished by God. We are all His dear creatures. Division among us does not come from God. We are created to love one another as brothers and sisters, help one another, and bless one another. We reap what we sow. God will treat us as we treat others.

The quest is on. Humans are now searching every inch of the planet for treasures of every kind. Wisdom is necessary to distinguish between rubbish and riches. Global telecommunications systems let interested ones see what is being uncovered. All that is hidden will be seen. There is no place to hide. Evil traits are openly available to discerning people. People hurt and are crying out for answers to ancient conflicts. Everyone needs God's loving protection. Our Blessed Mother reminds us that if believers sincerely live their faith, the whole world will become holy.

Time is God's gift to the lonely, thirsty, and dying world. Everyone is invited to the Eternal Wedding Feast. Mary's Son has power to provide more than enough for everyone.

The good news is that human hearts are tabernacles for no other presence than God's love. Hearts filled with divine love make a new earth that is God's Holy House of Prayer. Love dissolves gates that block Paradise. The fiery sword of the cherubim guarding the way to the Tree of Life is Truth.[35] That light of love flickers now in caves of faithfulness hidden in crevices of the planet earth. Soon the light will be a burning wind that consumes the world we now experience. People are sick of evil. The triumph of Mary's Immaculate Heart is a fire of love that eventually will consume the reign of evil. Our Blessed Mother directs our eyes to Jesus Christ who brings Heaven to earth. Awareness of God, reunion with "I AM WHO AM" is Paradise regained.

Mary's role as Mother of the human race, the Second Eve,[36] is steeped in the Incarnation of her Divine Son. God's only begotten Son Jesus Christ is her baby boy.[37] Through him, with him and in him, God's people belong to Mary in a relationship ever ancient and ever new that is being disclosed globally. Our Blessed Mother has all the goods of the earth to give us for our happiness. God's will is her delight. As mother of our eternal life, Mary is judicious in gift-giving.

Mary never leaves our side during our pilgrimage on earth though she will not interfere in our lives uninvited. Mary, our Mother will always take care of us, in this life and the next. She invites all of us to rest quietly under the mantle of her motherly love. That love will never fail us. Everything we do occurs in her presence and the presence of God. We are slow learners. We have been in training for thousands of years and the time of our visitation is at hand. We are beginning to recognize the time of our visitation.

Whenever God allows Mary to appear physically in apparitions, there is much grace for those who choose to participate. Pilgrimages to such holy sites free our souls from attachments to the earth and its limitations. Our Blessed Mother is always present in a special way for those who visit her dear Son Jesus in the Blessed Sacrament.

I am always present in a special way for those who visit my dear Son Jesus in the Blessed Sacrament.
Pray always: "Sacred Heart of Jesus most loving, I place my trust in Thee."
In that way, you find the peace that passes all understanding.
Pray much for your country.
Pray for your family.
I am your Mother Most Faithful.
I am always here for you.
Rely upon the love of my Son, the Savior of the world.
Those who disregard His ways taste deeply of the sorrows of the earth.
Cling to me now. I am your Mother Most Faithful.

The Icon of the Mother of God of Kazan—Patroness and Protector of all Russia

"Icons underline the Church's fundamental mission to recognize that all people and all things are created and called to be 'good' and 'beautiful.'"

—Orthodox Patriarch Bartholomew I of Constantinople, October 11, 2008, The Vatican Sistine Chapel in an address to the Roman Catholic World Synod of Bishops[1]

PART III

Gate of Heaven

SUPERNATURAL LOVE

"The fear of the Lord is the beginning of wisdom.
Fools despise wisdom and instruction."[1]

$\mathcal{N}$*ot everyone* understands Mary. Misogynists have trouble identifying with her. Some who have little or no faith find her contemporary appearances too challenging. Seculars need to see and hear Mary in some way to accept her reality. Our minds can be a labyrinth with many avenues of deception. Our bodies last only until death do us part. Transcendent reality is just as real as the walls around us. We are and can experience much more than our five senses report. Mary our Spiritual Mother shows us her secret way. Her presence among us is rightfully clothed in the mystery of mysticism.

The Patriarchs foreshadowed Mary, Mother of the Redeemer in types and figures. Prophets foretold the Blessed Virgin Mary's divine mission. The Psalms teach us that God's secrets (including Mary) are reserved for those who fear Him: it is a great gift of unmerited grace to have sincere awe of God. Who would have more wonder than the Mother of the Word made flesh? Medieval Jewish scholars produced the Kabala that gives us mystical systems of understanding such divine revelation. God's glory is hidden.[2] Consequently, God-fearing people actively pursue the essence of wisdom, understanding, and knowledge that flow forth from the Holy Spirit. The Blessed Mother, true spouse of the Holy Spirit, is described by the Evangelists and graciously saluted by the angels.[3]

The past is gone. Time is precious. The future is not ours. Only the present moment belongs to us. Our Blessed Mother asks us to take control of the present moment. Focus on problems only at the time we can do something about them. Enjoy God's blessings each moment. Remain awake to God's opportunities in the present moment only. Marg's sweet voice of peace guides us every day. Her grace makes of our souls a sanctuary reserved for God alone. Mary brings divine techniques that focus on our personal dignity as children of God. Suffering and sorrows pass away. The Blessed Mother awakens our spiritual perception of events: they in themselves are not stressful. As we look more closely at events, that knowledge guides our reactions to reality. Wisdom replaces tension with tranquillity as we take control over our reactions to events moment by moment. Mary brings us pristine faith and Herculean trust. With those gifts, supernatural love is possible.

As you shall discover in this section, Mary intervenes in history to help people listen to the inner voice of love deep within each moment. As it was in the past, so it is today. Our response to our Blessed Mother Mary enriches our lives. Mary brings us to her Son who loves us beyond all telling. His words are eternal life.

Listen to My Mother's messages carefully.
Follow her guidance.
Surrender totally to My will in all things.
Never be afraid. Fear is lack of trust.
I made you for Myself. I redeemed you. You are Mine.
Only you have the power to refuse Me.
No one, nothing can take you away from Me but you.
Always choose wisely. Pray for wisdom.
Seek forgiveness in all your failings.
I never withhold forgiveness to those who seek.
To be like Me you must forgive.
If you are like Me, you will be able to find Me to choose Me.
Allow My Mother to bring you to Me.
Experience all things through Me, and in Me, and with Me.
I am your Savior. There is no other.

CHAPTER 9

Mystical Rose

"That the God of our Lord Jesus Christ, the Father of glory, may give unto you the spirit of wisdom and of revelation, in the knowledge of him . . ."[1]

SAINT THERESA OF AVILA

Mary is the mentor of Dr. Theresa of Avila. Our Blessed Mother's trusted friend Theresa of Avila is also a wonderful spiritual guide for us. She lived in difficult times. Her homeland of Spain had many problems, not the least of which was the Inquisition. This great lady was called up before the Inquisitors who found no error in her writings and teachings. Dr. Theresa, daughter of an affluent Jewish entrepreneur and a devout Catholic mother, was a zealous reformer.[2] Her followers are all over the world today and her spiritual writings are without peer.

Visionary Lucia of Fatima and Pope John Paul II are just two of Dr. Theresa's more illustrious devotees. Mother Teresa of Calcutta and Mother Angelica, Saint Therese of Lisieux and Saint Padre Pio are also part of that mystical cadre. If you truly desire to enter deeply into the mysterious realms of God's divine presence throughout creation, you would be wise to befriend Saint Theresa of Avila. She is our big sister in faith.

Dr. Theresa (one of only three women Doctors of the Church) advises us to pray much as God draws us closer to the Heavenly

Mother He chose for us before He made the world. In her spiritual classics, *Interior Castle* and *The Way of Perfection*, Dr. Theresa shares advice and tutelage for receiving and implementing our Blessed Mother's supernatural secrets.

"Any good you may gain [from Mary's sacred secrets] will depend upon how well you profit by what you hear [see, experience, learn]."

Lest we worry needlessly about apparitions, visions, interior locutions, and all supernatural phenomena flowing from the Heavenly Kingdom, Dr. Theresa identifies three validating characteristics by which we can discern authentic, God-given spiritual gifts.

1. There is power and authority in the words: for example, "Fear not, it is I."
2. Tranquillity, joy, and praise well up in our soul flowing from the spiritual gifts.
3. Authentic words authorized by God do not quickly vanish from our memory.

Dr. Theresa points us to Sacred Scripture, which commands us to test all spirits. She firmly cautions us against indiscriminately seeking apparitions, visions, interior locutions, and supernatural phenomena.[3] We, however, discard such divine gifts at our own peril. She counsels us:

"The safest thing is to will only what God wills, for He knows us better than we know ourselves and He loves us. Let us place ourselves in His hands so that His will may be done in us. If we cling firmly to this maxim and our wills are resolute, we cannot possibly go astray."

Dr. Theresa, a woman of much practical wisdom, offers compelling reasons for us to refrain from seeking specific spiritual gifts for ourselves rather than graciously accepting the ones God chooses for us.

1. We lack humility when we ask God to give us what we have never deserved.

2. Before the Lord grants such favors, He gives the soul a high degree of self-knowledge.

3. Anyone who asks for visions, apparitions, and miracles is certain to be deceived. When someone has a great desire for something, the imagination is easily inflamed; he persuades himself he is seeing or hearing or obtaining what he desires.

4. It is presumptuous to try to choose our own spiritual path because we cannot tell what path is best for us. God knows why He created us and what he desires of us. Let God choose our path. He loves us.

5. The trials of those who receive such supernatural gifts are very great . . . very heavy . . . of many kinds. Will you be able to bear them?

6. The very thing from which you expected gain may only bring you loss. Saul lost by becoming a king.

Dr. Theresa, personally aware that our Blessed Mother is God's powerful gift to us, says the best rule is to seek always to live in total harmony with God's loving plan for our life's journey on earth. She suggests we remind ourselves to do this every day. It is helpful in difficult moments to trust God's big picture in our life when events, situations, people, and things disappoint. Our Blessed Mother is our greatest resource in such moments.

It is comforting to be aware that there is no more merit for receiving all supernatural gifts: quite the contrary, for such a person bears a greater obligation to serve. However, we do live in Mary's times. To disregard our Blessed Mother's loving guidance is the height of stupidity because it causes unnecessary suffering.

Theresa was blessed with many glorious spiritual gifts. One of her most remarkable visions was the following, which occurred shortly after she received the Sacrament of Reconciliation:

"She saw herself being clothed by Saint Joseph and Our Lady in a pure white garment, and was given to understand that she was cleansed of her sins. Christ's earthly parents assured her she was not to fear failure, but that both they and God would be served in her convent. Our Lady then placed around Theresa's neck a jeweled cross of such beauty that everything earthly looked 'like a smudge of soot.' "4

Dr. Theresa reminds us that many a saintly person has never received an extraordinary, supernatural favor of the kinds you find in this book.5 The mere fact that such supernatural gifts are possible is a gripping inspiration to seek for the heights of union with God's love. One never knows how a prayer will be answered. Simply let the spiritual gifts and miracles of those who surround us or have gone before us fill you with loving wisdom, unflinching courage, heightened faith, and exquisite hope.

Never be afraid to ask with faith and hope for all your needs and wants. God is generous. God is rich. God wants only the best for us. Knowledge of amazing favors granted through our Blessed Mother's intercession helps us strive to attain a high degree of perfection in the virtues.

Treasure Dr. Theresa's caveat:

"[T]hose who earn the virtues at the cost of their own toil have earned much more merit. . . . Souls fired with love accept adversity with joy simply because they desire God to see that they are not serving Him merely for remuneration. . . . [T]he nature of love invariably finds expression in works of a thousand kinds."6

There are infinite ways the Lord communicates Himself to souls. Quite often, and especially in these times, it is through Mary.

1. God gives spiritual gifts when a soul is afflicted [consider Saint Norbert].
2. God gives gifts when a soul, [or the world, a nation, city, or place] is about to be visited by some heavy trial [consider the apparitions of Our Lady at Fatima, Medjugorje, and Rwanda].
3. God gives some of these gifts for God's own delight—and to comfort a soul [consider Padre Pio, Pope John Paul II, Mother Teresa of Calcutta, and Mother Angelica].

INTELLECTUAL VISIONS

Contained within God is all wisdom and knowledge. An intellectual vision occurs when God suddenly reveals a truth about Himself.[7] (Imagine Mary's amazement when the Angel Gabriel communicated to her God's desire for the Incarnation.) Dr. Theresa explains to us that an intellectual vision is information communicated directly to our intellect that reveals reality to our soul in the Light of God [Truth]. Such information remains engraved upon our soul. She personally received the following spiritual knowledge from God by means of intellectual visions:

1. All sins are committed within God for we dwell in God. God does not cast us out when we sin.
2. Imitate God. Endure everything for greatly have we offended God's perfection. Forgive everything for God does and we live in God.
3. God is Sovereign Truth.
4. Study earnestly to walk in truth. Be careful never to lie about anything whatsoever. Constantly walk in truth in the presence of God and man.
5. Seek truth in everything.
6. Never desire to be better than we are.
7. Attribute to God what belongs to God and to us what is ours.
8. The Lord dearly loves the virtue of humility. Mary is humble because she knows God. The more we know God the more humility is a fiber of our soul. Humility is not an external characteristic. Humility is a sign of our relationship with God. Humility cannot be ascertained with the senses. Humility is a condition of the soul.
9. Since God alone is Sovereign Truth, to be humble is to walk in truth.[8]
10. We all suffer the misery and pain of our personal limitations. That is the ultimate self-knowledge. No limits can

be set on God. He can raise our soul to the heights of love, the richness of abundance in a single moment.

11. Never offend God—He can torment us as well as comfort us.[9] Two deadly perils on the spiritual journey are offending God and excessive rejoicing [after all, he who exalts himself *will* be humbled; better we humble ourselves than wait for God to correct us]. Courage is necessary. We need to stay centered in God's mercy at all times.

12. We need wisdom to stay out of spiritual trouble. The Blessed Mother, Seat of Wisdom is our best advocate during our spiritual journey on earth.

Dr. Theresa, who saw these places, describes Purgatory[10] and hell.[11] She says that souls in Purgatory endure adversity with patience and resignation. They shall not be disappointed. Souls in hell, to the contrary, have no patience and resignation. They have none of the contentment and delight that comes from God.

EACH SOUL IS AN INTERIOR WORLD

Dr. Theresa reveals a sacred secret, a wonderful mystery she learned at Mary's knee:

"Each of us possesses a soul, but we do not prize our souls as creatures made in God's image deserve and so we do not understand the great secrets they contain.[12] Each soul is an interior world wherein are many and beauteous castles . . . within each soul is a [sacred Seventh] castle for God. . . . Here in this [sacred Seventh] castle [a "Second Heaven," the heights and depths of all that is and was and ever will be], a soul feels called to enter into its own center . . . it is affected only in its higher part.[13] . . .

"The Seventh Castle, a 'second Heaven' is . . . an abiding place in our soul where God and our soul are alone together.[14] . . . In the 'Seventh Castle' God reveals these secrets. . . .

"[A] . . . soul in sin is not capable of enjoying the Light of God. Such souls are in [a] self-made prison—they are spiritually deaf and dumb. They deserve great pity. They need God's mercy. Pray much for them. This is the best kind of almsgiving. You could lose [such a person's] chains with your prayers."[15]

Dr. Theresa helps us understand better our need for Mary's help. Since we are all sinners, whether we are so aware or not, we greatly benefit from Mary's intercessory prayer surrounding, protecting, and lifting us into the loving light of God's omniscient presence. It is kinder, easier, and simpler to allow Mary's compassionate, maternal care when we hurt and need goodness and peace than to wallow in our own misery.

THE SEVENTH CASTLE

Dr. Theresa reveals certain mysteries (secrets) that our Blessed Mother shared with her to help us prepare and, with God's grace, enter the Seventh Castle:

1. The Blessed Mother asks us to cast our eyes upon Christ.
2. The Holy Rosary is a powerful spiritual tool for recognizing Jesus Christ.[16]
3. Focus upon Jesus Christ as God while praying the Holy Rosary. In that way, we will encounter true humility.
4. As long as we focus on our earthly nature, we remain quite materialistic and will not succeed in disengaging ourselves from cowardice, laziness, and fear. A materialist is content with low standards. Only Christ can free us from such baseness.
5. The Holy Rosary helps us to know ourselves and understand God's ways.
6. When we are absorbed in worldly affairs, honors, and ambitions, though we truly desire to be close to God, we fail more than we succeed.

7. We desperately need our Blessed Mother, the saints and angels as intercessors. Their prayers for us become like incense on our behalf before God's Throne.

8. All our help comes to us from God through His mercy.

9. Mary, Mother of Divine Mercy is God's exquisitely gentle gift of mercy to us.

10. Often we are so busy on the material plane that very little light of God's Love penetrates our souls. Our senses are so heightened that they force us to close our spiritual eyes to everything but the demands of the physical world. Our possessions, quotas, goals, and aspirations consume so much of our time that we feel unable to free ourselves. In such cases, the Holy Rosary is our lifeline to God's mercy.

11. Those who are able to remain faithful to the daily recitation of the Holy Rosary grow spiritually strong enough to put aside all unnecessary business and simplify life. Attachments to people, places, and things become less burdensome. But there is more.

12. It is well and good to shed outward attachments though we must become free of inward things as well.

13. All too often, cares that do not belong to us consume us.

14. The Holy Rosary helps us to grow in the love of God and of our neighbor.

Should we be so blessed as to be invited into the Seventh Castle, Dr. Theresa describes what happens there:

"In this seventh dwelling place the union [with God] comes about in a different way: our good God now desires to remove the scales from the soul's eyes and let it see and understand, although in a strange way, something of the favor He grants it. When the soul is brought into that dwelling place, the Most Blessed Trinity, all three Persons, through an intellectual vision, is revealed to it through a certain representation of the truth. First there comes an enkindling in the spirit in the manner of a cloud of magnificent splendor; and these Persons are

distinct, and through an admirable knowledge the soul understands as a most profound truth that all three Persons are one
substance and one power and one knowledge and one God
alone. It knows in such a way that what we hold by faith, it
understands. . . . Here all three Persons communicate themselves to it [the soul], speak to it and explain those works of the
Lord in the Gospel: that He and the Father and the Holy Spirit
will come to dwell with the soul that loves Him and keeps His
commandments."[17]

Dr. Theresa offers us three spiritual directives from our Blessed
Mother to help us along the path of life in God:

1. Refrain from indiscreet zeal [fanaticism], which may do us
   great harm.
2. Refrain from looking for faults in others; we lose our peace
   this way. Let each one look to himself or herself.[18] Be watch-
   ful.[19]
3. Refrain from judging anyone. Any judgment of another
   by one in a body is a nontruth. Only God can judge a human. Mary never judges God's people. She loves. She cor-
   rects. She guides. God alone judges. We cannot change
   anyone.[20] But we can always pray for others. God can
   change anyone, anything at any time.

Finally, we grow in awareness that we all are lost sheep. Our
coats are thick. Shearing is painful. Christ's peace is the only remedy
for all the pain in the world.

Theresa of Avila reminds us:

"[T]he Lord does not look so much at the magnitude of anything
we do as at the love with which we do it . . . offer the Lord whatever interior and exterior sacrifices we are able to give Him . . .
and He unites it with His offering to the Father for us from the
Cross, . . . so that it may have the value won for it by our own
will, even though our actions in themselves are trivial."[21]

Dr. Theresa shares this rule:

"You cannot enter the [interior] castles [of your soul] by your own efforts; the Lord of the Castle Himself must admit you to them. . . . He is a great lover of humility. . . . [O]nce you have been shown how to enjoy the [seventh] castle, you will find rest in everything, even in the things which most try you, and you will cherish a hope of returning to it which nobody can take from you."[22]

Our Blessed Mother, Mother of the Prince of Peace and Source of Peace on earth is a blessing to people, nations, and events.[23] Theresa of Avila remains one of Mary's most astute pupils. Lucia of Fatima, Pope John Paul II, Mother Teresa of Calcutta, Mother Angelica, Archbishop Fulton Sheen, Father Walter Ciszek, Saint Padre Pio, and Saint Jose Maria Escriva were great students of the wisdom of Dr. Theresa of Avila. Through them the world has benefited much from Dr. Theresa's understanding of Mary's sacred secrets. As we allow our Blessed Mother to care for us, she who is our hope and our gift most graciously carries us into the depths of the Seventh Castle.[24]

The mystical world of God where angels and saints, pure beings of light and love dwell, more present than the walls of our rooms, is accessible to all who love. Our life on earth is about becoming sensitive to that reality.

BLESSED LOUIS AND BLESSED ZELIE MARTIN

Saint Therese of Lisieux, a Doctor of the Church, is popularly known as The Little Flower. Formed at a young age in the ways of Dr. Theresa of Avila, Saint Therese of Lisieux promised to spend her heavenly life doing good deeds upon the earth. Her diary, *Story of a Soul*, is a masterpiece of spiritual wisdom. She was the youngest of five daughters of Louis and Zelie Martin. Her parents had exquisite knowledge of the spirit world and communicated it to their children so effectively that all five of their daughters entered a nearby

Carmelite Convent in Lisieux, France. Here the Martin girls dedicated their lives to the spiritual guidelines outlined by Dr. Theresa of Avila. From the cradle, Louis and Zelie inspired their daughters to retain the memory of Heaven and helped them grow in awareness of the spiritual world all around them.

Louis, a jeweler by trade, fashioned expensive baubles for the rich. His wife, Zelie, a working mother, was considered the finest lace maker in France. Few understood how Zelie and Louis could create such beautiful works of art. Perhaps the eyes of their souls were focused on the glories of the kingdom of God where all is beauty. This holy couple prayed together and fasted frequently as a spiritual discipline. Their devotion to Our Lady of Mount Carmel was an inspiration to their children, neighbors, and even their customers.[25] They mastered many spiritual secrets imparted to them by our Blessed Mother. Through disciplined prayer and loving intimacy with Mary, they became spiritually agile at listening to the Lord deep in their souls while at the same time being totally engaged in the duties of their home, family, work, and community.

Zelie and Louis Martin effectively combined service to Jesus with adoration of Jesus.[26] They were fortunate people who could hear trumpets on the horizon. Knowing Christ would come for them when they least expected, they seized each moment with fortitude and courage. Children of the light, they stayed alert lest they miss the time of their visitation.

Zelie died at a young age of breast cancer when Therese was only four years old. Louis persevered, eventually enduring the loss of his daughters who left home one by one to become "brides of Christ" (as professed Carmelite Sisters are popularly known). Long-suffering Louis died of complications of Alzheimer's disease. His family, caring for him to the end, surrendered every hardship and sorrow of that disease to God's providence.

The prayers and sacrifices, joys and sorrows of Zelie and Louis Martin and their children continue to bear sweet fruit throughout the world. Zelie and Louis were beatified by Pope Benedict XVI in October 2008. The Martin family—mother, father, and five daughters—are admired and emulated wherever the sun shines.

BLESSED TERESA OF CALCUTTA

Mother Teresa of Calcutta was totally devoted to Mary, and a blessed friend of Saint Theresa of Avila. Following in Dr. Theresa's footsteps, she truly became the hands and heart of the Immaculate One in a world of sinners. There is no doubt that this unique founder of the Missionaries of Charity had a personal and mystic relationship with the Holy Mother of God.

The Missionaries of Charity originated in 1950 as a small diocesan religious community. Today, Mother Teresa's organization is worldwide and includes men and women contemplatives as well as an order of priests to serve members.

Mother Teresa learned from our Blessed Mother that every moment of our lives on earth has eternal significance. And so she set out to make every moment eternally valuable. Born in Albania on August 26, 1910, Mother Teresa became an Indian citizen in 1950. She lived and worked among the poorest of the poor in the slums of Calcutta and the richest of the rich throughout the world. She tutored England's Princess Diana in the ways of hands-on charity and held First Lady Hillary Clinton's hand during a Missionaries of Charity dedication of their newest orphanage in Chevy Chase, Maryland. Mother Teresa found her way to the president of Bulgaria to seek his help in opening a Missionaries of Charity orphanage in his nation, and she often addressed world leaders in their pursuits of social justice. She also gathered the dying from the streets and held them in her arms as death claimed them.

This petite woman, who during her life on earth stood no more than five feet tall, won the Nobel Peace Prize in 1979. She gave the award money, $192,000, to the poor in India. When asked by the Nobel Committee what could be done to promote world peace, she responded: "Go home and love your family." Mother Teresa, in her Nobel Lecture said, "A person that is shut out, who feels unwanted, unloved, terrified—the person who has been thrown out from society—that poverty is so egregious that I find it very, very difficult."[27] She remains a spiritual giant recognized throughout the world for her work among the sick and poorest of the poor. She was awarded the Presidential Medal of Freedom by President Ronald Reagan at a White House ceremony in 1985. She was beatified (first rung on the ladder to sainthood) on October 19, 2003. Pope John Paul II knew Mother Teresa of Calcutta well. At her beatification ceremony in Rome's Saint Peter's Square, he lauded her as one of the most relevant personalities of our age and an icon of the Good Samaritan. "Her life," he said, was "a bold proclamation of the gospel." The Pope explained that her love for the Holy Eucharist, for prayer, and for the poor left an example for all of us. John Paul II waived the waiting period in the case of Blessed Teresa of Calcutta. She died September 5, 1997, and was beatified by Pope John Paul II on October 19, 2003.

Raised in the Ottoman Empire in a place known as Skopje, Macedonia, she was baptized Gonzha (Agnes) Bojaxhiu. Her father was a contractor who provided well for his wife and three children. Agnes, the youngest, was deeply grieved with the sudden and unexpected death of her father. She attended public school and at age eighteen entered the Sisters of Loreto in Dublin. One year later, in 1929, Agnes was sent to the Loreto novitiate in Darjeeling, India. Carrying the name of her famous mentor, Saint Theresa of Avila, Sister Teresa as a young nun was assigned to a girl's high school in Calcutta. There she taught geography and history to wealthy young ladies.

It was 1946, just after World War II. Sister Teresa, who was quite familiar with the requests of Our Lady of Fatima, was riding on a train in India when she heard what she later described as "a call within a call. The message was clear. I was to leave the convent and help the poor while living among them."

Sister Teresa studied nursing, received permission to leave the Sisters of Loreto, traded her religious habit for the ordinary dress of a poor Indian woman, a white sari and sandals, and followed Christ into the slums to care for the sick and the poor. Soon she opened a school for poor children and befriended her neighbors. Before long, volunteers joined her and formed the core of the Missionaries of Charity. Donations followed. In 1952, the city of Calcutta gave the Missionaries of Charity a former hostel that Mother Teresa promptly converted to a home for the destitute and dying. Gradually, care was extended to orphans, abandoned children, the aging, alcoholics, and street people.

During the following four decades Mother Teresa struggled relentlessly on behalf of the sick and poor. Her love and energy sent her crisscrossing the globe pleading for support and inviting others to see the face of Jesus in the sick and poorest of the poor. Mother Teresa learned from Our Lady that we can do no great things, but only many small things with great love.

Shortly before her death, Mother Teresa told me to listen more carefully to the voice of the Lord and His Blessed Mother when I inadvertently ran into her in an alcove of the U.S. Congress, where she was resting in her wheelchair shortly after having received the Congressional Medal of Honor.[28] She was insistent that the Lord awaits all of us every day in the Blessed Sacrament. She said, "Adore Him. Show Him your love. Ask everyone to find Jesus in the Blessed Sacrament. He gives us the strength to follow God's will for us on earth." As I was leaving the hall, I encountered her once again, sitting in her wheelchair. Mother handed me a pouch of Miraculous Medals to distribute in her name. And I did, on the floor of the New York Stock Exchange. Several weeks later, traders flocked to the pouch like bees to honey when word spread that I had medals from Mother Teresa.

Mother Teresa of Calcutta believed that God desires to speak to all of us. "Blessed are those who have ears to hear," she said. God surely has great plans for all of us. True happiness is hidden in His ways. Our Blessed Mother guided Mother Teresa's ways, leading her ever deeper into the Heart of her Son, the Savior of the world who is the delight of all delights. Mother Teresa left her mark on India and the world.[29] She learned through experience that with Mary's help, we all may know better the ways of God our Father in Heaven.

Blessed Teresa of Calcutta said,

"Let us ask Our Lady to make our hearts 'meek and humble' as her Son's was. It is so very easy to be proud and selfish, so easy; but we have been created for greater things. How much we can learn from Our Lady! She was so humble because she was all for

God. She was full of grace. Ask our Lady to tell Jesus, 'They have no wine,' the wine of humility and meekness, of kindness and sweetness. She is sure to remind us, 'Do whatever He tells you.' Accept cheerfully all the chances she sends you. We learn humility through accepting humiliations cheerfully."[30]

SAINT PIO OF PIETRELCINA AND SAINT JOSEMARIA ESCRIVA

There are many saints, most of whom remain unknown to us. Two twentieth-century Catholic priests whose worldwide followers sincerely struggle to become hidden saints are Saint [Padre] Pio of Italy and Saint Josemaria Escriva of Spain. The former was a Capuchin Franciscan who not only bore the wounds of Jesus in his body for all to see, but also was known to bilocate,[31] do hand-to-hand combat with demonic forces,[32] and engage his Guardian Angel as a mighty coworker. Saint [Padre] Pio constantly encouraged people to turn to Mary in every need. He said of our Blessed Mother:

> "She springs like a ray of light from the Mind of God: everything is in relation to her, every grace passes through her hands: only she can capture the torrents of love that flow from the Heart of God, only she is worthy to correspond to them: most tender Mother grant that I may love Him; pour into my heart that love which burned in thine; purify my heart that I may be able to love my and thy God: purify my spirit that I may be able to adore Him in spirit and truth: purify my body that I may be His living tabernacle."

Saint Josemaria Escriva was a practical priest for spiritually dangerous times. He knew Our Lady as Mother Most Consoling, Mother Most Faithful. Saint Josemaria traveled the world teaching people to live happily in the conscious presence of God at all times, and to sanctify every thought, word, and deed for the glory of God. His down-to-earth spiritual guidance continues to attract religious and laypeople all over the world. He believed that saints are men and women of God, souls identified with Jesus Christ; not supermen, just ordinary people who choose to love the Lord and one another. He said:

> "Let's not deceive ourselves: in our life we will find vigor and victory and depression and defeat. This has always been true in the earthly pilgrimage of Christians, even those we venerate on the altars. Do you remember Peter, Augustine or Francis? I have never liked biographies of saints which naively—but also with lack of sound doctrine—present their deeds as if they had been confirmed in grace from birth. No. The true life stories of Christian heroes resemble our own experience: they fought and won; they fought and lost. And then, repentant, they returned to the fray."[33]

Saint [Padre] Pio and Saint Josemaria believed our Blessed Mother has enough virtue to share with all her children. The best of mothers, her offspring need only come to her protection. However, she is quick to let us know that virtue untested is no virtue at all. Often, we realize that our Blessed Mother has much more confidence in us than we have in ourselves.

MOTHER ANGELICA (RITA RIZZO)

An amazing lady and true daughter of the Holy Rosary who did not miss the time of her heavenly visitation was born in the slums of Canton, Ohio, on April 20, 1923. A group of newly immigrated Sicilians used black-handled revolvers to rule the neighborhood where her family lived. "Mob slayings were a common occurrence in southeast Canton. . . . This ethnic ghetto—where hookers tapped bordello windows to attract their johns; where shopkeepers lived across the street from female assassins; where parish priests tried to lead small-time husbands to a better life; where the profane mingled with the sacred, and everyone struggled to make ends meet—this was the world that awaited Rita Rizzo's coming in 1923."[34] Her father did not want her or her mother, Mae.

The stigma of divorce and the poverty of the depression combined to form a rack upon which Rita and her mother managed to survive. Though they lived in rat-infested hovels, Rita seemed cheerful and unaware that her life was unbearable. By the time she turned sixteen, Rita was diagnosed with malnutrition. At age seventeen, Rita was employed at a factory and spent most of her meager paycheck on her mother, who was recovering from a nervous breakdown.

In December of 1941, when Japan attacked Pearl Harbor, war jobs came to Canton and Rita found higher-paying work, but her health was gone. Shortly thereafter, Rita met a miracle worker stigmatic.[35] Rhoda Wise became a friend and confidante of young Rita, whose heart pounded with joy at the stories of Jesus and His Blessed Mother that Rhoda told her. Not only did Rhoda claim that she had visions of Jesus and Mary, but she claimed she also knew and often saw Saint Therese, the Little Flower.

One can only imagine what the impressionable young Rita Rizzo thought as she witnessed the following: "On Good Friday in 1942, what appeared to be blood spilled from gashes on Wise's forehead. Over the next few years, she would intermittently suffer Jesus Christ's Passion: profuse bleeding from her head, hands, and feet between noon and three o'clock on Fridays. Unknown to her devotees at the time, Wise had offered herself as a 'Victim Soul' (like Saint Therese of Lisieux) for the good of priests and religious. Her idea, rooted in Catholic tradition, was that her personal suffering offered to God in union with Christ's sacrifice on the cross could compensate for the spiritual failings of others."[36]

After witnessing such life-changing mystical experiences, Rita began to pray more. She now knew that mystical experiences with saints, our Blessed Mother, and the Lord Jesus Himself were really quite natural. And she was mysteriously healed from a stomach ailment that she attributes to the intercessory prayer of Saint Therese and Rhoda. Rhoda loved to tell Rita about Jesus truly present in the Blessed Sacrament. She explained how lonely Jesus is as so few know Him, love Him, serve Him, or seek His help and protection. Yet Rhoda assured her, all we have and do and hope comes from His Sacred Heart filled with pure love for poor sinners. With that knowledge, Rita could hardly wait to get to the local Catholic church each day to rest in adoration before the Blessed Sacrament. She truly wanted to learn from Jesus who knows all things, can do all things, and loves us beyond our capacity to comprehend.[37]

By age twenty-one, Rita burned with the desire to become a nun in the Adoration Monastery at 40th and Euclid in Cleveland. As her farewell to her mother, Rita advised her to "attach yourself to God alone who is patiently waiting for all your love. A cloister, my mother, is a heaven on earth. It is the *greatest* privilege given to man on earth. . . . We belong first to God then to our parents."[38]

Rita became a Franciscan nun of the Most Blessed Sacrament, a French Order of Poor Clares whose founders (in 1854) received messages from God. She wanted her whole life to be for Jesus, with Jesus, and in Jesus.[39] The religious order is dedicated to the Blessed Virgin Mary under her title The Immaculate Conception. Each nun in perpetuity would therefore be consecrated to the Mother of God under that title and would bear the name Mary in some form. The Religious Order's mission would always be to adore Jesus in the Blessed Sacrament in a spirit of perpetual thanksgiving, making reparation for man's ingratitude toward God. In 1868, the Religious Order legally became a Pontifical Institute answerable only to the Holy See in Rome. Sister Mary Agnes, a devout woman from Vienna, Austria, founded the first American branch of the order in Cleveland in 1921.

Few could fathom the mystery of God that lay hidden in the heart of Rita Rizzo on November 8, 1945, when she officially became a professed "bride of Christ."[40] Thereafter, Rita would be known as Sister Mary Angelica of the Annunciation. With a photographic memory and a hearty appetite for the mystical teachings of Saint Theresa of Avila, and the missionary zeal of Saint Therese of Lisieux, the young nun grew in her appreciation for God's ways in the world. And yet the ways of men never intimidated Sister Angelica: she kept her tough skin and possessed an uncanny ability to hold tough in times of adversity. One particularly interesting dialogue with Christ that Mother Angelica would cherish involved her difficulties in the early days of her monastic life. She suffered physical ailments and endured vexations caused by the rigors of cloistered life.

One cold winter night, Angelica drew the slot for eucharistic adoration at three a.m. Arriving in the chapel, feet and knees sore from overwork, Angelica mumbled to the Blessed Sacrament: "Jesus, what do You think I am, a horse?"

"No My beloved, you are My bride," responded the Lord. Angelica would never again complain [much] about the rigors of monastic life.[41]

As the years passed, Angelica became crippled with severe back and leg pain from failed spinal surgery. But she never lost a moment of time in spite of her leg brace. When her monastery in Canton needed trees for a Marian grotto, Angelica called a mob leader and asked for almsgiving: she told him to get checks from "all the boys" (gangsters). "I'm going to put their names on a piece of parchment, roll it up, and put it inside the statue of Our Lady. . . . Nobody's going to see it; it'll be buried in concrete, like you're going to be one of these days if you don't straighten up. . . . I need people like you to buy these trees so that one day, if you're ever in a lot of trouble, you'll remember the Lord and His Mother."[42]

In 1961, as Vatican II went onto the drawing board, subsequently to be reckoned with throughout the world, Rome appointed Angelica abbess of a new monastery in racially tormented Birmingham, Alabama, where Catholics composed less than 2 percent of the population. Under Mother Angelica's guidance, Our Lady of the Angels Monastery became a place of joy, family delight, and deep, directed, heartfelt prayer. Her approach to monastic living eliminated "public talk of faults and humiliating penances. Mother Angelica pioneered a monastery where there was 'no longer an isolated individual, seeking self alone, but a togetherness . . . one in will, in purpose, in love.'"[43] Formalism and regimentation were washed away by a family spirit centered around each one's desire for deep communal union with God. Mother Angelica believes monasteries should be homes of holiness modeled after early Christian communities.[44]

In the early 1970s, thanks to Father Robert De Grandis, an Italian Josephite priest serving as pastor at a nearby black parish, Mother Angelica was introduced to the Charismatic Renewal.[45] Now alive with the Holy Spirit, Mother was invited to speak to groups of every religious persuasion. Soon Mother Angelica hosted a ten-minute radio show, *Journey into the Scripture.* Then Mother Angelica began writing pamphlets and books for the public. She said of her work, "We use the talents we possess to the best of our ability and leave the results to God. We are at peace in the knowledge that He is pleased with our efforts and that His providence will take care of the fruits of those efforts."[46]

Mother Angelica is world famous as the founder and guiding star of the Eternal Word Television Network (EWTN).[47] She told her viewers, "I want you to listen to this network because you want to get closer to the Lord. I want you to listen to this network because we have serious times and people all over the world are suffering."[48] Her television network is broadcast throughout the world. From such humble beginnings, Mother Mary Angelica of the Annunciation was named the most influential Catholic woman in America by *Time* magazine in 1995. This little soul, totally consecrated to the Mother of God in perpetuity, initiated dazzling evangelism that has touched every continent.

Mother Angelica's joy is contagious. And her commitments are solid. She relied on the Lord for everything. She watched and waited with Him in the Blessed Sacrament. How well she would know His voice and His ways.

All joy flows from My joy.
I am the Source of all that Creation is.
My joy is complete when it rests in your heart,
your longings and your goals.
Flee now to the Mountain of Peace and abide with Me in Serene
Stillness little children of My Heart.
It pleases Me that you study the Bible.
My Word is enough for you for the moment of truth
flows only from Me.
Flee from the rooftops where men chatter in the breeze of curiosity
and miss the time of their visitation.
Flee from the winds of confusion, the seas of debris and the
paths of avarice that destroy the stillness of
My Presence in the world.
I am all around you.
I nurture and sustain you on the sweetmeat of My Love.
Bless Me little children of My Heart.
Bless My creation. Bless My Ways.

Image of Mother of Sorrows in Jerusalem at the Church of the Holy Sepulchre

CHAPTER 10

Tower of Ivory

Jesus said to his Disciples: *"He that hath my commandments, and keepeth them; he it is that loveth me. And he that loveth me shall be loved of my Father: and I will love him, and will manifest myself to him."*[1]

RUSSIA'S NEW ERA

The rich heritage of Russia as "Mary's Garden" continues to be unveiled at the dawn of the twenty-first century. After the brutal massacre at Ekaterinburg, Siberia, of Czar Nicholas II and his family in 1917,[2] Lenin ruled and was followed by Stalin who governed as an autocrat for thirty years. The Russian Civil War from 1918 until 1922 claimed eight million lives. And things went from bad to worse as Walter Ciszek[3] experienced firsthand. World wars, the Cold War, and its ensuing nuclear Balance of Terror impoverished the nation, the people, and the morals of Russia. Now, a trendy upscale mall is just across the street from Lenin's Tomb in Red Square and ancient places of worship are being restored. After enduring decades of Soviet poverty, Russians want to make up for lost time.

Traffic jams, unheard of in Communist times, include Lamborghinis, Masaratis, Bentleys, Rolls-Royces, Ferraris, Aston Martins, and Porsches that honk and pass in a mad rush to glittering pleasure palaces, while stylish young people flock to chic boutiques at Red

Square. Though greed and corruption are supposedly widespread, and the rules of law and finance may be in their infancy, consumerism is flourishing in Russia and innate spirituality is growing more public. One of the side effects of global commerce is more freedom for Russians in fashion and expression. In the old days, under totalitarian rule, no one dared wear a cross or profess belief in God. Such an "opiate of the masses," as religion was branded in Soviet days, was a guarantee of persecution, imprisonment, and, in extreme cases, death.

Russia is changing quickly. The population now includes new-moneyed billionaires. There are upwards of ten million Internet users—generally highly educated people under thirty-five who work for large companies and organizations and are well paid. Known as an "advanced" audience, they are immune to the communist and nationalist ideology widespread in low-income sections of Russian society. Russia's Internet users are the elite of society today, and they will determine the country's destiny tomorrow.[4]

It has been observed that Moscow bears the "sinister magic of a city that reveals its true colors at night."[5] In 2008, Moscow at night was described as "a fairy tale with menace. A Cinderella who doesn't leave the Kremlin at midnight could lose more than a glass slipper."[6] Addicts roam the streets while thieves and prostitutes vie with one another for their prey. Harleys and Hondas race through the streets, speeding ahead of Mercedes and Bentleys to luxurious restaurants and clubs that compete to duplicate the grandeur of the Russian aristocracy of old. Afloat in petrodollars, Moscow is the most expensive city in the world. It boasts more billionaires than any other place on earth. Nothing is too much where billion-dollar deals are commonplace. The majority of Russians, however, are poor.

People all over the world have prayed faithfully and consistently for the spiritual conversion of Russia, in response to our Blessed Mother's request to the three children at Fatima in 1917. And for good reason: Russia is the "Garden of Mary." It has been so named since it was Christianized over one thousand years ago.

THE ROMANOFF FAMILY

Russian public and international policy neglected the Mother of God and the Gospel of her Divine Son in the early days of the twentieth century, with heinous consequences. No one was spared the terrorist-driven downfall of the Russian Empire, not even the family of Czar Nicholas II. His wife, Empress Alexandra,[7] a granddaughter of Queen Victoria of England, received a prophetic warning about the fate of her family and the Russian people. In December 1916, an elderly nun renown for holiness who was said to be more than 107 years old, addressed the Czarina: "Here is the martyr Empress Alexandra. Tell the Czar to beware the 1st of March."[8] One year later, the Czar abdicated the sacred throne of holy Russia. From that moment until his assassination, abomination followed him, his family, and the people of Russia.[9]

The Czar, his wife, children, and close associates were brutally murdered under the cover of night in the basement of their house-prison in Siberia. Nicholas and Alexandra, their five children, and faithful courtiers were mercilessly shot but the bullets did not kill them. The terrorists then battered them, using their bayonets to stab the suffering first family of Russia and beat them to death with rifle butts. The revolutionaries slaughtered them, and stripped, burned, and left their remains to rot. Every Russian tasted the bitterness of this brutality steeped in atheism and felt deprivation, degradation, desolation, despair, and spiritual death for more than seven decades.

SERVANT OF GOD WALTER J. CISZEK

Life in Soviet Russia was truly difficult for Jesuit Walter Ciszek. The American missionary priest was falsely arrested, imprisoned, and tortured in Moscow's dreaded Lubyanka. He was held there in solitary confinement for five years with no trial, no representation, and no contact with the outside world. Father Walter Ciszek, S.J., was officially listed as dead in 1947—his Jesuit colleagues thought he had died in the bowels of the Soviet prison system. But he had much more to accomplish for God in Russia and great suffering to patiently endure for God's holy people.

During his seminary years in the late 1920s, Walter undoubtedly learned of the apparitions of Our Lady of Fatima, and her global request for prayers and penance for the spiritual conversion of Russia. In response, Walter, who was consecrated to our Blessed Mother from a young age, felt a call deep in his soul to join the Russian missions. Pope Pius XI, aware of the three secrets of Fatima, sent out a request, especially to the Jesuits, seeking priests to serve in Russia. Walter Ciszek wholeheartedly volunteered to become a missionary in Russia. Consequently, he left home and family to study at the newly opened Russian Center in Rome. After ordination, his first assignment in Eastern Europe ended in 1941 when Germany invaded Russia. There were refugees everywhere. They needed priests and Father Ciszek was willing to help.

Walter accompanied some labor brigades to the Soviet Union to minister to their needs. The great majority of people traveling with him in the unheated boxcar were Jews escaping from German-occupied lands where their very lives were threatened. Everyone in the boxcar—men, women, and children—were on their way to the Urals where a big Soviet lumber combine was hiring cheap labor.

Life was hard for all the refugees in the Soviet work camps. Cruel overlords allowed no religious observance for anyone. That meant Walter, himself working as a laborer, could do nothing but pray and sacrifice silently for his fellow sufferers. Hunger, sickness, cold, fatigue, total lack of privacy, and unimaginable stress were the lot of the people working in the labor camps.

Walter worked and prayed and helped others as best he could under such difficult living conditions. His comfort in personal desolation was the First Principle and Foundation of Saint Ignatius Loyola, founder of his religious order, the Society of Jesus.

"Man is created to praise, revere and serve God our Lord, and by this means to save his soul. The other things on the face of the earth are created for man to help him in attaining the end for which he is created. Hence, man is to make use of them in so far as they help him in the attainment of his end, and he must rid himself of them insofar as they prove a hindrance to him. Therefore, we must make ourselves indifferent to all created things."[10]

Because word got out that Walter, an American citizen, was a Jesuit Catholic priest, the NKVD (Soviet Secret Police) arrested him—on June 22, 1941—and sent him to Lubyanka Prison in Moscow where terror, torture, and summary executions were common occurrences.[11] Accused of being a Vatican spy, he was most severely treated. Walter patiently endured five years of solitary confinement, excruciating interrogations, and every kind of torture. Many believe it is miraculous that he survived; so few did. His cell contained an iron bed upon which he was permitted to sleep for only a few hours during the night. The rest of the time, he was forced to stand or lean against the walls, or pace back and forth. A toilet bucket with a lid was the only other object in the cell. Walter endured the confinement, thirst, starvation, filth, pain, cold, darkness, intense heat, and eerie silence through constant prayer, especially the prayers of the Mass he knew by heart. In lieu of his breviary prayers (his captors had confiscated all his personal belongings) he prayed many rosaries daily: at least one in Russian, one in English, one in Latin, and one in Polish.

His captors tantalized him, suggesting he become an Orthodox priest: they even offered to find a Soviet wife for him. His price for such a concession—freedom under their dominion and some measure of dignity—was that he would be forced to denounce the Pope, and all vestiges of Roman Catholicism. The Jesuit refused. After even more egregious torture, he was offered the opportunity to go to Rome as a Soviet spy. Walter Ciszek chose heinous death rather than betray his vows.

For some reason he never understood, he was not sent immediately before a firing squad, as were other uncooperative prisoners of Lubyanka. Because his interrogators could not break him, even with the threat of death, they decided instead to subject him to highly undesirable work under the cruelest of conditions. Father Walter Ciszek, S.J., was sentenced to fifteen years at hard labor in the prison camps of Siberia. Few if any survived such an ordeal; for most it was a long, slow, tortuous death sentence. History confirms that Walter Ciszek's only "crime" was to have been an American missionary Catholic priest unfortunate enough to be caught serving and ministering to refugees in a Russian work camp during World War II.

God brings good out of everything. Walter learned an extraordinarily valuable spiritual lesson during his sufferings in Russia: that man's sole purpose is to do the will of God. As he wrote:

> "Not the will of God as we might wish it, or as we might have envisioned it, or as we thought in our poor human wisdom it ought to be. But rather the will of God as God envisioned it and revealed it to us each day in the created situations with which he presented us. His will for us was the twenty-four hours of each day: the people, the places, the circumstances he set before us in that time. Those were the things God knew were important to him and to us at that moment, and these were the things upon which he wanted us to act, not out of any abstract principle, or out of any subjective desire to 'do the will of God.' No, these things, the twenty-four hours of this day, were His will; we had to learn to recognize His will in the reality of the situation and act accordingly. We had to learn to look at our daily lives, at everything that crossed our path each day, with the eyes of God; learning to see His estimate of things, places, and above all people, recognizing that He had a goal and a purpose in bringing us into contact with these things and these people, and striving always to do that will—His will—every hour of every day in the situations in which He had placed us."[12]

Walter was finally exchanged in 1963, and came home to the United States after twenty-three agonizing years in Soviet prisons and labor camps in Siberia. By 1965, he was at work at the Pope John XXIII Center at Fordham University in New York, where he was much sought after as a spiritual director and adviser. His family and religious superiors wanted to know how he had endured under such horrendous suffering when so few others survived.

Some knew about Walter Ciszek's profound devotion to our

Blessed Mother. Of course, as a Jesuit, he was following in the footsteps of Saint Ignatius of Loyola, whose love for Our Lady is a deep component of the Jesuit charism. He finally wrote about his travails behind the Iron Curtain in *With God in Russia*.[13] But later, pondering the godly lessons he was privileged to learn serving as a missionary in Soviet Russia, he wrote one of the most beautiful spiritual treatises ever produced: *He Leadeth Me*.

Walter Ciszek's love for Our Lady was publicly revealed and rewarded at his death on the great feast of her Immaculate Conception, December 8, 1984. Those who had the opportunity to know him during those nineteen years after his release from Russia learned from a holy man. Walter Ciszek summed up his entire life as an opportunity to embrace God's will. His challenge was to cherish God's will enough to perform whatever assignments God chose to give him with the highest possible valor. Considered a saint in the truest sense of the word, his missionary zeal for the Russian people is a grace for all of us. A sacrificial beneficiary of Mary's gifts, Walter bore sincere love for those who severely persecuted him. Of his fellow sufferers in the labor camps he wrote:

> "The kingdom of God will grow upon earth, will be brought to fulfillment, in the same way it was established: by the daily and seemingly hidden lives of those who do always the will of the Father. It was this faith that impressed me so much in the . . . believers [of every sect] I met in the Soviet Union . . . Hampered by difficulties and every form of subtle persecution, restricted by law, they nevertheless retained their belief in God and all that it meant in practice. Their prayers and their sufferings can only foreshadow, I know, a future harvest of faith in this land once known as Holy Russia. The kingdom of God survives and is spread by the active and unshakable faith of such people as these; it remains, too, in the hearts of the masses who know instinctively there must be more to life than the future promised by communism. No one knows better than those who are constantly attacking that faith how firmly its seeds remain planted in Russia; only God in His providence knows how soon it will flower."[14]

Walter Ciszek's cause for canonization is underway at the Vatican, where he is officially known as a "Servant of God." His perseverance in suffering and heroic work to lead others into the heart of divine love are harbingers of the great coming of God's Kingdom on earth.

THE ICON OF HOPE

Hopefully life for everyone in Russia will continue to improve. Human tributes to the Mother of God are dazzling jewels in the Russian consciousness. Shrines, icons, monasteries, churches, basilicas, and even rustic altars dot the landscape of the Russian Empire. On June 26, 2004, the *Los Angeles Times*[15] reported that the day prior,

> "a chain of people stretched for up to a mile around the Church of the Savior in central Moscow, where the Virgin of Tikhvin icon—considered a protector of the nation since the 14th century—returned this week after a 60-year hiatus in the United States . . . The return of the icon of Our Lady of Tikhvin is a convincing indication that the macabre period in Russia's history is finally coming to an end."[16]

VLADIMIR PUTIN

Russian leader Vladimir Putin is baptized, and though he was high ranking in the KGB under the Communist regime, it is said he has a monk as a spiritual director. In summer of 2004, Mr. Putin announced that the Russian government will do all it can under his watch to allow the renaissance of Christianity in Russia. He said his administration would facilitate the full-scale revival of the Russian Orthodox Church.[17] More than thirteen thousand churches have been built or rebuilt in the last fifteen years alone.

Time magazine named Vladimir Putin "Person of the Year" in its December 31, 2007, issue, and referred to him as "Tsar of the New Russia":

"Russia is central to our world—and the new world that is being born. If Russia fails, all bets are off for the 21st century. And if Russia succeeds as a nation-state in the family of nations, it will owe much of its success to one man, Vladimir Vladimirovich Putin."[18]

Putin's paternal grandfather cooked for both Lenin and Stalin. His father fought in World War II and afterward worked in a train-car factory. His modestly educated mother was believed to be a devout Orthodox Christian who loved her son dearly and sacrificed much for him. His familiar name, Volodya, fell sweetly from her lips. Putin's most admired leader is Peter the Great, not Stalin or Lenin.

Putin attended Leningrad State University and dreamed of becoming a spy. He joined the KGB (Soviet Intelligence Agency) and was trained in counterintelligence. He worked undercover in East Germany doing espionage work on both NATO and certain German politicians. When the Berlin Wall crumbled in 1989, Putin's KGB career fell with it. Next, Putin ran the Russian Statistical Office that granted foreign investment rights and registered businesses. He then worked in Moscow in the Kremlin and became head of the Federal Service (FSB), the successor to the defunct KGB. Subsequently he became Yeltsin's fifth prime minister in seventeen months and finally president of Russia.

Time magazine reporter Adi Ignatius interviewed Putin[19] and said of the experience, "[T]alking to the Russia President is not just exhausting but often chilling." Putin, fifty-five years old, and his wife, Lyudmila, who before her marriage to Mr. Putin was an airline stewardess, have two daughters, now in their twenties. They live in a compound some twenty-five miles outside of Moscow. His mansion, hidden deep in a forest, is carefully guarded by heavily armed snipers hidden in trees.

Putin is about five feet six inches tall. He is sturdy, having reached black belt status in judo, and keeps in shape by swimming an hour each day. Putin eats quite moderately and is not publicly known as a carouser. He likes classical music, particularly Brahms,

Mozart, and Tchaikovsky, and even enjoys the Beatles song "Yesterday."[20]

It is said Putin does not use e-mail, and though he was raised in an atheist country, he claims to be a believer who reads the Bible and respects the Russian Orthodox Church. When asked by *Time* magazine editor in chief John Huey what role faith plays in his leadership, Putin replied, "First and foremost, we should be governed by common sense. But common sense should be based on moral principles first. And it is not possible today to have morality separated from religious values."[21]

MOTHER OF RUSSIA

Our Lady promised at Fatima that God would be greatly glorified by the Russian people. And she asked all her children throughout the world to pray for the conversion of Russia. Certainly the Russian population has had its share of suffering. Devotees of our Blessed Mother continue to pray for them. A most precious, and prescient Marian spiritual treasure of the Russian people is the ancient, most sacred Icon of the Mother of God of Kazan. This revered Russian image depicts the Blessed Virgin holding her Divine Infant Son, whose tiny face graces her left cheek. The Infant's right hand is raised toward His Mother in a gesture of benediction. The sacred icon is covered with a "Rizza" of precious silver, richly gilded and made to form the outline figures and dress. Only the faces of the Blessed Virgin and that of the Divine Infant are visible. The silver "Rizza" dates from the seventeenth century. This covering is encrusted with more than a thousand diamonds, emeralds, oriental rubies, sapphires, and pearls. Most of these precious stones have graced the icon for centuries. Their prime significance is their attestation of the great veneration in which this icon is held by the people of Russia and throughout the world. This hallowed icon represents the Mother of God as Patroness and Protector of all Russia. The icon's origins and history are deeply rooted in the spirituality of true Russians.

A thousand years ago or so, Russia was only a small farming region in eastern Europe. Over the years, people of diverse ethnic and cultural backgrounds have settled there. Many have kept their ancient customs and language, even into the twenty-first century. More than three hundred languages and dialects are in use in the former Soviet Empire. Most of the people who settled in Russia were poor and uneducated. They loved working the land, from which they derived their entire livelihood. Life was often harsh, backbreaking, and uncertain for the Russian people. Yet with faith powerful, deep, and enduring, they began to refer to the soil as "Mother Russia" from century to century.

The Icon of the Mother of God of Kazan is a vital cultural expression of that collective soul of the Russian people during the last thousand years. Legend has it that it bears an exacting replica of the Mother of God and her Infant Son. Faithful Russians cling to Mary, the God-bearer, Theotokas, Mother of God who brings their Savior Redeemer to them. God's special graciousness to Russia, it is believed, resides in the Icon of the Mother of God of Kazan, and God's presence is said to powerfully manifest in that unique spiritual treasure.

On Sunday, August 22, 2004, Pope John Paul II publicly stated that he would finally allow the Mother of God of Kazan icon that had been hanging in his private apartments for years to return to the Russian people. Few doubt Pope John Paul II's personal belief in the power of the Mother of God of Kazan icon. Though he wanted to bring the sacred icon to Russia himself, he was not invited to do so.

As long ago as the year 1101, the icon was venerated throughout Russia with pilgrims traveling vast distances on foot to pray before it. In that holy presence, they claimed to experience the powerful "presence" of Almighty God. It is not the icon itself that contains God's "presence." Rather, the sacred image awakens spiritual memories planted deep in our souls.

The fame of the Icon of the Mother of God of Kazan continued to grow. Folk dances, songs, and festivals in many cultures and languages throughout the vast lands of Russia commemorated the mystical beauty and miracles of the icon. Its fame, however, was just beginning.

Centuries rolled along yet the mystique of the Icon of the Mother of God of Kazan continued to grow in popularity and mystery. Gradually the icon, now lavishly endowed in a sanctuary especially built for it and maintained by the Czar, was revered throughout the Russian Empire under the title "Patroness and Protector of Holy Mother Russia." Miracles and cures attributed to the powerful "presence" within the icon increased and continued.

Peter the Great actually carried the holy and miraculous Icon of the Mother of God of Kazan as a banner. With the Icon of the "Patroness and Protector of Holy Mother Russia" as his insignia, he was seemingly invincible. When he transferred the capital from Moscow to Saint Petersburg, Czar Peter personally carried the Icon of the Mother of God of Kazan. With great homage and immense reverence, the Czar crossed the vast stretch of Russian soil that separated the two cities. Faithful Russians lined his path along the entire length of the way. Some sang prayerful songs. Many cheered and applauded as the holy icon passed before them in the hands of Czar Peter. Fervent demonstrators represented their heartfelt devotion to the Mother of God of Kazan as "Patroness and Protector of Holy Mother Russia" by attiring themselves in their finest native folk dress, bearing banners and flowers manifesting their culture, language, and ethnic origin. Only when Peter the Great enshrined the sacred Icon of the Mother of God of Kazan within his city, in a small wooden chapel on Posadskoy Bolshoy Street, on Saint Petersburg Island, was the official transfer of the capital complete.

In 1712, this chapel was renamed the Church of Our Lady of Kazan. In 1720, the icon was transferred to the Cathedral of the Holy Trinity. But by 1727, the icon was considered truly miraculous and was transferred back to the Church of Our Lady of Kazan, now renamed the Church of the Nativity of the Mother of God. So prolific were the cures wrought by the icon's presence that it was carried to the homes of the sick and the dying. In 1737, a new and more beautiful church on the main street, Nevsky Prospekt, became the shrine for the miraculous Icon of Our Lady of Kazan.

Centuries later, Emperor Napoleon prepared to conquer Russia. He expected an easy victory. But Napoleon misjudged the humble faith of the Russian people. He laughed scornfully when he heard that huge numbers of Russians were gathering before the sacred and revered Icon of the Mother of God of Kazan. Constant prayer vigils were formed before the icon (located in the presence of the Blessed Sacrament) to implore the intercession of the Mother of God on behalf of Holy Mother Russia.

"Stupid superstition!" mocked Napoleon and his generals. Napoleon, highly skeptical of legends of spiritual power emanating from such inanimate objects as icons, was pleased that gullible Russians were afraid of him. Napoleon heard reports that men, women, and children throughout the Russian Empire were praying, fasting, and singing ancient songs commemorating the miraculous powers of the Icon of the Mother of God of Kazan. They spoke prayers taught to them by their ancestors in preparation for war.

No true Russian believed Napoleon's might was strong enough to take from them by force their lands protected by Theotokas, the Patroness and Protector of Holy Mother Russia. Their faith was strong. They believed that her Son is God Incarnate. God rewarded their faith. His power saved Russia, and Napoleon was defeated by the elements. As his troops retreated across the snow-covered Russian tundra, marching to the delectation of howling winds, the Russian people were lifting their voices in praise and thanksgiving throughout the vast empire. God's kindness to them in their victory was attributed to the intercession of the Mother of God and the sacred, most powerful "presence" in the Miraculous Icon. Again, God revealed our Blessed Mother as "Patroness and Protector" of Holy Mother Russia.

During the reign of Czar Alexander I, a magnificent cathedral modeled after Saint Peter's in Rome was constructed at Red Square in Moscow to house another sacred Icon of the Mother of God of Kazan. This icon, however, did not enter Moscow amid a glorious display of devotion such as witnessed the procession to Saint Petersburg by Peter the Great. No one is certain exactly how or why the icon came to Moscow, yet the faithful came to venerate the icon in the Moscow cathedral. And a mysterious and powerful "presence" extended blessings to Russians who treasured and venerated it. Faith-filled fervor of the Russian people surrounding the mysteriously powerful icon diminished during the time of Rasputin, and seemingly ended at the Russian Revolution of 1917.

The Bolsheviks were particularly irritated with the spiritual influence of icons concerning the "soul of the Russian people." While intellectuals (perhaps unknowingly mimicking Napoleon) made sport of the "superstitious" faith of the masses, the aristocracy remained indifferent. Consequently, in a massive act of violent terror, anarchists destroyed the cathedral housing the Most Blessed Sacrament and the sacred Icon of the Mother of God of Kazan at Red Square. Revolutionaries celebrated. They expected to prove by this senseless act of destruction that indeed, God does not exist. Leninists loudly mocked the Russian people's faith as they scorned the Blessed Sacrament and the sacred Kazan Icon. In 1917, the sacred icon was gone. Circumstances surrounding its disappearance remain unknown.

Bolshevik revolutionaries desecrated the Saint Petersburg Basilica and turned it into a museum of history. Sacred tabernacles, icons, adornments, church vessels, and vestments were sold or destroyed. No one talks about details, but the miraculous Icon of Our Lady of Kazan eventually turned up in Poland. And in 1935, it came to England after a South African industrialist obtained it. By 1950, F. A. Mitchell-Hedges of Farleigh Castle, Reading, England, acquired the miraculous icon. His heir, Miss Anna Mitchell-Hedges, desired to restore the Icon of Our Lady of Kazan to the Church. It was brought to the United States for veneration in Orthodox churches. Later the icon was displayed in the Russian Orthodox Pavilion at the New York World's Fair (1964–1965). Subsequently, the holy icon remained in a bank vault in England.

By 1970, John M. Haffert, lay leader of the Blue Army Fatima Apostolate in the United States obtained the sacred image. He arranged its enshrinement at Fatima in the Byzantine Chapel, once again in the presence of the Most Blessed Sacrament. It remained there until Pope John Paul II personally took it to his own suite of rooms in the Vatican during the last days of his life.

After nearly a century in the West, the Mother of God of Kazan Icon was displayed beside Pope John Paul II during his weekly general audience in the Paul VI Hall, at the Vatican, on Wednesday,

August 25, 2004. The Pope officially presented the Mother of God of Kazan Icon to Cardinal Walter Kasper, president of the Vatican office for relations with other Christian denominations, who was chosen to head the delegation going to Moscow on August 28 to return the icon to the Russian Christian Orthodox Church on the feast day of the dormition of the Blessed Virgin Mary. In his reporting on the event for the *New York Times*, Jason Horowitz pointed out that "a tiny 12-by-10-inch copy of a Russian icon brought more attention than the masterpieces of Michelangelo and Bernini surrounding it."[23]

> ". . . The copy disappeared from Russia to the West sometime after the Bolshevik Revolution. It was bought by a Catholic group in the 1970s and later given to the Pope, who has said that it watched over his daily work. . . . 'What is important is that it is being revered,' said Archdeacon Vsevolod Borzak. 'In the end we have the same roots.' "[24]

No one really knows which icon is the miraculous one—the disappeared Moscow Icon of Our Lady of Kazan, or the Saint Petersburg icon enshrined in the Basilica of Our Lady of Kazan in Saint Petersburg.[25] The travels of the Holy Icon of Our Lady of Kazan are but pieces of God's mosaic.

Consider the following coincidence. Simultaneously with the desecration of the shrines housing the Icon of the Mother of God of Kazan in Moscow and Saint Petersburg by fanatic revolutionaries in 1917, Mary appeared to the children at Fatima. During her visits at Fatima, Mary asked God's faithful throughout the world to pray for His suffering people in Russia and to pray for the spiritual conversion of that nation. People everywhere did as our Blessed Mother asked.

And so it happened that in 2004, Pope John Paul II sent the Sacred Icon of the Mother of God of Kazan home to Holy Mother Russia. There is a connection between spiritual gifts and material prosperity that overfill a country when its people honor our Blessed Mother. Many have ears to hear the great God of Abraham.

Come little children of My Heart.
Come to the Mountain of Peace where all glistens in the silence
of My Presence.
Come little children of My Covenant with My people.
I am the Alpha and the Omega.
Dwell in My Presence for I am the Faithful One who
hears every sigh,
knows every desire
and provides from the reservoir of My unconditional love for
each of you.
You shall not want little children of My Heart.
You are Mine.
Do not fear. All is well.
I AM WHO AM.

Replica Image of the Black Madonna, Our Lady of Czestochowa in the Church of Saint Maxmillan Kolbe in Poland

CHAPTER 11

House of Gold

Blessed be the Lord, the God of Israel, for he has visited and brought redemption to his people.[1]

Throughout the centuries, people of every faith and culture have had personal experiences with Mary. The Blessed Mother was present in the upper room at Pentecost.[2] During her life on earth, the apostles and early disciples saw Mary in many circumstances, and even by the mystery of bilocation (being physically present in two places at one time).[3] Tradition holds that she spent her old age with the family of Saint John in Ephesus, which was a thriving center of commerce and culture at that time.

Basilicas, grottos, shrines, and churches, some of which remain, commemorate sites where ancient bilocations, visions, and meetings with the Blessed Virgin occurred. All over the world there are places marked by magnificent cathedrals as well as humble primitive altars that memorialize heavenly experiences people claim with the Blessed Mother through the ages. The handed-down history of such places recounts miraculous favors granted to ordinary people coming in faith to such sites. Some of the places where Mary revealed Heaven on earth remain shrines of great repute with amazing spiritual power.

Everything about our Blessed Mother is centered in love. Love is the key to the Heart of God. Mary helps us unlock the portal of true love hidden deep within us. Spiritual vision gives us eyes to see loving possibilities in every circumstance. Heaven is only for those who truly know how to love and be loved. Such Olympian skill is won at great cost to the ego.

SAINT EDITH STEIN

Thirteen-year-old Edith Stein was a strong-willed teenager in Breslau, Germany, who decided to rebel against her family's devout Orthodox Judaism. The youngest of eleven children, she was born on the Day of Atonement, October 12, 1891. High strung, independent, and precocious, Edith was a hypersensitive child with a gifted mind who loved to dance. From age thirteen to twenty-one, she actively included herself among fashionable, socially suave intellectual atheists. She claimed no belief in the existence of a personal God.[4]

In 1911, Edith enrolled at the University of Breslau, concentrating on the emerging discipline of psychology. All the while, she watched her intensely spiritual mother whose complete absorption in God, rather than any religious rituals or ceremonies, was both magnificent to Edith and completely confusing.

Edith became a phenomenologist and an educator. Along the way, she was deeply influenced by Christian friends and peers who sincerely believed that Jesus Christ is the Messiah. She would eventually say that "Christian philosophy was awakening like Sleeping Beauty from its centuries-old sleep." Academics activated a deep sense of social justice in Edith. She would later write: "My own strong sense of social responsibility led me to an active participation in the struggle for women's suffrage."[5]

During World War I, Edith volunteered at a military hospital and was later awarded a medal of valor for her efforts. War and suffering were patient and relentless teachers that Edith Stein did not escape. Later she went back to her studies and was awarded her doctoral degree summa cum laude.

One of her professors was well-known Max Scheller, who taught her that religion alone makes the human being human. "He placed humility at the foundation of all moral endeavors and argued that the sole purpose of this endeavor was to lead the individual to the loss of self in God—and on to the new resurrection."[6] About the same time, Edith discovered prayer. Coupled with intellectual curiosity, prayer led her to Mary. And Mary introduced Edith Stein to the miracle of the Word Made Flesh. The reality of the Incarnation opened the young seeker's heart to the heights of God's loving presence in all that is.

Edith Stein's hunger for union with Christ led her to the writings of Dr. Theresa of Avila, which ultimately led her to the loving kindness of Mary who brings Jesus: "What Edith Stein found in Theresa's autobiography was the confirmation of her own experience. God is not a God of knowledge, God is love. He does not reveal His mysteries to the deductive intelligence, but to the heart that surrenders itself to him."[7] Edith's spiritual awakening intensified as she submerged herself completely in the writings of Theresa of Avila. Theresa herself had had a similar experience when she read Saint Augustine's autobiography. Augustine wrote:

"Thanks be to God for giving me the life that rescued me from such an awful death. After all the kindness I had received from you, my God, the hardness of my soul was almost unbelievable. I seem to have been almost totally powerless, as if bound by chains that were keeping me from making a total surrender to God. . . . Then I began to understand that I wasn't living but wrestling with the shadow of death. . . . My soul was totally worn out; all it wanted was rest."[8]

As Edith became comfortable with truth, she discerned a call deep in her soul to give herself totally to Jesus Christ. Her spiritual mentor, Theresa of Avila pointed the way for her to the Carmelite Convent in Cologne, Germany. In that monastic enclosure, Edith learned to let her intellect rest in solitude and silence. Theresa of Avila, Our Lady's astute pupil, promises her Carmelite nuns and priests: "Once one has tasted a single drop of the water of this [heavenly] kingdom, he is repelled by the taste of anything earthly. Imagine what it must be like to be completely immersed in it."[9]

Edith Stein, ever the intellectual, found the wisdom of Dominican Scholastic Doctor Saint Thomas Aquinas refreshing. After a mystical experience of the truth of God, Thomas Aquinas referred to his immense theological writings as mere straw in comparison to who and what God truly is. He said:

> "Faith is the way to likeness to God which is the goal of the human person; yet faith must always remain a dark way because the truths of faith cannot be grasped by the unaided workings of the human intellect. For this they require divine illumination, and this in turn demands the cooperation of the will. What sets the will in motion is love. Contrary to the intellect, 'The perfection of love does not consist in a certainty of knowledge but in an intensity of being seized.' Whereas faith . . . aims at an object that is absent, love by its very nature is ordered towards the incomprehensible, to God, who himself, is love."[10]

Edith continued to work on her books and papers from behind convent walls. Learning from Mary, she wrote that spiritually mature women are a major source of healing for the world. Viewing the interconnectedness of people and nations after World War I, she wrote: "If a woman's vocation is the protection of life and the preservation of the family, she cannot remain indifferent as to whether or not governments and nations assume forms which are favorable to the growth of the family and the well-being of the young."[11]

When Edith Stein took her vows as a cloistered Carmelite nun in Cologne, Germany, she chose the name Mary (as all Carmelites receive) Teresa (for her spiritual mentor Saint Theresa of Avila) Benedicta of the Cross. At this time, persecution of Jews in Germany was real and it was frightening. Many heard her say of such crimes: "One day this will all have to be atoned for." Though Edith had an offer to teach in South America where she could have escaped the horrors of anti-Semitism, she instead followed her call to religious life. She said of that decision: "I did feel a great sense of calm, knowing that I was coming into the harbor of God's will."[12]

In 1937, as the safety of Jews in Germany disintegrated, plans were considered by which Edith would be transferred to the Carmelite Convent in Palestine. On April 21, 1938, Edith Stein pronounced her solemn and final vows at the Cologne Carmelite Convent. By

November, synagogues were burned, Jewish citizens were forcefully driven from their homes and their businesses were confiscated. Some of Edith's siblings immigrated to America. Palestine refused to accept Sister Theresa Benedicta of the Cross. Consequently the Superior of Edith's convent arranged for her transfer to the Dutch convent of Echt. Edith left under the cover of darkness on December 31, 1938.

The following spring, on Passion Sunday, 1939, Edith Stein made a personal offering of herself as a victim to God on behalf of the Jewish people for peace throughout the world (the elimination of war), and holiness for her family.[13] She spiritually surrendered herself, by a conscious act of her will, delivering herself over to the Eternal Father for poor sinners. Edith Stein chose to be a ransom with Jesus and Mary.

By 1940, the Germans occupied Holland. The Gestapo seemed to be everywhere. Complete extermination of the Jews was the political agenda of Hitler's military operation. On Sunday, August 2, 1942, all Jews who had converted to Catholicism in Holland were arrested, including members of religious orders. On August 7, SS commandos ruthlessly herded Edith Stein, the professed Carmelite nun now known as Sister Mary Theresa Benedicta of the Cross, along with her Jewish neighbors and friends, into a train heading east. All of them were sacrificed in the gas chambers at Auschwitz on August 9, 1942.

Edith Stein was a mystic and an intellectual. In her, the merging of Judaism and Christianity as a single redemptive unity came to life. Born on the Day of Atonement, she is forever a baptized German Jew and canonized saint who drank deep of the cup of her people's suffering and fulfilled her destiny of atoning love in death. She proved that supernatural faith is stronger than death; supernatural hope gives meaning to life and supernatural love lives forever.

MARY'S APOCALYPTIC PRESENCE

Mary's apocalyptic presence among us now is a sign of the immortality promised by Christ to those who love. Mary brings us awareness of the larger reality of the cosmic whole. Her wisdom allows us to develop deeper respect for the gift of our lives and all life around us. The Blessed Mother's presence is a harbinger of the cosmic triumph of human history in Christ the Savior. We can absolutely hope Mary's presence with us now will turn the tide in this time of infamy.

Mary brings secrets of God's loving providence to all faiths and cultures. Mary graciously helps everyone who belongs to her to live the way Jesus showed us when He, too, walked the earth. As we respond to her secrets unfolding in the world, we receive gifts that enable us to do whatever her Son tells us.[14] Mary among us now is part of the miracle of peace.

Humanity bears weapons of mass destruction. If they are used, portions of the earth become a wasteland, unfit for human habitation. Exactly whose victory will that be? Experience teaches us that there are other ways to resolve conflicts besides violence and terrorism. Jesus tells us: *"Love your enemies, do good to those who hate you."*[15] His Mother reminds us:

Cling to Jesus little ones.
Those who find me come to Jesus in my arms.
I am Mother of all the lost children of our Father.
I care for you as you allow.
Please live your faith perfectly dear little followers of Jesus.
As you live your faith perfectly, all will find
the Path to Paradise.
Jesus is the Path. Jesus, my Son is God Incarnate.

OUR LADY OF THE CASTLE

"And whence is this to me that the mother of my Lord should come to me?"[16]

Marian messages, visions, and apparitions are great cosmic gifts that enrich the earth's inhabitants. Consider the following excerpt of an interview at Oliveto Citro, Italy, in October 1989. Two brothers who grew up in Chicago were present the first night of what would become ongoing apparitions of the Blessed Mother, referred to as Our Lady of the Castle. Mary appeared with the Christ Child in her arms at Oliveto Citro, Italy, beginning on May 24, 1985. Teenagers at the time, the young men [who wish to remain anonymous] shared some of their personal recollections with the author.

Q. How old are you D——?
A. Seventeen.
Q. Where were you born?
A. Chicago.
Q. When did you move to Oliveto Citra, Italy?
A. My family moved back to Italy in 1984 after my grandfather had a heart attack.
Q. Have you personally seen the Blessed Mother?
A. Yes. Several times.
Q. What have you seen?
A. Mary with the Infant Jesus.
Q. How do you know for certain that it was the Mother of Jesus and her Son whom you think you saw?
A. There is no possibility of doubt.
Q. In what way is there no possibility of doubt?
A. It's hard to explain. Jesus is a baby, but more than that. He is the Son of God.
Q. What does that look like?
A. I don't know how to explain.
Q. Can you remember the first time that you had this experience?
A. Yes. I will never forget.
Q. How old were you at the time?
A. Thirteen.
Q. Please tell us what you remember.
A. It was May 24, 1985. It was dark, between 10:00 and 10:30 at night. My brother and I were hanging around with our friends. We were very, very scared.
Q. Why were you frightened?
A. It suddenly got really dark. Black—no stars, moon, no light at all. The wind was howling. In the distance, near the ancient castle, we could hear a baby crying. The castle door was creaking. It was real weird.

Q. How did you feel?

A. We were really scared. We ran down the hill—in the dark—away from the castle. We were so scared—all the darkness—weird sounds—we started to yell. But then we decided some guys might be trying to scare us. So we each picked up a few rocks to protect ourselves. One of my friends threw the first rock up the hill through the castle gate. But the rock didn't hit anything solid. It turned around in midair and bounced back through the gate at us—

Q. How strange!

A. Scary! We knew right away normal rocks don't do that. We got even more scared. Then the rock began rolling on the ground. In the meantime, the baby kept crying. Loud cries. And the wind was howling.

Q. But you said it was pitch black, totally dark. How could you see the rock?

A. A weird, flashing kind of eerie light in the dark was shining on the rock. My friend picked up the rock and threw it again. This time he threw it really hard through the gate.

Q. What happened?

A. Suddenly there was a huge ball of light in the gate of the castle. It began to get bigger and bigger. Then it exploded and we saw a Beautiful Lady, like a Queen standing in the light with a baby in her arms. Angels were all around her and the baby.

Q. What did you do when you saw this amazing scene?

A. I was so scared that I fell on my knees.

Q. Do you remember what happened next?

A. Yes. Some other kids ran up to the gate. They saw it, too. We were all very scared. And we were all very happy.

Q. What did the Beautiful Lady look like?

A. She was . . . heavenly . . . I can't describe her the right way. She was young. Sixteen or seventeen. Maybe not. She was not my contemporary.

Q. What do you mean by that?

A. I don't really know how to explain it. She was young-looking but eternal. She held the baby in her left arm. He was wrapped in a white blanket.

Q. How did you know the baby was a boy?

A. I just knew. I had no doubt. And I knew He was God. I was stunned.

Q. Can you describe the infant?

A. Yes. There was light all around Him and the Beautiful Lady. His eyes . . . I can still remember them . . . somehow I can't explain . . . they were filled with knowledge and power and . . . love. He wore no shirt or shoes. There was so much light around Him. I can never forget the light all around Him. He had a rosary in His right hand. And He was sobbing with sorrow.

Q. Sorrow?

A. It's hard to describe. It was tearing my heart out of me to see His pain. It was kind of the sorrow of deep, wounded— The Beautiful Lady from Heaven kept trying to comfort Him. She was covering and soothing Him. Singing to Him.

Q. How old do you think the baby was?

A. He was tiny. But those eyes . . .

Q. What about his eyes?

A. So much love. So much sorrow. So much compassion. So much pain. His eyes were looking at all of me.

Q. What does that mean?

A. I don't exactly know. He knew me. He's always known me. He loves me. He was sorrowful for me! Hurting for me!

Q. You could see all that in his eyes?

A. You would just have to see for yourself. I can't explain it.

Q. Did the Beautiful Lady speak to you?

A. No. Not to me. I saw her speak to my brother C——and to my friend P——. They were the only ones who heard her speak. The rest of us only saw her and her divine Infant. I can never forget the Infant. It's like I always knew Him, but I had forgotten Him. Then, when I saw Him, I realized how much He loves me. Maybe He was crying because I didn't always remember Him. I don't know. He knows everything!

Q. C——, did you see the same things your brother has just told us about?

A. Yes. I saw Jesus' Mother and the Christ Child, too.

Q. Did you know for certain that it was the Blessed Mother, and the Christ Child?

A. Yes.

Q. Did the Beautiful Lady speak to you?

A. Yes.

Q. What did the Lady say?

A. She said: "Peace to each of you young men."

Q. Were you afraid?

A. Yes. There was a lot of brilliant light around Jesus and His Mother. There were angels with them—the most powerful beings I ever saw. The Blessed Mother had a crown, like a halo of light with twelve stars.

Q. How do you know there were twelve stars of light?

A. Because when I was looking, I counted them. The Infant knew what I was doing.

Q. How do you know that?

A. There are lots of things that are different with them [the Blessed Mother and Child] than with just normal people.

Q. What were the angels like?

A. You just know they were holy. Powerful. They were small in size but that didn't affect their strength. They are stronger than any human.

Q. What did the angels look like?

A. They were like beings of light.

Q. How could you tell that they were holy?

A. I knew better than I know trees have leaves. Some things you just know but can't explain. The Blessed Mother and Christ Child, and the angels were filled-over with love.

Q. What does love look like?

A. It is just something you know. Like you know the sky is the sky. I can't explain it.

Q. What were the stars in the Beautiful Lady's crown like?

A. They were golden light that was twinkling.

Q. Did the Beautiful Lady wear a veil?

A. Yes. A long blue veil. It came all the way down to the bottom of her dress.

Q. What color was her dress?

A. White. A kind of shining white with gold. She was standing on a cloud. There was a brilliant light all around the Christ Child, the Blessed Mother, and the angels. There were lots of clouds around them, too.

Q. How long did you see all this?

A. We stayed until about midnight. We saw the Christ Child, the Blessed Mother and the angels the whole time.

Q. What did you do during that time?

A. We looked.

Q. That was quite a long time to look. How did you know for certain that it was the Blessed Virgin Mary and the Infant Jesus?

A. At first I did not know what was going on. Things were happening. Behind the Beautiful Lady there was an orangish-red cloud. I learned it was the devil.

Q. How do you know it was the devil?

A. The Blessed Virgin Mary told us. She said that wherever she appears, the devil is always seething nearby. He hates the Blessed Mother. She told us there is a fierce battle for souls going on now all over the world. The Blessed Mother said most people today don't even know they are fodder in a great spiritual battle.

Q. What else did the Blessed Mother tell you?

A. She told us her Son Jesus is the Savior of the human race. She told us to turn to Jesus, the Savior. She said His pain is great because so many people forget or do not know how to turn to Him for salvation.

Q. What did you do then?

A. I looked mostly at the Infant Jesus. I was stunned at His power.

Q. What kind of power?

A. His love for us. It's stronger than all the nuclear bombs in the world. It's bigger than all the planets.

Q. How do you know that?

A. You just have to experience it for yourself.

Q. What were you doing as you looked at the vision?

A. I don't know. At first the orangish-red cloud was not there. It came after awhile. I knew it was the devil.

Q. Are you certain of that?

A. Yes.

Q. How do you know?

A. The Blessed Mother told me.

Q. What did the devil look like?

A. He took the form of a small man, about one meter high. He was covered with ugly warts of varying sizes. He had small arms, small legs, and big, hideous black eyes that looked like holes. He jeered at the Blessed Mother. She wouldn't let him near her Infant. He was laughing at us and screaming at us and even trying to spit at us.

Q. No wonder you were frightened. What did the Blessed Mother say to you about this creature you just described?

A. She told me not to be afraid because her Son Jesus has given us all we need to overcome his power over us.

Q. He has power over us? In what way?

A. The Blessed Mother said the warts were all the unconfessed sins of the people of Oliveto Citra. The devil was mocking and claiming the people whose sins gave him power over them.

Q. The Blessed Mother explained this to you?

A. Every sin of every person in our town gives the devil power over the people and the town.

Q. Did that frighten you?

A. Yes. Very much.

Q. Why? How did you know the "warts" you saw were really the sins of the people in the town?

A. Because I could see my sins hanging on that hideous creature. He knew I recognized them. He insulted me. He said some bad things to me.

Q. And you, D——, what did you see?

A. I could see my sins, too.

Q. You young men both "saw" your sins with your eyes in those "warts"? How can you see a sin with your eyes? What do sins look like?

A. Sins are hideous. My sins are really ugly. I saw bad choices I've made in my life hanging on that devil. I was crying.

Q. Why were you crying?

A. Because I saw, actually experienced the pain I've caused, especially to people I really care about.

Q. How did this awareness make you feel?

A. I was afraid, ashamed, filled with guilt. That devil knew things about me I tried to hide. But he knew. It gave him power over me. He said I was worthless. He was making me feel despair.

Q. We all make mistakes. Weren't you being hard on yourself?

A. Not when the devil has power over you. You can't imagine how terrible his power is. His anger is so violent you can't stand it! His cruelty is . . . worse than a thousand R-rated violent war movies. He didn't want to let me go. I was feeling hopeless.

Q. What did you do?

A. I was trying to pray to the Christ Child. We all were. The Blessed Mother comforted us. She said we weren't worthless. She said her Infant Jesus can remedy all the mistakes I ever made. She told us all the sins and mistakes of all the people are the reason why her Infant Jesus came to the earth. She asked us to allow *her* to give us to Jesus so that He would take away our sins.

Q. Did you do that?

A. Yes.

Q. Did that make you feel better? Was the devil then less terrifying?

A. The devil is always terrifying. The Blessed Mother said the devil has always hated her, too. She promised she always brings Jesus to us when we call to her. I started calling to her right away.

Q. Then what happened?

A. The Blessed Mother said: "If you young men pray to Jesus, you will be saved. Remember, only Jesus can save you from your sins."

Q. What did you do?

A. I started to pray to Jesus right away. I prayed harder than I ever prayed before. The Blessed Mother folded her Infant's hands and they prayed together. Very, very fervently.

Q. Why were you praying so hard?

A. I wanted to. I needed to pray. I was trying to pray. I couldn't stop crying.

Q. How did you pray?

A. I prayed to Jesus to save me from my sins.

Q. Why?

A. Because I could see how destructive my sins are to me and to people I love. I needed to pray. I wanted to pray then and I've wanted to pray ever since.

Q. Did you tell the others to pray?

A. They already knew. We were all crying.

Q. Why?

A. We were all seeing our sins hanging on that orangish-red devil. We all prayed for a long time. We were crying a lot. We saw poor people in the world who do not know how to pray to Jesus. We heard them crying everywhere. We saw how much is wasted on the earth. We saw people who are poor and abandoned because no one cares about them. No one helps them. People who are in a position to change bad situations don't do anything and the devil just gets more and more in control of the earth and its riches.

Q. You "saw" all that?

A. That and lots more, too.

Q. Did praying make you feel less afraid?

A. I don't know.

Q. What happened to you as you were praying with Jesus and His Blessed Mother?

A. As we were praying, Jesus let us see how much we can do to make God's ways happen on the earth.

Q. Did Jesus speak to you about this?

A. Not with words. He didn't need to.

Q. Did the Blessed Mother say anything about this?

A. Yes. The Blessed Mother said that Jesus is how we are saved from our sins. Real prayer brings us light to see the truth about ourselves. Good prayer helps us understand our responsibilities and opportunities in situations around us.

Q. Did the Blessed Mother ask you to pray more?

A. The Blessed Mother said God commands us to pray, not her. Prayer makes us healthy in every way.

Q. Did you ask the Blessed Mother why you were seeing her and her Infant Jesus?

A. Yes. The Blessed Mother told me it is God who lets us see her.

Q. Has this experience changed your life?

A. Yes. Totally. Before I didn't go to church very often. I didn't pray much. Now I go to church every Sunday and receive the Holy Eucharist. I pray a lot. I go to confession whenever I make mistakes.

Q. How frequently do you go to confession?

A. Often. I don't want anything to be unconfessed.

Q. Does confessing your sins make a difference?

A. Confessing to the priest is like confessing to Jesus. When he says: "Your sins are forgiven you" the devil has no power over us.

Q. Do you young men continue to see the Blessed Mother and the Christ Child?

A. (D——) No.

A. (C——) Yes.

Q. Do you continue to experience the presence of the devil?

A. A year ago, on May 24, the devil was up there by the gate again. He was bugging pilgrims who came here.

Q. The devil was bothering pilgrims?

A. Yes. He took the form of the Blessed Virgin Mary. He talked to people. He told people not to pray. He told people not to love one another, to keep grudges. He said the poor deserve to be poor. He told people not to pray much, just to live for themselves, be happy. He said not to fast. He told people they need to eat to be healthy for strength. He told people they were already good enough, and had already done enough.

Q. Please wait a moment. Are you telling me that the devil appeared here in this village masquerading as the Blessed Virgin Mary?

A. That's *exactly* what I'm telling you!

Q. Why would God allow such a thing?

A. I don't know.

Q. Tell me what you recall about this deceptive apparition.

A. The devil was pretending to be the Blessed Virgin Mary. He was not beautiful . . . though he looked like a woman, he was eerie, beautiful in a cruel way . . . really frightening. This strange apparition continued to tell all the people who were looking to be selfish. He wanted them to bow down and worship him. He told people to look out for themselves, take what they could to be happy now and not to worry about other people—or even heaven.

Q. Were people aware that this creature was not the Blessed Virgin Mary?

A. The longer the apparition lasted, the more obvious it was that something wacky was going on. This Madonna was tough, not gentle. She was greedy—you could see it in her eyes—she wanted power and importance. She was flaunting herself, a real show off. We weren't fooled because we had seen the real Madonna.

Q. How blessed you are. Did you try to help others?

A. We didn't need to. The devil's disguise didn't work for long. When he started telling people to have a good time, saying "Why suffer? Jesus already did that on the cross," we knew it wasn't God's Blessed Mother. Suddenly his disguise fell off him and he laughed at us. The devil raged out at us and screamed to the people not to think about God or our family or friends.

Q. The devil said all that while taking the form of the Blessed Virgin Mary?

A. Yes.

Q. Do you know whether people realized it was not the Blessed Virgin Mary?

A. There was a lot of confusion. There was no peace. No one was able to pray much. People were in very bad moods. The apparition was basically ugly. The messages were ugly, too. There was a lot of cruel behavior everywhere.

Q. Do you think everyone there knew it was a false apparition that day?

A. People knew something was very wrong.

Q. Why do you suppose God allowed that to happen?

A. We wondered about that. I don't know why. Maybe to get us to recognize the difference between what is from Heaven and what is from hell.

Q. Did you believe in hell before these mystical experiences happened here?

A. Maybe not.

Q. Do you believe in hell now?

A. I do.

Q. Has that recognition changed how you behave?

A. It has changed how I think and live.

Q. Are there messages at Oliveta Citra from Heaven?

A. Yes. It's about Jesus.

Q. In what way?

A. If only everyone in the world could see Him, see who He really is, then everyone would know the truth.

Q. What can you do about that C——?

A. The Blessed Mother told me God wants all of us to pray and pray a lot. Jesus wants us to love one another. Share. Take care of the sick and the poor. Sacrifice. Do good things for others that nobody knows about.

Q. But you said the Infant Jesus didn't speak to you.

A. He didn't need to use words. He communicated a lot to me that night that I can never forget.

Q. Did the Blessed Mother ask for a shrine to be built here?

A. No. Just this small place of prayer. She wants us to pray, ask the angels to help us. I saw how powerful they are.

Q. What about your family?

A. Our family, too.

Q. Do pilgrims come here to Oliveta Citra from other places?

A. Yes. They come from America, Canada, South America, Mexico, France, Spain, Germany, the Philippines. They come from everywhere.

Q. Do they see the Blessed Mother and the Infant Jesus?

A. Some do and they see the Angels.

Q. Is there any special time that the Blessed Mother and the Christ Child appear?

A. They sometimes appear at night during the rosary. But there is no set time. A lot of people see them in the mornings, too.

Q. Do the Blessed Mother and the Infant Jesus come here every day?

A. Yes.

Q. Do you know how long they will appear here?

A. No.

Q. What do these visions mean to you?

A. Jesus Christ is a real person. He is the only one who can save us from our sins.

Q. What is the most important thing you have learned from this encounter with Jesus and His Mother?

A. If you could just see Jesus once, you would try hard to love everyone and everything. You can't imagine how much He loves each of us!

Q. Anything else?

A. Yes. We need to be really careful how we live our life.

Q. Anything else?

A. Yes. We need the church.

Q. Why?

A. We need the sacraments Jesus gave us. There is no place else to find them.

Q. Do you know why you were given these celestial experiences?

A. No.

Q. Do you know why the Lord Jesus and His Mother have come to your village?

A. Not really. Maybe so we won't lose our souls. Most of us were probably on the wrong path spiritually because we didn't know how much God loves us. We didn't know how destructive to us our sins are.

Q. Anything else?

A. Nothing compares with Jesus' love. I want to experience that again. Nothing else really matters.

Spiritual riches are everlasting. Everybody is made in the image and likeness of God and our union with God is perfect love. The Blessed Mother's gift to us is Jesus who is God. Mary, our mother, prays for each of us before the Throne of God. She knows how much we need Jesus, our Savior. The Blessed Mother's presence in the world of our times continues to be a sign of God's unfathomable faith in us, God's immutable love for the human race. Mary assures us that God wills only the very best for His people: we are sacred and destined to live in loving relationship with God and one another forever. Peace, joy, and the fullness of love flow abundantly from the Hand of God. There is no other source. Mary's life in God and her presence with us show us that abiding peace, deep joy, and unconditional love are the consummate human expression of union with God.

To rebel against the loving Plan of God is to make ourselves God's enemies. Rebellion on our part drives God's protection from our lives. History teaches us that withdrawal of God's blessing is His response to rebellion. Poverty, pain, hardship fill the vacuum. No cruelty flows from God's Hand for God is love. When human rebellion (behavior contrary to God's Law of love) scorns God's protection, calamity runs rampant and deprivation, degradation, desolation, despair, and death take over our lives. In these times, Mary's presence and work in the world remind us that without God's protection, rudeness, indolence, lewdness, licentiousness, greed, depravity, corruption, debauchery, vice, sickness, poverty, violence, war, and torture reign. Deviancy sweeps the innocent onto its path.

People of every race, creed, and nation are listening and watching for our Blessed Mother who brings God's mercy to impossible situations. The poor, the abandoned, the oppressed, and the downtrodden who pray see and hear Mary, Comfort of the Afflicted with eyes and ears of faith. Our Mother of Good Counsel is known to surprise presidents, monarchs, popes, corporate leaders, military leaders, bureaucrats, and civil authorities. Where Mary is honored, spiritual and material life flourish.

Truth reveals that everyone on earth is needy in some way, regardless of material wealth and power. Jesus showed us just how broken we are when He cried out from the cross: "Forgive them Father. They know not what they do." Jesus Christ chose to need Mary, His Mother Most Loving. She shared her strength, faith, and trust in God's abiding, omniscient love from the stable in Bethlehem to the cross on Calvary. The Blessed Mother, who revealed Jesus to the shepherds and Wise Men continues to reveal Him to us. She suffered with her dying Son at His crucifixion while fearful followers hovered in hiding. Christ's Mother, Seat of Wisdom, helps us to love. Her presence with us is an inestimable sign of God's providential mercy for the human race.

My name, dear children, is Wisdom.
I sit at the foot of the throne of the Trinity with all my children.
We are the sweetmeat of God's love and
His fathomless generosity.

I am His daughter dear children.
I am His love. I am His wisdom.
I am His Mother.
I am the House of the Lord.
No one who seeks my help is left unaided.[17]
Everyone who asks is included in my motherly care.[18]
If you pray with all your hearts, you will find luminous happiness
in God's Plan for us.[19]

The Virgin of Guadalupe

CHAPTER 12

Refuge of Sinners

"For God so loved the world, as to give his only begotten Son; that whosoever believeth in him, may not perish, but may have life ever-lasting."[1]

Christian faith holds that all things were created and exist in Jesus Christ. Mary's Son Jesus is actively present throughout the cosmos and calls to each of us by name. Consequently, the progressive fulfill-ment of the vast galaxies comes through our supernatural faith, su-pernatural trust, and supernatural love of the Word of God. Since everything and everyone—past, present, and future—is rooted and united in Christ for whom all things were made, the world and its history belong to Christ. Everything is held together in Christ. We are mysteriously in union with Him.

All of us pray for poor sinners. All of us sacrifice for poor sinners and all of us love poor sinners because we are the sinners for whom we pray, sacrifice, and love. If we can go a step higher and do likewise for others, we know we are growing in Christ's ways. If we go even a step higher and offer our lives in union with Jesus, His divine atone-ment and our meager acts become one.

Our true path into the depths of Christ is the way of the Incar-nation. At the heart of the Incarnation is Mary, our true Mother Most Faithful. Jesus, not clinging to His divinity, took human form in and through and with Mary. We, too, if we would be like Jesus, are invited to humbly descend into Mary's Immaculate Heart. Such descent for us is from the lofty pinnacle of our self-centered pride. To do so, we must leave behind all the golden calves that weigh us down. There is a mighty reward for us: victory over the difficult toil of pain and suffering that attach to us as we journey on the earth.

THE SECRETS OF GOD

The secrets of God that Mary knows are for those who fear Him.[2] Alienation from the secrets of God causes our life to degenerate to trivial pursuits that do not penetrate the depths of our souls. The courage to seek holiness above all else is necessary for individuals and families and nations.

Mary received the Messiah in human flesh and transmitted Him to all generations. She want us to know her ways:

> *I am the patient, long-suffering mother.*
> *I do not interfere in my children's lives.*
> *Only those who pray and seek me find me.*

Those who find Mary learn that not only is God in Heaven above, but Mary's Son Jesus is upon the earth below. Praying at Mary's knee is the story of Divinity bending low to lift us up to the highest heights. The relationship between God and His creation is sourced in revealed truth: with the Archangel Gabriel, we can all say: *Hail Mary, full of grace, the Lord is with thee: blessed art thou among women.*[3]

The nature of the relationship between creation and the divine source from which it emanates is a paradox: the transcendence of God and the inability of human reason to grasp our Creator. God's divine energy, Light from Light devolves from higher spiritual planes to lower ones. Mary not only bore the Son of God, begotten, not made, consubstantial with the Father, but she cared for Him, nursed Him, raised Him, and stood in solidarity with Him beneath His cross as He made the ultimate atonement for all of us. That is why Mary, our Spiritual Mother is so central to our spiritual journey.

It is useless to fear the cross of Christ: suffering, just like joy and happiness, is part of everyone's life on earth. Christ's crucifixion does not represent the triumph of darkness. On the contrary, His cross is the symbol of progress and our victory won through errors, disappointments, mistakes, and extreme hard work. Everyone suffers on earth, and everyone dies. Each of our sins—and we are all sinners—contains the seed of its own punishment. Repentance is the elixir of new life. Repentance in Christ frees us from the spiritual consequences of those sins. Jesus is the sinner's delight because He saves us from eternal punishment for our sins. Through faith in Christ who atoned for us, we receive mercy, forgiveness, justification. We can whine and cry and die as cowards do. Or we can believe that Christ suffered and died for our sins so that we can love and pray and praise and die as heroes do. The choice is ours. Our suffering, in union with Christ on the cross, is the arrow that shoots us into the glorified world to come.

Wisdom tells us we come to earth with a moral imperative to make the world better during our brief sojourn here. We must struggle to overcome all that can defile our integrity. The secrets of Mary help us to understand that we can only live well if we grasp not only the meaning of life, but also the meaning of death. On a superficial level, human death is a fragmentation of our personal unity: the existence we have labored to create for our self over our lifetime. But that is not the end of our personal life story. The resurrection of Christ reveals that death is our passage to eternal life. It is the necessary precondition for the final unique synthesis by which God, in Jesus, puts us back together again. Everything of value in our life will be purified and transformed. To the extent that our life on earth and the crosses (suffering) assigned to us are carried and endured in union with Christ, God will glorify the fragments of the attempted unity we have sought to achieve with our best efforts. God will lovingly put all the pieces of our life back together again but in a higher synthesis in which we enjoy a more intimate, closer union with the one, true God of Love and all His creation.[4]

Mary is forever the mother of the life of Jesus in us. Wherever our Blessed Mother has appeared on earth, there are always extraordinary graces and blessings, physical, psychological, and spiritual cures and healings for those who choose to participate. When Jesus walked the earth, no one who approached Him was turned away. Our Blessed Mother, who has perfect access to her Divine Son, brings every one of us who comes to her to Jesus in a most personal and familial way. She is truly our Spiritual Mother Most Powerful.

Jesus sends His Holy Mother to us because we truly need her. She is always near us, but most especially in times of difficulty and suffering. When Mary appears, the cross is real, but a wonderful resurrection of all that is bright and beautiful and marvelous is imminent if we but persevere.

The apostles and disciples of Jesus noted that the crucified Christ was totally healed when they saw Him after His resurrection, but He kept the marks of the wounds of his hands, feet, and side. Our Lady knows that when we are healed, as Christ wants us all to be, we, too, do not lose our wounds, but only their negativity and pain. Healed places in our bodies, minds, and spirits become powerful and glorious harbingers of the heavenly life to come. We are all called to be part of the Triumph of our Blessed Mother's Immaculate Heart. With such knowledge, it is valuable to look more closely at priceless clues that make our earth journey more enjoyable.

THE SECOND COMING OF CHRIST

One of the most valuable mystical gifts the world cherishes in fullness is the Divine Mercy revelation of the Lord Jesus and His Blessed Mother to Saint Faustina in the 1930s, in Lagiewniki, near Krakow, Poland.[5] Pope John Paul II was a great devotee of this revelation and died on the Feast Day of Divine Mercy, celebrated annually on the first Sunday after Easter. He spoke often of his burning desire that the message of God's merciful love, proclaimed through Saint Faustina, be known to all the peoples of the earth so that all hearts may be filled with hope. The Lord's message of Divine Mercy is "the spark which will prepare the world for His final coming."[6]

There is valuable information regarding the Second Coming of Jesus Christ in the *Diary of Saint Faustina Kowalska: Divine Mercy in My Soul*.[7] Jesus and Mary disclosed this knowledge to her on behalf of all of us in her convent in Poland as the Second World War loomed on the horizon.

"March 25, 1936. In the morning, during meditation, God's Presence enveloped me in a special way, as I saw the immeasurable greatness of God, and at the same time, His condescension to His creatures. Then I saw the Mother of God who said to me: 'O how pleasing to God is the soul that follows faithfully the inspirations of His grace! I gave the Savior to the world; as for you, you have to speak to the world about his great mercy and prepare the world for the Second Coming of Him who will come, not as a merciful Savior, but as a just Judge. O how terrible is that day! Determined is the day of justice, the day of divine wrath. The angels tremble before it. Speak to souls about this great mercy while it is still the time for [granting] mercy. If you keep silent now, you will be answering for a great number of souls on that terrible day. Fear nothing. Be faithful to the end.' "[8]

The warning that Saint Faustina passes on to us should surprise no one familiar with Scripture. Earlier, in 1934, the Lord Jesus appeared to Sister Faustina and asked her to make certain that all of us know the following.

"Write this: before I come as the just Judge, I am coming first as the King of Mercy. Before the day of justice arrives, there will be given to people a sign in the heavens of this sort: All light in the heavens will be extinguished, and there will be great darkness over the whole earth. Then the sign of the cross will be seen in the sky, and from the openings where the hands and the feet were nailed will come forth great lights which will light up the earth for a period of time. This will take place shortly before the last day."[9]

"In February of 1937, Jesus Christ appeared again to Sister Faustina and said: 'Souls perish in spite of My bitter Passion. I am giving them the last hope of salvation; that is, the Feast of My Mercy. If they will not adore My mercy, they will perish for all eternity. . . . [T]ell souls about this great mercy of Mine because the awful day, the day of justice is near.' "[10]

In December of 1936, Jesus appeared to Sister Faustina and said:

"Speak to the world about My mercy; let all mankind recognize My unfathomable mercy. It is a sign for the end times; after it will come the day of justice. While there is still time, let them have recourse to the fount of My mercy; let them profit from the Blood and Water which gushed forth for them."[11]

In June of 1937, Jesus appeared to Sister Faustina and said:

"Let the greatest sinners place their trust in My mercy. They have the right before others to trust in the abyss of My mercy . . . toward tormented souls. Souls that make an appeal to My mercy delight Me. To such souls I grant even more graces than they ask. I cannot punish even the greatest sinner if he makes an appeal to My compassion. On the contrary I justify him in My unfathomable and inscrutable mercy. . . . [B]efore I come as a just judge, I first open wide the door of My mercy. He who refuses to pass through the door of My mercy must pass through the door of My justice."[12]

In 1938, Christ said to Sister Faustina:

"Know that between Me and you there is a bottomless abyss that separates the Creator from the creature. But this abyss is filled with My mercy. I raise you up to Myself, not that I have need of you, but it is solely out of mercy that I grant you the grace of union with Myself."[13]

Shortly thereafter, Jesus told Sister Faustina:

"In the Old Covenant I sent prophets wielding thunderbolts to My people. Today I am sending you with My mercy to the people of the whole world. I do not want to punish aching mankind, but I desire to heal it, pressing it to My Merciful Heart. I use punishment when they themselves force Me to do so; My hand is reluctant to take hold of the sword of justice. Before the Day of Justice I am sending the Day of Mercy."[14]

Scripture reminds us that we cannot know the day or the hour of Divine Judgment. It is of some value to look to others who have been in a position to have more refined knowledge of the Second Coming of Christ. One such person is the late Pope John Paul II who called himself the "Pope of the Divine Mercy." The Pontiff believed that the Divine Mercy of Jesus Christ can rebalance the world of the Third Millennium.

Perhaps the following message from Jesus to Sister Faustina best sums up the heights and depths of Mary's secrets that prepare us for the second coming of her Son Jesus. After all, her finest gift to us is our Savior.

Jesus said:

> "How very much I desire the salvation of souls! . . . I want to pour out My divine life into human souls and sanctify them, if only they are willing to accept My grace. The greatest sinners would achieve great sanctity if only they would trust in My mercy. The very inner depths of My being are filled to overflowing with mercy, and it is being poured out upon all I have created. My delight is to act in a human soul and fill it with My mercy and to justify it. My kingdom on earth is My life in the human soul. I Myself am the spiritual guide of souls—and I guide them indirectly . . . and lead each one to sanctity by a road known to Me alone.[15]

The image of Christ as the Divine Mercy was painted in 1934 in Vilnius, Lithuania, and exhibited there in 1935 at the Shrine of the Mother of Mercy. During World War II, the sacred image was hidden. By 1986, it was once again available for veneration. The Divine Mercy image is intended to be a source of inspiration and grace. Those who contemplate the image see the Risen Christ extending one hand in blessings for the world, and the other touching the wound in His side from which blood and water gushed forth as mercy for all.[16] The mystical meaning of the Divine Mercy image is the love and forgiveness of God made man in Jesus Christ the Redeemer.

MIRACLES OF DIVINE MERCY

In a southern state in the United States, a hardened criminal awaited
execution on death row. His behavior was obviously evil. A young
lawyer was assigned to the case who did not believe in capital punishment. He tried his best, at great personal sacrifice, through every available legal means, to have the criminal's death sentence commuted. As
each appeal was exhausted, the inmate's chance for life diminished. At
the height of his frustration, the lawyer received a telephone call from
a nun he did not know. She asked to have a meeting with the condemned criminal. The lawyer quickly assured her that the warden on
death row would never allow such a meeting. But the nun persisted
and begged him to ask the warden for the meeting. The lawyer be-
grudgingly agreed. To his shock, the warden readily acquiesced.

Before the date of execution, the nun met with the heavily guarded
criminal. She gave him an image of Jesus Christ, the Divine Mercy
and asked him simply to look at the image as often as possible. The
meeting lasted less than two minutes. Several weeks before his execution, the criminal, born and raised in the dregs of Appalachia, requested baptism. On the day of his execution, he stood between the
prison minister and his attorney. Holding the image of Divine Mercy
to his heart, he praised the mercy of Jesus Christ and begged forgiveness of all whom he had harmed. His attorney was stunned, as were
those who had known the hardened man during his incarceration.

When the executed criminal's lawyer attempted to find the nun
who had insisted upon seeing his late client, he was told the young
woman was confined to a nearby nursing home. Surprised, he decided
to return the well-worn image of the Divine Mercy to her. He found
her terribly crippled and in the final stages of advanced multiple scle-
rosis. The illness had come upon her quite suddenly after her visit to
death row. The lawyer patiently explained to her the spiritual events
surrounding the final hours of the condemned man's life. "Souls are
expensive" responded the suffering nun. She was thirty-three years old.

•   •   •

A million people were slaughtered in the genocide of Rwanda at the close of the twentieth century. Today, there is a Divine Mercy Shrine there and great need for survivors of the atrocities to find forgiveness and mercy for the murderers. Our Lady appeared in Rwanda at Kibeho during the 1980s to forewarn the largely Catholic population.[17] Her messages were poorly disseminated and unheeded. Now, with more light and peace in the area, healing and renewal are possible. Our Lady of Kibeho, Mother of Divine Mercy asked the entire world to pray for the people of Africa, and for everyone on earth.

The Lord Jesus told his apostle of Divine Mercy, Saint Faustina: "I am Love and Mercy itself. When a soul approaches Me with trust, I fill it with such an abundance of graces that it cannot contain them within itself, but radiates them to other souls."

In these times, our Blessed Mother is calling all people to become Apostles of Divine Mercy.[18] Christ said:

"I have opened My Heart as a living fountain of mercy. Let all souls draw life from it. Let them approach this sea of mercy with great trust. In the Cross, the fountain of My Mercy was opened wide by the lance for all souls. No one have I excluded. The graces of My Mercy are drawn by means of one vessel only, and that is trust. The more a soul trusts, the more it will receive. . . . I never reject a contrite heart. Sooner would heaven and earth turn into nothingness than would My Mercy not embrace a trusting soul."[19]

God is unchanging. His love for the human race is beyond telling. There is no other life but life in God. All else is illusion: the dark kingdom of destruction, depravity, despair, death. We are rediscovering that peace is the harbor of truth. Truth is God's unfathomable love for the human race.

CELESTIAL PETALS IN THE PHILIPPINES

The late Benedictine Father Rene Laurentin, a French theologian and preeminent Mariologist, was highly skilled at discernment of authentic apparitions of the Blessed Virgin Mary and wrote extensively about them. I could not have known when I read his description of Our Lady's apparitions to Teresita Castillo, a novice at the Carmel of Lipa, in the Philippines, that one day I would meet Teresita. At the conclusion of my interview with her, my husband and I, along with several of the nuns who were present, personally experienced a shower of red rose petals, bearing the imprint of the face of Christ, mysteriously falling upon us in the parlor of the Carmelite Convent where the apparitions occurred in 1948.[20] The origin of the rose petals was not understandable with human reason. My husband continues to marvel; not only at the mysterious shower of rose petals, but also that he is one of the few males ever permitted in the convent garden of apparitions.

Rene Laurentin wrote:

"On September 13, 1948. Teresita Castillo, a novice at the Carmel of Lipa (Philippines), was walking in the garden of her convent. Suddenly she saw a 'beautiful woman' who was smiling with her hands together in prayer, holding a golden rosary around her right hand. She was wearing a white dress, tightly belted; her bare feet rested on a small cloud 20 inches off the ground. 'Be faithful and come back here, whether it's raining or not,' Teresita heard her say. 'Who are you, Beautiful Lady?' [asked Teresita of the apparition] Our Lady answered, 'I am your Mother, my little one.'

"On September 14, 1948, the Virgin awaited her in the same place, with her arms wide open. 'I wish to have this place blessed tomorrow,' she said and blessed the nun before she disappeared again. The next day, around 3:00 PM, the auxiliary bishop of Lipa and the chaplain of the Carmel came to bless the place. Teresita saw the Virgin again with open arms. '. . . Take a piece of paper and a pencil, and write down the following,' said the apparition. 'My daughters, I ask you to believe in me, and to keep this message a secret for yourselves. Love one another like true sisters. Pay me visits here regularly; keep this place sacred and respected. Pick up the rose petals. I bless you all.'

"After this apparition, a rain of rose petals fell and was seen by all the people present.

"The following October 3rd, a 'rain of rose petals' occurred again. On Friday, November 12, 1948, Teresita saw the Virgin after Mass. Our Lady said: 'Pray intensely, my daughters, because of persecutions. Pray for priests. What I ask in this place is the same thing I asked in Fatima. Do penance for those who do not believe. This is my last apparition here.'

"People began hearing of cures, . . . On December 6, 1948, an official report was sent to Bishop A. Verzosa, of Lipa. The prelate blessed the place, appointed an investigatory commission, and declared that the Virgin was at the origin of the 'rain of petals.' "[21]

THE VIRGIN OF GUADALUPE

Though I have written of Our Lady of Guadalupe in other books, these unique visions of Mary provide rare, ever new, and fresh glimpses into the sacred kingdom of God's kind providence. As far as is known in these times, the image of the Blessed Mother on Juan Diego's ancient *tilma* [poncho] is the only known heaven-sent icon of the Blessed Virgin Mary that exists on earth. It now hangs on display in the great Basilica that was constructed on Tepeyac hill in Mexico City. Approximately seven million pilgrims come from all over the world each year to the great Basilica of Our Lady of Guadalupe. No one who comes there in faith is ever disappointed.

Pope Benedict XVI, on the Feast Day of Our Lady of Fatima, May 13, 2005, placed the entire Church in the maternal hands of the Virgin of Guadalupe during a visit to venerate her image in the Vatican Gardens.[22] The Pope prayed in Spanish before the image.[23] "Holy Mary, under the advocacy of Our Lady of Guadalupe, . . . encouraged by the love you inspire in us, we again place our lives in your maternal hands." Placing a floral offering at the foot of the statue, the Holy Father recited a Hail Mary and prayed: "You who are present in the Vatican Gardens, reign in the hearts of all in the world. With great hope, we come to you and trust in you."

MARY'S SPECIAL PROTECTION

Jesus Christ grants His Blessed Mother the privilege of offering her special protection to those who allow her to be their maternal advocate before God.[24] Mary among us is an unmerited gift of Christ's Divine Mercy. Mary leads us into the beauty of God's peace so that we may experience His serenity.[25] God's serenity is patience, forgiveness, true love. God's serenity is ours when we are able to love and serve one another in God and for God and with God.

Mary is here for us to illumine God within us and around us.[26] Our Blessed Mother helps us to joyfully embrace God's ways, live in His love, defend His will, share His bounty, and protect His creation.[27] Our Lady keeps our lives filled with God's marvelous gifts.

As Saint Louis de Montfort wrote three hundred years ago in his spiritual classic, *True Devotion to the Blessed Virgin*:

"Mary is the fruitful Virgin, and in all the souls in which she comes to dwell she causes to flourish purity of heart and body, rightness of intention and abundance of good works. Do not imagine that Mary, the most fruitful of creatures who gave birth to a God, remains barren in a faithful soul. It will be she who makes the soul live incessantly for Jesus Christ, and will make Jesus live in the soul."

Our Blessed Mother knows us. Her love for us is total. Her words are our hope and our delight.

You have nothing to fear little children.
Rest serene upon the Heart of Jesus.
He is your light, your life, your joy, your peace,
your living reality.
All that is not of Jesus, for Jesus, with Jesus
passes away.

His love is your ransom. His life is yours.
Play little ones.
Play in the courtyard of my joy.
Enjoy my presence and my blessing.

Wisdom is a great gift worthy of our highest efforts. The moment of our own personal Apocalypse is set. We know not the day, nor the time that each one of us will be called before the Throne of God to render an accounting of our time on earth. God's mercy is for those who fear Him. To know God is to be filled with joyful awe and wonder at the majesty of our loving God. Such is the beginning of wisdom.

Wisdom teaches us to review our past only in the light of God's mercy. We all can pray with confidence in God's mercy. He hears His children's pleas. He honors even our most modest attempts to love. God redeems mistakes and disappointments that haunt our memory. God has entrusted supernatural gifts of wondrous glory to fragile human vessels. Christ is at work in the world even if it is tarnished by some who have betrayed their human dignity. Jesus promised to be with us until the end of time. And so will He be.

REPENTANCE IS THE ELIXIR OF
NEW LIFE IN GOD

In Jesus, God has provided a remedy for all the evil in the world. If we try constantly to remain faithful to God's ways, we will fly into God's Heart where nothing created will disturb our life with God. Sacred Scripture and life experience assure us that God is love. God alone can reveal to us exactly what that means. God is eternal. So also are we, but do any of us really know ourselves as eternal beings created to love and be loved?

The Blessed Mother discloses to us that if we truly desire to be happy on this earth, we keep for ourselves only what we need, and we share what we keep. The Blessed Mother reminds each of us to be Good Samaritans. She asks those who know her to be witnesses of her loving presence to all God's people.

In our inner depths, every one of us has knowledge of our Blessed

Mother. In her care, we played before the Face of God before He made the world. We all long to open an inner door and return to our Home in the depths of love and peace and holiness. The key to that door is truth. Truth is visible, but only in the Light.

Our Blessed Mother urgently calls everyone to pray fervently for the gift of wisdom. Ever our Loving Mother, she begs us to firmly believe in God who is our light and our strength. To do so requires courage and patience. Our Blessed Mother graciously reminds us that God commands firm moral leadership. She reminds us that failure to honor God's commandments is a sign that we do not love God. Those who do not love God do not honor God. Devastation of all we hold dear is the consequence of such darkness. We reap what we sow. Divine Mercy is our finest hope. Repentance is the elixir of new life in God.

God comes and dwells in those who keep the commandments.[28] Our Blessed Mother forewarns us that all too soon where God does not dwell, there will be no life. Love begets love. Goodness begets goodness. Justice begets justice. Evil begets evil. Our Blessed Mother tells us there are days ahead we cannot fathom. Divine Mercy is our gift. God alone makes all things bright and beautiful forever.

If we would be truly happy, we strive to become highly sensitive to God's presence in our lives. One way is to offer Him more loving sacrifices. God sees everything. Though God does not need anything, our small sacrifice is our heartfelt gift of love. We cannot outdo God in generosity. He lovingly rewards even the most petite gift. Truth teaches us by experience that we really must either gently surrender into God's Kingdom of Love, or bear the grief of separation from all that is good and decent and beautiful and life-giving forever.

Because we are prone to miss the time of our personal visitation, that sublime moment when God bends low to whisper divine secrets to us and around us, Holy Wisdom leads us to our Blessed Mother. Every culture, tribe, and civilization is aware of her, though some do not yet know her name. Many ponder her faithfulness, her gentleness, her profound kindness. Many seek intimate relationship with the merciful mother who blesses all God's creation. Our Blessed Mother asks us to meditate on the loving sacrifice of our older brother Jesus on the cross to receive the spiritual gift of intimacy with her. Confusion is of the world, not of Heaven. When we act without faith in the unseen world all around us, we lose our spiritual light. Darkness encloses our mortal bodies and we experience reality merely by means of our five senses. Encased in human bodies, we can become quite unbalanced. The truth is that we do live before the Face of God who is visible to the eyes of our immortal soul. Faith is our physical access to that reality. Our Blessed Mother is here with us now to help us voluntarily rid ourselves of all that is not of God. She dwells with us as we watch and wait for Him.

Revelations of God come to us when we least expect. Our Blessed Mother's very life shows us that silence is a gift. Pray for the gift of silence. Silence is a prayer when we are awaiting God. Say nothing. Think nothing. Just wait. God will come when we least expect. Then we will experience His love. We will feel His peace come into our bodies. Mary's silence was contemplation. She lived on the earth immersed in the symphony of God's presence. Mary wants to share that gift with us.

Hope promises us that God's Kingdom is all around us. We are invited to become aware of His Kingdom. God speaks in the silence of our hearts. We must spend more time alone with God if we desire to hear His voice. When our faith is strong, we prepare a place for God in our lives. We are invited to live in the Heart of Christ for all eternity. Jesus is the path of eternal life. Pray, listen for God's voice, praise Him, strive to sense His nearness, and become comfortable in His presence.

Be confident in God's power. God makes all things well, new, beautiful. The gift of hope sees God's love and mercy in everything. We really need to discipline ourselves so that we trust always in God's merciful kindness. If we trust God, we necessarily believe that evil does not triumph.

THE ELIXIR OF PEACE

If we believe that we *really do* belong to God and that God makes all things new, beautiful, and life-giving, we are able to allow everything in our lives to pass gently into God's hands. That is the elixir of God's peace that passes all understanding. Clinging to our Blessed Mother, we enjoy delight. Her words are a lullaby in the recesses of our memory. She soothes our fears, eases our burdens, and loosens our chains of sorrow. She helps us to let go of the pain we harbor for misfortunes not of our making. Nothing happens to a soul that God our Father does not allow. Mary knows all the sorrow we harbor. She helps us trust God's power to remedy all our pain, suffering, and every need. In that way, we become capable of supernatural love.

Humans have acquired the means of annihilating one another and indeed the entire planet. But our Blessed Mother promises that prayer, penance, and spiritual fasting will bring peace. We all have a stake in making that happen in whatever way we can. God, in His infinite love, has allowed us the freedom to choose good or evil. A person who does not pray, who does no penance, who does not fast is helpless to distinguish between good and evil. We are becoming aware of these present dangers.

He who made the world still governs it. When we look at the big picture and see the earth against a cosmic background, there is a larger drama unfolding now, birthing a new freedom for humanity.[29] Our simple yes to God's will allows us to enter into the safety of the Almighty who has His own design and purpose for all things. The heart open to God is stronger than any weapon.[30] Awareness heals, renews, and wisely restores. Our Blessed Mother *is* the Queen of Peace. She says we are on the path of peace.[31] We are all created to enjoy God's blessings.

ASSIGNMENTS

We can strive to be proactive. With Mary's help, we are able to ascend the mountain of supernatural faith, trust, and love. Some suggestions include:

1. Accept our Blessed Mother's strength as a pledge of her power to protect her own.
2. Do not accept into our sacred persons the bitter potions of the devil. He froths and rages to destroy the beauty of Mary's presence in our families, cities, nations, and, indeed, the world.
3. Flee from what assails the integrity and serenity of God's love for each one. Abandon fear, loneliness, and self-destructive ways.

4. Do not return to places of iniquity, which have injured our serenity in the past.

5. Live simply and peacefully in the depths of our Blessed Mother's love.

6. Forgive and we shall be forgiven. God's love is the light of the world. If we have enough faith and trust in God, we can love under any circumstances. When we love, we forgive all wrongs. Compassion is the companion of those who love.

7. Honor the commitments we have made.

8. Refine our goals. We must diligently perform our obligations with dedication. If we remain unfaithful to our responsibilities in small things, we shall forfeit participation in larger responsibilities.

9. Pray more. Make a commitment to pray about everything. Learn to pray always.

10. Give our Blessed Mother many small renunciations of our sensual appetites. Our sacrifices deposited in Our Lady's hands are currency our Blessed Mother uses to obtain gifts for us from her Son.

11. Learn to love the Holy Rosary—our lifeline to eternal life.

12. Help others. Be faithful day and night.

13. Consciously strive to avoid negativity at all times.

14. Choose to believe and we will be able to believe.

15. Trust God's love. Trust begets love. Love begets peace.

16. Allow authentic love to dwell in every thought, word, and deed.

17. Bless everyone and everything.

18. Pray always: *"The Lord bless thee, and keep thee. The Lord shew his face to thee, and have mercy on thee. The Lord turn his countenance to thee and give thee peace."*[32]

TRUTHS OF THE UPPER WORLDS

The unique spiritual journey we each experience on the earth brings us, and all aspects of our personal reality, into harmony with the divine purpose for which everything has been created.

These are wondrous, celestial matters that no human mind can penetrate.

Our Blessed Mother reveals to us the essence of God: truths of the upper worlds that both astonish and frighten us when we venture too close. These realms are accessible only by supernatural faith. Even the highest spheres of human reason are impotent in the light of perfect truth. Mary learned from her Divine Son. Mary understands Christ as only His Mother knows. She remains His vessel, loving us for Him and teaching us the glories of God hidden from all ages. Mary, the Queen Mother pure and holy, is the Living Torah of all people. Her prophetic wisdom is sourced in God the Creator who chose her before He made the earth to be His human Mother and our Spiritual Mother.

The secrets of Mary take us beyond the boundaries of mere human reason. Through her, Heaven transmits infinite light to earth. Those who choose to become faithful sons and daughters of Mary Most Holy advance quickly in wisdom and holiness. Seekers who remove themselves from the brilliant tutorials that Mary provides become sightless in the dark. Higher souls live on light. They must have the revealed illumination of God to exist. Though hidden from the world, Mary is the spiritual mentor of those who are able to receive her light.

Mary is the God-bearer. One never worships the God-bearer. Only God is worthy of worship. When we kneel before our Blessed Mother, we kneel before the light that flows through her to all God's children. Mary, bringing God to mankind, is the mother of our life in God. In the past, Mary's presence remained available only to a few highly privileged individuals of great spiritual refinement, some of whom have been identified in this book. In these times, seekers all over the world are experiencing supernatural faith as they encounter Mary.

Our Blessed Mother is here to nurture us to the supreme heights of spiritual wisdom. Mary helps us to pray with delight. She invites us to sing and dance amid the profusion of God's goodness, graciousness, and providence. We humans are animated from within. As we learn to embrace the ways of Mary's Son, we experience the resurrection of all that dies in Christ. With Mary, we dwell in the springtime of supernatural hope.

Great minds bend to the mysteries of God's presence. As the rains water the earth with new life, so the Living Water nourishes mankind with divine truth. Mary's Son makes all things new in countless manifestations of supernatural love. We can only conclude therefore that this generation is close to the completion of the world.

Mary, Mother Most Faithful

My dear little children
Thank you for allowing me to be with you.
My Son is Love.
I am the Mother of Love.
Cling to me dear children. Cling to my love.
My love is strength. My love is union with God.
Live in stillness.
My Son comes when you least expect Him.
Will you be awaiting Him?
Those who are busy about the things and ideas of the world miss
His visitation.
They weep and wail but they find Him not.
Call Him dear children. Call to Him day and night.
Look for Him everywhere, in every circumstance of your lives.
Those who seek Him find Him. He longs to be found.
Jesus is Love Incarnate.
A heart filled with love is the resting place of the Holy
Trinity.
Such a heart is the treasure of the Holy Trinity.
Such a heart is the earthen vessel of the Holy Trinity.
In prayer, united to obedience to
God's Word and God's will,
my children are capable of love.

The Kingdom of Heaven is within.
Dear little Princes and Princesses of
the Kingdom of Heaven,
enter into that Kingdom now.
Accept the Kingship of my Divine Son Jesus.
Jesus is Lord of the Cosmos.
His children are royalty by His blood.
Be my children little ones.
I am Queen of Heaven. I am Queen of the earth.
Be my children for I am Queen of the Cosmos.

Praise the Holy Trinity dear little ones.
He who is mighty has done great things for

us and holy is His Name.
Blessed are you dear little ones of my heart for
I am the Mother of God
and Mother of each of you who come to me.

Call to my Son. Love my Son. Obey my Son.
Be like my Son.

Vision of Lucia of Fatima: God the Father, Christ on the cross, the dove representing the Holy Spirit. Mary stands at the right hand of her son, Jesus. Angels of the Eucharist appear on either side of the tabernacle.

The Woman Clothed with My Son has come for her children.
Her ways are not the ways of the world as you know it.
That world is passing away before your eyes.
The mortification I want is a renunciation of all those
things in the world
not of Jesus or for Jesus or through Jesus.
The joyful laughter of My children is
a carillon ringing in Paradise.
The time to cry is passing. The time to laugh is coming.
Through the messages of Mary the power of
evil is diminishing.
Though evil seems strong, it is unmasked.
My beloved daughter Mary will be known and
loved by all My children.
All families are Marian families.
The day is coming when the entire world will be
a Marian family before My Face.
I am reclaiming My kingdom on earth.

Pray and fast.
Choose My Kingdom.
Live in My Kingdom.
I AM WHO AM

Image of Mary, Spiritual Mother of the
Human Race

Afterword

It shall come to pass, in the last days, (saith the Lord,)
I will pour out of my Spirit upon all flesh:
and your sons and your daughters shall prophesy,
and your young men shall see visions,
and your old men shall dream dreams.
And upon my servants, indeed, and upon my handmaids
will I pour out in those days of my spirit,
and they shall prophesy.
And I will shew wonders in the heavens above,
and signs on the earth beneath:
blood, fire, and a vapour of smoke.
The sun shall be turned into darkness,
and the moon into blood,
before the great and manifest day of the Lord, come.
And it shall come to pass,
that whosoever shall call upon the name of the Lord,
shall be saved.[1]

Appendix 1

SPECIAL PRAYERS TO MARY

These prayers, in some cases, have resulted in scientifically authenticated miracles.

HAIL MARY

*Hail Mary, full of grace. The Lord is with you. Blessed are you
among women and blessed is the fruit of your womb, Jesus.
Holy Mary, Mother of God, pray for us sinners now and
at the hour of our death. Amen.*

MEMORARE

*Remember O most gracious Virgin Mary that never was it known
that anyone who has fled to your protection,
implored your help or sought your intercession
was left unaided.
Inspired by this confidence,
I fly unto you O Virgin of Virgins my Mother.
To you do I come,
before you I stand, sinful and sorrowful.
O Mother of the Word Incarnate,
despise not my petitions
but in your mercy hear and answer me.
Amen.[1]*

DEAREST BLESSED MOTHER

Dearest Blessed Mother, be thou my true mentor
During this pilgrimage here on earth.
And stand by my side
When death draws near
To lead me to that encounter of all encounters.
At your side may the Lord Jesus say to me:
"Well done good and faithful servant.
Enter into the kingdom prepared for you
From all ages". Amen.

THE MYSTERIES OF THE HOLY ROSARY

Five Joyful Mysteries
1. The Annunciation
2. The Visitation
3. The Nativity
4. The Presentation
5. The Finding of the Child Jesus in the Temple

Five Luminous Mysteries
1. Christ's Baptism in the Jordan
2. Christ's First Miracle at the Wedding Feast of Cana
3. Christ's Proclamation of the Kingdom Within
4. Christ's Transfiguration
5. Christ's Institution of the Holy Eucharist

Five Sorrowful Mysteries
1. Christ's Agony in the Garden
2. Christ's Scourging at the Pillar
3. Christ's Crowning with Thorns
4. Christ Carries His Cross
5. Christ Is Crucified

The Five Glorious Mysteries
1. Christ's Resurrection
2. Christ's Ascension
3. The Descent of the Holy Spirit
4. The Assumption of Mary into Heaven
5. The Crowning of Mary Queen of Heaven and Earth

Appendix Two

SOME REPORTED APPARITIONS OF
THE BLESSED VIRGIN MARY[1]

1830 Paris, Rue-de-Bac to Saint Catherine Laboure

1836 Paris, Our Lady of Victory to Rev. Genettes

1840 Blangy, France, to Sister Justine Bisqueyburu

1846 LaSalette, France, to Melanie Calvat and Maximim Giraud

1858 Lourdes, France, to Saint Bernadette Soubirous

1871 Pontmain, France, to Eugene and Joseph Barbadette

1876 Pellovoisin, France, to Estelle Faguette

1879 Knock, Ireland, to fifteen people

1904 Poland to Saint Maximilian Kolbe

1917 Fatima, Portugal, to Blessed Jacinta, Blessed Francisco, and Lucia

1918 San Giovanni, Italy, to Padre Pio stigmatist

1920 Verdun, Quebec, Canada, to Emma Blanche Curotte

1920s Millbury, Massachusetts, United States, to Eileen George

1922 Montreal, Canada, to Georgette Faniel, stigmatist

1925 Tuy, Spain, to Sister Lucia of Fatima

1932 Beauraing, Belgium, to five children

1933 Banneaux, Belgium, to Mariette Beco

1937 to Saint Faustina Kowlaska

1945 Amsterdam, Holland, to Ida Peerdeman

1947 Montichiari, Italy, to Pierina Gilli

1947 Tre Fontane, Rome, to Bruno Cornacchiola

1948 Lipa, Philippines, to Terisita Castillo

1952 India to Rev. Louis M. Shouriah, S.J.

1954 Seredne, Ukraine, to Anna

1954 Ohio, United States, to Sister Mildred Neuzil

1961 Garabandal, Spain, to four children

1964 San Damiano, Italy, to Mama Rosa Quattrini

1968 Italy to Mama Carmela Carabelli

1968 Cairo, Egypt, to thousands

1970 Vladmir Prison, Russia, to Josyp Terelya

1972 Milan, Italy, to Rev. Stefano Gobbi

1973 Akita, Japan, to Sister Agnes Sasagawa

1974 Ninh Loi, Vietnam, to Stephen Ho Ngoc Ahn

1976 Betania, Venezuela, to Maria Esperanza and others

1980 Cuapa, Nicaragua, to Bernardo Martinez

1980 Escorial, Spain, to Amparo Cuevas

1981 Medjugorje, Bosnia, to six children

1981 Kibeho, Rwanda, Africa, to six girls and one boy

1982 Damascus, Syria, to Mirna Nazour stigmatist

1983 San Nicolas, Argentina, to Gladys Quiroga de Motta

1985 Ballinspittle, Ireland, to two O'Mahoney women

1985 Carns Grotto, Ireland, to four girls

1985 Oliveto Citra, Italy, to children and many people

1985 Naju, Korea, to Julia Kim stigmatist

1985 Switzerland to Vassula Ryden

1985 Cleveland, Ohio, United States, to Maureen Sweeny

1985 Ohlau, Poland, to Casimierz Domanski

1987 Terra Blanca, Mexico, to three children

1987 Bessbrook, Northern Ireland, to Beulah Lynch & Mark Trenor

1987 Seredne, Ukraine, to Maria Kizyn and thousands

1987 Cuenca, Equidor, to Patricia Talbot

1987 Rome, Italy, to Sister Anna Ali

1987 Conyers, Georgia, United States, to Nancy Fowler

1987 Midwest, United States, to Mariamante

1988 Cortnadreha, Ireland, to Christine Gallagher

1988 Phoenix, Arizona, United States, to Estella Ruiz

1988 Scottsdale, Arizona, United States, to nine young people

1989 Toronto, Canada, to Zdenko "Jim" Singer

1989 Marlboro, New Jersey. United States, to Joseph Januszkiewicz

1990 Denver, Colorado, United States, to Theresa Lopez and Veronicxa Garcia

1990 Chicago, Illinois, United States, to Joseph Reinholtz

1990 Santa Maria, California, United States, to thousands

1990 Litmonova, Slavakia, to two young girls and a young boy

1991 Mosul, Iraq, to Dina Basher stigmatist

1992 Steubenville, Ohio, United States, to Tony Fernwalt

1993 Belleville, Illinois, United States, to Ray Doiron

1994 Emmetsburg, Maryland, United States, to Gianna Sullivan

1995 Budapest, Hungary, to Sister Natalie stigmatist

1995 Dong Lu, China, to ten thousand

1996 Pittsburgh, Pennsylvania, United States, to Virginia

1998 New York, New York, United States, to Maria Almieda

2000 Washington, D.C., United States, to Mark

2000–2001 Assuit, Egypt, to thousands

2000 Prince Edward Island, Canada, to Rev. Doucette

2001 Hilversum, Netherlands, to Agatha Moiki

2001 Long Island, New York, United States, to Mary Reilly

2002 Gettysburg, Pennsylvania, United States, to Mary Ellen Lucas

2007 Johannesburg, South Africa, to Francesca Zackey

2007 Albania, to Valmira Malaj

Appendix Three

CONSECRATION TO JESUS THROUGH MARY

In the presence of all the heavenly court I choose you forever dear Mother of Jesus as my own Blessed Mother. I deliver and consecrate to you my body and soul, my goods, both interior and exterior, and even the value of all my actions, past, present, and future; imploring you to make full use of everything that belongs to me, according to your great wisdom, for the greatest glory of God, my eternal salvation and the salvation of poor suffering souls everywhere. Amen[1]

Notes

PAGE XVII

1. Quoting Pope John Paul II in the presence of 1,500 bishops in Rome, October 8, 2000.

INTRODUCTION

1. Matthew 7:7–11.
2. John 19:25–27.
3. John 2:1–11; John 19:25–27.
4. Luke 1:31–33; Council of Ephesus, 416; Second Vatican Council, 1962.
5. Dogma of the Roman Catholic Church: *Munificentissimus Deus*, 1950. "We pronounce, declare and define it to be divinely revealed dogma: that the Immaculate Mother of God, the ever Virgin Mary, having completed the course of her earthly life, was assumed body and soul into heavenly glory." See also Stephen J. Shoemaker, *Ancient Traditions of the Virgin Mary's Dormition and Assumption* (London: Oxford University Press, 2002, 2006).
6. Archbishop Donald J. Wuerl, *The Catholic Way* (New York: Doubleday, 2001), pp. 67, 131. "In the final resurrection our bodies will be transformed. . . . Each will rise as the same person, in the same flesh made living by the one Spirit. But the life of those who have risen will be richly enlarged, enhanced, deepened," p. 133. See also Jovian P. Lang, O.F.M., *Dictionary of the Liturgy* (New York: Catholic Book Publishing Company, 1989).
7. Luke 1:28. Pope Pius IX, December 8, 1854, Dogma of the Roman Catholic Church:, *Ineffabilis Deus*.
8. "[T]he most Blessed Virgin Mary, in the first instant of her Conception, by a singular grace and privilege granted by Almighty God, in view of the merits of Jesus Christ, the Savior of the human race, was preserved free from all stain of original sin." Dogma: Papal Bull, *Ineffabilis Deus*, as quoted in Michael O'Carroll, C.S.Sp., *Theotokas: A Theological Encyclopedia of the Blessed Virgin Mary* (Collegeville, Minn.: The Liturgical Press, 1982), p. 179.
9. John 1:1–5, Council of Nicaea, A.D. 325: Nicene Creed.

10. John 14:21.

11. Matthew 16:17.

12. John 15:16.

13. John 2:1–11.

14. Luke 1:47.

15. Deuteronomy 5:6–21. Zenit.org, quoting Professor Scott Hahn, reported on December 25, 2002: "Jesus himself, as a faithful Jew, kept the Fourth Commandment and honored His mother. Since Christ is our brother, she is our mother too. Indeed, at the end of John's Gospel, Jesus named her as the mother of all of us beloved disciples. So we too have a duty to honor her. If we look back into the biblical history of ancient Israel, we discover that the Chosen People always paid homage not only to their king, but also to the mother of the king. The gebirah, the queen mother, loomed large in the affections of Israelites. In Matthew's Gospel especially, we find Jesus portrayed as the royal Son of David and Mary as the queen mother. The Wise Men, for example, traveled far to find the Child King with his mother. We find the mother of the Son of David portrayed in a similar way in the Book of Revelation, Chapter 12. There she is shown to be crowned with 12 stars, for the 12 tribes of Israel. The New Testament writers, you see, were careful to show us Mary's important place in the kingdom, and how we should love and honor her."

16. Deuteronomy 5:6–21.

17. In that way we are like the Wise Men who traveled far to find the Child King in the arms of His Mother. Matthew 2:1–11.

18. John 19:25–27.

19. Saint Louis de Montfort, *True Devotion to Mary* (Rockford, Ill.: Tan Books and Publishers, 1985), p. 33. Pope John Paul II lived and taught this process, *"Totus Tuis Maria."*

20. Luke 2:19.

21. "Mary has received from God a great dominion over the souls of the elect; for she cannot make her residence in them as God the Father ordered her to do, and as their mother, form, nourish and bring them forth to eternal life, and have them as her inheritance and portion, and form them in Jesus Christ and Jesus Christ in them, and strike the roots of her virtues in their hearts and be the inseparable companion of the Holy Ghost in all His works of grace—she cannot, I say, do all these things unless she has a right and a dominion over their souls by a singular grace of the Most High, who having given her power over His only and natural Son, has given it also to her over His adopted children, not only as to their bodies, which would be but a small matter, but also as to their souls. Mary is the Queen of Heaven and earth by grace, as Jesus is the King of them by nature and by conquest. Now as the Kingdom of Jesus Christ consists principally in the heart of the interior of man—according to the words 'The Kingdom of God is

within you.' (Luke 17:21)—in like manner the Kingdom of our Blessed Lady is principally in the interior of man: that is to say, his soul." Saint Louis de Montfort, *True Devotion to Mary*, p. 22.

22. 1 Acts 2:17–21; Isaiah 44:3; Joel 2:28, 1:32; Romans 10:13.

23. Genesis 9:9–11.

24. "And God said: This is the sign of the covenant which I give between me and you, and to every living soul that is with you, for perpetual generations. I will set my bow in the clouds, and it shall be the sign of a covenant between me, and the earth" (Genesis 9:12–16). See Hebrews 8:6–13 re Christ the mediator of the new covenant. And "I [God] will put my laws in their minds, and I will write them upon their hearts. I will be their God and they shall be my people . . ."

25. See notes 6 and 7 supra.

26. Luke 1:48.

27. Saint Louis de Montfort said of Mary: "Because Mary remained hidden during her life she is called by the Holy Spirit and the Church 'Alma Mater,' Mother hidden and unknown. So great was her humility that she desired nothing more upon earth than to remain unknown to herself and to others, and to be known only to God. In answer to her prayers to remain hidden. . . . God was pleased to conceal her from nearly every other human creature in her conception, her birth, her life, her mysteries. . . . Her own parents did not really know her; and the angels would often ask one another, 'Who can she possibly be?' for God had hidden her from them, or if He did reveal anything to them, it was nothing compared to what He withheld." Treatise on *True Devotion to Mary*, #2 and #3.

28. See Cardinal Tarcisio Bertone, Foreword by Pope Benedict XVI. *The Last Secret of Fatima* (New York: Doubleday, 2008) for the official Vatican position concerning Our Lady of Fatima.

29. *Wall Street Journal, Washington Post, USA Today, New York Times, New York Post, Chicago Sun-Times, Los Angeles Times, Fort Lauderdale Sun, Newsweek,* and *Time* cover story (2005)—to name only a few—have featured Mary's apparitions and messages.

30. Cardinal Tarcisio Bertone, *The Last Secret of Fatima*, p. 10.

31. Journalists are trained to report facts as they happen. Consequently, responsible media have allowed Our Lady's presence among us to be more widely known than ever before. That is good. It is truly not the business of the Church to judge mystical phenomenon as the deposit of faith closed with the completion of Holy Scripture. However, the Church, in its wisdom, has and will continue to "approve" certain apparitions that illumine a specific tenant of faith. A brilliant example is the apparition of Our Lady of Lourdes to Saint Bernadette Souberous in 1858, four years after the Papal promulgation of the Dogma of the Immaculate Conception. Our Lady identified herself at Lourdes to illiterate, uncatechised fourteen-year-old Saint Bernadette as "The Immaculate Conception."

32. Father Tomislav Pervan, O.F.M., Pastor of Saint James Church, Medjugorje, sent a global e-mail from Medjugorje on April 8, 2008, confirming that ecclesial jurisdiction over Medjugorje has been removed from the local and national ordinaries and totally shifted to Rome, under the direct supervision of the Vatican. The national commission headed by Cardinal Vinko Puljic is subject to higher church authority and must receive all instructions regarding Medjugorje from the Vatican. See www.medjugorje.org.

33. See my books *The Visions of the Children*, Revised and Updated (New York: St. Martin's Press, 2007), and *Queen of the Cosmos*, Revised Edition (Orleans, Mass.: Paraclete Press, 2006), which contain personal interviews with the six visionaries (and locutionists) concerning Our Lady's Medjugorje apparitions, messages and secrets.

34. See Janice Connell, *Queen of the Cosmos* and *The Visions of the Children*.

35. Author's interview with Rev. Joseph Augustine DiNoia, O.P., in Rome, during Legatus Pilgrimage, September 2005.

36. Ezekiel 37:1–11.

37. Matthew 23:39.

38. John 1:14; Luke 1:26–35; Matthew 1:18–21. Pope Benedict XVI explains: "God is Logos and God is Love—to the point that he completely humbled himself, assuming a human body and finally, giving himself into our hands as bread, . . . We know that God is not a philosophical hypothesis, he is not something that perhaps exists, but we know him and he knows us. And we can know him better and better if we keep up a dialogue with him. . . . This is why it is a fundamental task of pastoral care to teach people how to pray and how to learn to do so personally, better and better."

39. From the prayer "Hail Holy Queen."

40. Those alive at this time in history.

41. See my book *Angel Power* (New York: Ballantine Books/Random House, 1995).

42. 1 Corinthians 2:9.

43. Genesis 3:15.

44. Isaiah 9:7.

45. Pope Benedict XVI, in his first Encyclical, *Deus Caritas Est (God is Love)*, says of Mary: "Men and women of every time and place have recourse to her motherly kindness and her virginal purity and grace, in all their needs and aspirations, their joys and sorrows, their moments of loneliness and their common endeavors. They constantly experience the gift of her goodness and the unfailing love which she pours out from the depths of her heart. The testimonials of gratitude, offered to her from every continent and culture, are recognition of that pure love which is not self-seeking but simply benevolent."

46. Matthew 18:3.

PAGE XXXIII

1. Pope Benedict XVI, in his first Encyclical *Deus Caritas Est*, explains it this way: *"Mary's greatness consists in the fact that she wants to magnify God, not herself. She is lowly: her only desire is to be the handmaid of the Lord (cf. Luke 1:38, 1:48). . . . The Magnificat—a portrait, so to speak, of her soul—is entirely woven from threads of Holy Scripture, threads drawn from the Word of God. Here we see how completely at home Mary is with the Word of God, with ease she moves in and out of it. She speaks and thinks with the Word of God; the Word of God becomes her word, and her word issues from the Word of God. Here we see how her thoughts are attuned to the thoughts of God, how her will is one with the will of God. Since Mary is completely imbued with the Word of God, she is able to become the Mother of the Word Incarnate. Finally, Mary is a woman who loves. How could it be otherwise? As a believer who in faith thinks with God's thoughts and wills with God's will, she cannot fail to be a woman who loves. We sense this in her quiet gestures, as recounted by the infancy narratives in the Gospel. We see it in the delicacy with which she recognizes the need of the spouses at Cana and makes it known to Jesus. We see it in the humility with which she recedes into the background during Jesus' public life, knowing that her Son must establish a new family and that His Mother's hour will come only with the Cross, which will be Jesus' true hour (cf. John 2:4; 13:1). When the disciples flee, Mary will remain beneath the Cross (cf. John 19:25–27); later, at the hour of Pentecost, it will be they who gather around her as they wait for the Holy Spirit (cf. Acts 1:14). . . ."* . . . In the saints one thing becomes clear: those who draw near to God do not withdraw from people, but rather become truly close to them. In no one do we see this more clearly than in Mary. The words addressed by the crucified Lord to his disciple—to John and through him to all disciples of Jesus: "Behold, your mother!" (John 19:27)—are fulfilled anew in every generation. Mary has truly become the Mother of all believers."

PAGE XXXV

1. Mary's School of Prayer is a place of joy and light. Pope Benedict spoke of his vision for such Prayer in the following way: "[N]ot only does this spiritual dimension exist but it is the source of all things. . . . To this end, we must increase the number of these schools of prayer, for praying together, where it is possible to learn personal prayer in all its dimensions: as silent listening to God, as a listening that penetrates his Word, penetrates his silence, sounds the depths of his action in history and in one's own person; and to understand his language in one's life and then to learn to respond in prayer with the great prayers of the Psalms of the Old

Testament and prayers of the New. . . . This intimate being with God, hence, the experience of God's presence, is what makes us, so to speak, experience ever anew the greatness of Christianity, and then also helps us to find our way through all the trivialities among which, of course, it must also be lived and—day after day, in suffering and loving, in joy and sorrow—put into practice."

PAGE XLV

1. Luke 1:46–55.

FOREWORD

1. John 2:1–11: *"There was a wedding in the town of Cana, in Galilee. Jesus' mother was present, and Jesus and his followers were there too. They ran out of wine, and the mother of Jesus said to him, 'They have no more wine.' He answered her, 'What is that to us? My time has not yet come.' Jesus' mother said to the servants, 'Do whatever he tells you.' Standing near were six stone jars, the kind used for Jewish rituals of purification. Each jar could hold twenty or thirty gallons of water. Jesus told the servants, 'Fill the jars with water.' They filled up the jars. 'Now pour some out,' Jesus said, 'and take it to the master of ceremonies.' They did this. The master of ceremonies tasted the water, now turned into wine; he did not know where the wine came from, but the servants knew. The master of ceremonies called the bridegroom and said to him, 'People serve the best wine first, and the less good wine later, when people have had more to drink; but you have kept the best wine until the last!' Jesus did this first one of his signs in Cana, in Galilee, and so he revealed his glory, and his followers believed in him."*

PART ONE

1. Matthew 16:26–27.
2. Scholar Jaroslav Pelikan remarks: "Even in a secular age . . . the Bible proves to be the unique antidote to cynicism and the source of inspiration for poets and philosophers, artists and musicians, and the countless millions all over the globe who turn to it every day and in their times of need. . . . [It] provides the subtext . . . for how we define our deepest hopes." Jaroslav Pelikan, *Whose Bible Is It?* (New York: Viking, 2004).
3. *Newsweek* poll on beliefs about Jesus at http://www.newsweek.com/id/55487.
4. *Catechism of the Catholic Church,* Second Edition (Citta del Vaticano: Libreria Editrice Vaticano, 1997), pp. 252–254, 258–262; 867.

5. Pope Benedict XVI, several years ago before he became pope, ventured: "One of the signs of our times is that the announcements of 'Marian Apparitions' are multiplying all over the world."

6. Corinthians 6:13–15, 6:17–20.

7. Scholarship and study of sacred texts are regarded as the highest form of learning: they are the privilege of the few.

8. Teaching of Saint Cyril of Alexandria.

9. Luke 1:48–50.

10. John 19:25–27

CHAPTER ONE: MOTHER OF GOD

1. Luke 1:26–38.

2. Christianity has taught this fundamental truth from its inception: more than a hundred billion Christians adhere to this truth. Most Americans believe the virgin birth is literally true, a recent *Newsweek* poll finds. "Seventy-nine percent of Americans believe that, as the Bible says, Jesus Christ was born of the Virgin Mary, without a human father, according to a new *Newsweek* poll on beliefs about Jesus." http://www.newsweek.com/id/55487.

3. Harvard minister Peter Gomes about Jesus' receiving a Protestant theologian at the pearly gates, as quoted in David Van Biema, "Hail Mary," *Time*, March 21, 2005.

4. From the Nicene Creed.

5. Ibid.

6. True prosperity is holiness: wholeness, integration of body, mind, and spirit, essential union with the God of love from whom all good things flow.

7. See *The Catholic Encyclopedia* (New York: Robert Appleton Company, 1911). Retrieved September 27, 2008 from New Advent: http://newadvent.org/cathen/11554a.htm.

8. Council of Ephesus, 437.

9. Though Patricius is not officially canonized, his sacramental death numbers him among the elect.

10. Saint Augustine, in his *Confessions*, spoke to God of his mother: "[Y]ou made her beautiful, an object of reverent love, and a source of admiration . . ."

11. Saint Augustine, *The Confessions* (Garden City, N.Y.: Doubleday, 1960).

12. Revelations 22:13.

13. William J. Walsh, *Heaven's Bright Queen* (New York: Carey-Stafford Company, 1904), p. 158. Popes throughout the centuries, beginning with Gregory IX in 1227, promulgate this devotion and affirm the indulgences carried with it. See *Bull Injuncti Nobis* (3 of the *nones of June, 1621*).

14. Saint Ambrose, a Doctor of the Church said of Mary: "May the life of Blessed Mary be ever present to our awareness. In her, as in a mirror, the form of virtue and beauty of chastity shine forth. She was virgin, not only in body, but in mind and spirit. She never sullied the pure affection of her heart by unworthy feelings. She was humble of heart. She was serious in her conversations. She was prudent in her counsels. She preferred to pray rather than to speak. She united in her heart the prayers of the poor and avoided the uncertainty of worldly riches. She was ever faithful to her daily duties, reserved in her conversations, and always accustomed to recognize God as the Witness of her thoughts. Blessed Be the Name of Jesus."

15. Pope Benedict XVI is reported to be a devotee and scholar of the spirituality of Saint Augustine.

16. Saint Augustine, *The Confessions,* p. 173.

17. Saint Augustine, *The City of God*, Introduction by Thomas Merton (New York: Random House, 1950).

18. Other notable canonized theologians have added their insights to the Eucharistic Presence of Christ. Among them, consider the following:

"The longer you stay away from Communion, the more your soul will become weak, and in the end you will become dangerously indifferent."—Saint John Bosco.

"The Eucharist is necessary to preserve the soul in the spiritual life of grace; for the soul, like the body, becomes gradually exhausted, if care is not to be taken to repair its strength. Jesus Christ gives Himself entirely to us, He unites His Sacred Body with ours; and, by this union, we become one and the same spirit with Him. As the food which we take nourishes our body, so the Holy Eucharist is the nourishment for our soul."—Saint John Baptist de la Salle.

"It is impossible that if one communicates daily, one should not gradually be delivered even from venial sins and from all attachment to them."—Saint Pius X.

"The Sacrament infuses into the soul great interior peace, a strong inclination to virtue, and great willingness to practice it, thus rendering it easy to walk in the path of perfection."—Saint Alphonsus Liguori.

"One of the most admirable effects of Holy Communion is to preserve souls from falling and to help those who fall from weakness to rise again. Therefore, it is much more profitable to approach the divine Sacrament frequently, with love, respect, and confidence, to keep them back from an excess of fear."—Saint Ignatius Loyola.

19. Augustinian expert Thomas Martin observes: "From 391 until his death in 430 he held in delicate balance the roles and tasks chosen for him: monk, priest-then-bishop, preacher and teacher, civic leader and judge, voice of the Church of Africa, prominent theologian, correspondent, polemicist, but above all a man 'intent upon God.' Throughout these four decades his voice and pen would never tire trying to explore and explain that mysterious bond that unites humanity to

God." Thomas F. Martin, O.S.A., *Our Restless Heart: The Augustinian Tradition* (Maryknoll, N.Y.: Orbis Books, 2003), p. 23.

20. Saint Augustine, *The Confessions*, p. 140

21. Ibid., p. 155.

22. Thomas F. Martin, *Our Restless Heart*, p. 35, quoting Saint Augustine.

23. Donald X. Burt, quoting Saint Augustine's Commentary on Psalm 41, 9. *Let Me Know You: Reflections on Augustine's Search for God* (Collegeville, Md.: Liturgical Press, 2003), p. 106.

24. *The Catechism of the Catholic Church*, Second Edition (Citta del Vaticano: Libreria Editrice Vaticano), states at (499); "The deepening of faith in the virginal mother-hood [of Mary] led the Church to confess Mary's real and perpetual virginity even in the act of giving birth to the Son of God made man. In fact, Christ's birth did not diminish his mother's virginal integrity, but sanctified it. And so, the liturgy of the Church celebrates Mary as *Aeiparthenos*, the 'Ever-virgin,'" p. 126.

25. Council of the Lateran, A.D. 649.

26. Archbishop Donald W. Wuerl explains: "When it came time for Mary to give birth, she remained a virgin before, during and after the birth of Jesus—a privi-lege granted to her to manifest that this was a unique moment in human history, the birth of Jesus who is God's Son as well as Mary's. The Church proclaims that Mary remained a virgin from the time of Jesus' conception on through his birth and afterwards. As the Catechism of the Catholic Church points out: the deepen-ing of faith in the virginal motherhood led the church to confess Mary's perpetual virginity even in the act of giving birth to the Son of God made man" (see Section 499). Donald W. Wuerl, *The Catholic Way* (New York: Doubleday, 2001), p. 66.

27. Council of Ephesus, Mary Mother of God, Nicene Creed., See also Donald W. Wuerl, *The Catholic Way*, p. 65.

28. Catechism of the Catholic Church, Section 495, as quoted by Archbishop Don-ald W. Wuerl, *The Catholic Way*, p. 65.

29. For further reading, see Richard Fletcher, *The Conversion of Europe: From Paganism to Christianity 371–1386 A.D.* (London: HarperCollins, 1997); Ian Wood, *The Mission-ary Life: Saints and the Evangelization of Europe 400–1050* (London: Longman, 2001).

30. Saint Dunstan in the 1913 edition of the *Catholic Encyclopedia*

31. Ibid.

32. Matthew 6:23–24.

CHAPTER TWO: MOTHER OF CHRIST

1. Matthew 1:18–23.

2. The sacrament of penance and reconciliation is defined in the Catechism of the Catholic Church thus: "Those who approach the sacrament of Penance obtain

pardon from God's mercy for the offense committed against him, and are at the same time, reconciled with the Church which they have wounded by their sins and which by charity, by example, and by prayer labors for their conversion. It is called the sacrament of conversion because it makes sacramentally present Jesus' call to conversion, the first step in returning to the Father from whom one has strayed by sin. It is called the sacrament of Penance, since it consecrates the Christian sinner's personal and ecclesial steps of conversion, penance and satisfaction. It is called the sacrament of confession, since the disclosure or confession of sins to a priest is an essential element of this sacrament. In a profound sense is it also a "confession"—acknowledgement and praise—of the holiness of God and of his mercy toward sinful man. It is called the sacrament of forgiveness, since by the priest's sacramental absolution God grants the penitent pardon and peace. It is called the sacrament of Reconciliation, because it imparts to the sinner the love of God who reconciles: "Be reconciled to God." (2 Corinthians 5:20) He who lives by God's merciful love is ready to respond to the Lord's call: "Go; first be reconciled to your brother." " (Matthew 5:24) *Catechism of the Catholic Church,* Second Edition (Citta del Vaticano: Libreria Editrice Vaticano), pp. 357, 358.

3. Saint Norbert, twelth century. As quoted at www.wordofGodeveryday.com, January 13, 2009.

4. Francis M. Geudens, "St. Norbert." In *The Catholic Encyclopedia,* Vol. 11 (New York: Robert Appleton Company, 1911). Retrieved September 7, 2008, from http://newadvent.org/cathen/11100b.htm.

5. Pope John Paul II, speaking to pilgrims in Baltimore, Maryland, 2005.

6. Rosita McHugh, *The Knights of Malta: 900 Years of Care* (Dublin, Ireland: The Irish Association of the Sovereign Military Hospitaller Order of Saint John of Jerusalem, of Rhodes and of Malta, 1996), p.1.

7. Ibid., pp. 79, 124.

8. Ibid., p. 142. Agnes, a Roman woman, became the first Abbess, receiving her habit of the Order from Brother Gerard. The Sisters worked in the hospitals of the Knights.

9. Rosita McHugh, *The Knights of Malta,* p. 133.

10. Msgr. John Dimech, *The Saints and Blessed of The Sovereign Military Order of Malta* (Maltese Association S.M.O.M.; printed at Portelli Print Nadur, Gozo).

CHAPTER THREE: MOTHER OF THE CHURCH

1. Pope Paul VI proclaimed officially that Mary is Mother of the Church on November 21, 1964, during the celebration of a Mass at the conclusion of the third session of the Second Vatican Council. He stated: "For the glory of the Blessed Virgin and our own consolation, we proclaim the Most Blessed Virgin Mary

Mother of the Church, of the whole people of God, faithful and pastors, and we call her most loving Mother." The Holy Father went on to express the hope that this title of Mary, Mother of the church would "lead Christians to honor Mary even more and to call upon her with still greater confidence." He decreed that "from now onward the whole Christian people should give even greater honor to the Mother of God under this most loving title."

2. Luke 1:39–45.

3. John 14:18.

4. Janice T. Connell, *Praying with Mary* (San Francisco: HarperSanFrancisco, 1997), pp. 139–143.

5. William J. Walsh, *Heaven's Bright Queen*, Vol. II (New York: Carey-Stafford Company, 1904), p. 26.

6. Ibid., p. 27.

7. Ibid., p. 312. (Slightly adapted.)

8. Ibid., p. 313. (Edited and adapted.)

9. Janice T. Connell, *Praying with Mary*; pp. 141–142.

10. William J. Walsh, *Heaven's Bright Queen*, Vol. II, p. 18.

11. Janice T. Connell, *Angel Power* (New York: Ballantine Books, 1995). In the broadest sense, angels are God's messengers.

12. John 14:6, 14:9, 14:11, 14:21, 15:9–10, 15:12.

13. Teaching of Saint Margaret Mary, Saint Louis de Montfort, and more recently, the late Pope John Paul II.

14. *"And the third day, there was a marriage in Cana of Galilee: and the mother of Jesus was there. And Jesus also was invited, and his disciples, to the marriage. And the wine failing, the mother of Jesus saith to him, They have no wine. And Jesus saith to her: Woman what is that to me and thee? My hour is not yet come. His mother saith to the waiters; Whatsoever he shall say to you. Do ye."* (John 2:1–5)

15. John 2:15.

16. Catholic News Service. Tsunami-Vailankanni (UPDATED), December 30, 2004.

17. Krishna Pakharel in New Delhi and Zahid Hussain in Islamabad. "Indian Leader Accuses Pakistan of Terror Role," *Wall Street Journal*, January 7, 2009, p. A7.

18. Where Mary is honored, gender bias eventually dissolves. A recent study published in the British Medical Journal, the *Lancelot* disclosed that in the last twenty years alone, as many as ten million Indian females have been eliminated before birth in modern India where Christianity is not yet well established. As quoted by Carla Power in "A Generation of Women Wiped Out," *Glamour* 104, no. 8 (2006):173. In 2002, the Bill and Melinda Gates Foundation underwrote a study that uncovered 628 girls for every 1,000 boys among children six and under, in only one area of Punjab.

19. See Appendix 3 for a sample prayer of consecration to Mary.

20. John 19:26–27.
21. Policy statement of David A. Leonard, Administrator, Saint Mary's Hospital, Surgery Center of Mayo Clinic, Rochester, Minnesota, Fall 1989.
22. Ancient title of Mary as God-bearer.

CHAPTER 4: MOTHER MOST ADMIRABLE

1. Acts 1:13–14.
2. Janice T. Connell, *Angel Power* (New York: Ballantine Books, 1995).
3. Seven apparitions of the Blessed Mother in Portugal in 1917. See Janice T. Connell, *Meetings with Mary* (New York: Ballantine Books, 1995), pp. 89–118.
4. Sister Lucia of Jesus and of the Immaculate Heart, *"Calls" from The Message of Fatima*, English Translation by Sisters of Monsteiro de Santa Maria and Convento de N.S. dp Bon Sucesso, Lisbon. (Secretariado dos Pastorinhos, Fatima, Portugal: The Ravengate Press, 2000), p. 51.
5. Sister Lucia of Fatima, op cit., pp 42, 43.
6. Hell has been described in many ways by mystics throughout the centuries. See Janice Connell, *Meetings with Mary*, p. 101, for a description of hell by visionary Lucia of Fatima.
7. Colossians 1:15
8. See the Vatican website for February 13, 2008.
9. Pope John Paul II in an interview published in the October 13, 1981, issue of *Stimme des Glaubens,* a German publication.
10. The official Message of Fatima released by the Roman Catholic Congregation for the Doctrine of Faith can be read on line at www.vatican.va/roman_curia/congregations/cfaith/documenta/rc_con_cfaith_doc. Skeptics question whether there is more to the secret that the Vatican withholds for diplomatic reasons.
11. See Cardinal Tarcisio Bertone, Foreword Pope Benedict XVI, *The Last Secret of Fatima* (New York: Doubleday, 2008) for the official Vatican position concerning the secrets of Our Lady of Fatima.
12. See Janice T. Connell, *Queen of the Cosmos,* Revised Edition (Orleans, Mass.: Paraclete Press, 2006), and *The Visions of the Children*, Revised and Updated (New York: St. Martin's Press, 2007), for in depth interviews with each of the Medjugorje visionaries and the locutionists.
13. During the Bosnian genocide, not a blade of grass was disturbed in Medjugorje, although surrounding towns and villages were ravaged by the war.
14. Author interview with Monsignor Joseph Murphy, National Shrine of the Immaculate Conception, 1990. Miracles include inexplicable healing of physical ailments; psychological infirmities; relationship difficulties; political, social, and economic problems.

15. The martyrs of Japan were canonized in 1862.

16. The process of conversion that Mary brings involves the distribution among the willing of special divine graces that open human minds and hearts to alternative means of dispute resolution. Her plan as Queen of Peace is to walk with us into a springtime of opportunity, a new way of thinking that respects the dignity and safety of each child of God on earth.

17. See Janice Connell, *Angel Power.*

18. The American couple wishes to remain anonymous.

19. For more information about this apparition, see Janice Connell, *Meetings with Mary*, pp. 119–146.

PART TWO

1. John 19:26, 19:27.

2. David Van Biema, "Hail, Mary," *Time*, March 21, 2005, p. 63.

3. Ibid., p. 64.

CHAPTER FIVE: QUEEN OF ALL SAINTS

1. Apocalypse 12:1.

2. See Janice T. Connell, *Meetings with Mary* (New York: Ballantine Books, 1995), pp. 129–146.

3. For more information about the apparition at Akita, see ibid.

4. July 13, 1917, at Fatima, Portugal.

5. Matthew 24:30.

6. Excerpted from Father Rene Laurentin and Father R. Lejeune, *Messages and Teachings of Mary* (Milford, Ohio: Riehle Foundation, 1988), p. 202.

7. Matthew 28:20.

8. Vatican City, October 15, 2007 (zenit.org).

9. Jelena Vasilj, as quoted in Janice T. Connell, *The Visions of the Children*, Revised and Updated (New York: St. Martin's Press, 2007), p. 159.

10. Pope John XXIII Journal, p. 170, as quoted in Peter Hebblewaite, *Pope John XXIII* (Garden City, N.Y.: Doubleday, 1985), p. 45.

11. Ibid., p. 55.

12. Ibid., p. 141

13. Ibid.

14. Ibid., p. 128.

15. Ibid.

16. Ibid., p. 143

17. Ibid., p. 150.
18. Seven practices of charity toward our neighbor, based on Christ's statement of the Last Judgment in Matthew 25:34. They are (1) Feed the hungry, (2) Give drink to the thirsty, (3) Clothe the naked, (4) Shelter the homeless, (5) Visit the sick, (6) Visit those in prison, (7) Bury the dead.
19. Pope John XXIII, Journal, p. 175.
20. Ibid.; Peter Hebblewaite, *Pope John XXIII*, op. cit. p. 186.
21. Ibid., p. 186.
22. Ibid., quoting Actes et documents, 10, p. 161, letter dated February 28, 1944, p. 193.
23. Ibid., p. 197.
24. Ibid., p. 234.
25. Ibid., quoting Khrushchev's interview with Norman Cousins, editor of the *Saturday Review* on December 13, 1962, p. 445.
26. Ibid., p. 468.
27. Prayer to Mary of Pope John XXIII: Hail Mary, hope of the world. "Hail holy and meek Blessed Virgin, filled with God's love, gentle and serene. Pray for us your children."
28. The conciliar document "Nostra Aetate" articulates Christian understanding of Islam: "The Church regards with esteem also the Muslims. They adore the one God, living and subsisting in Himself; merciful and all-powerful, the Creator of heaven and earth, who has spoken to men; they take pains to submit wholeheartedly to even His inscrutable decrees, just as Abraham, with whom the faith of Islam takes pleasure in linking itself, submitted to God" (zenet.org).
29. Janice T. Connell, *Meetings with Mary*, pp. 126–128.
30. Pilgrims in the Holy Land in March 1994 were told of this by local guides.
31. I have written about this in other works.
32. Acts 1:13–14
33. See explanation of this experience by Saint Theresa of Avila in Chapter 9.

CHAPTER SIX: QUEEN OF HEAVEN AND EARTH

1. Genesis 3:14, 3:15.
2. Matthew 14:1–11.
3. *USA Today*, June 4, 2002.
4. Revelation 12:1.The ancient image of Our Lady of Guadalupe is the only known divinely imprinted portrayal of Mary. For more on Saint Juan Diego, see Chapter 12. See also Janice T. Connell, *Meetings with Mary* (New York: Ballantine Books, 1995), pp. 51–55.
5. Matthew 25:31, 25:32.

6. A person who prays, who sacrifices and fasts, is able to distinguish more clearly between good and evil.

7. Both world leaders received messages from Medjugorje visionary Marija Pavlovic in early January 1988. These messages of peace were from Mary, Queen of Peace. Both leaders acknowledged respect for Mary's presence and their desire to be "peacemakers." See Janice T. Connell, *The Visions of the Children*, Revised and Updated (New York: St. Martin's Press, 2007), for more information.

8. This subjective, cosmic miracle is described in Janice T. Connell, *Meetings With Mary* as follows: "The sun shook and spun so fiercely that it seemed to explode and come tumbling down toward the people, who were terrified. But it stopped suddenly, and then went back to its normal position in the sky. It gave off colors of indescribable beauty, which shone down on the earth and all the people gathered at Fatima." People within a thirty-mile radius of the village of Fatima saw the phenomenon (p. 110).

9. Consider just one such example, the Battle of Lepanto, October 7, 1571.

10. Consider the Jesuit Retreat House at ground zero at Hiroshima. Not one of the priests suffered the least injury as they calmly prayed the rosary during the atomic bomb blast though everything around them was destroyed.

11. The late Czech bishop Pavel Hnilica traveled clandestinely throughout the Soviet Union during the late 1980s, at the request of Our Lady, saying Masses wherever he went, and performing the rite of consecration to the Immaculate Heart of Mary on behalf of Pope John Paul II. He was a confidant of Sister Lucia of Fatima, and pilgrims from all over the world whom he met at Medjugorje and other shrines.

12. Marian prayer groups for peace continue to spring up all over the world. Locations and websites of some are included in the Appendix of this book. If you desire to include your Marian prayer group for peace in future publications, please notify the publisher.

13. In his Encyclical *"Spe Salvi" (Saved in Hope)*, Pope Benedict XVI offers this insight: "[T]he Gospel is not merely a communication of things that can be known—it is one that makes things happen and is life-changing. The dark door of time, of the future, has been thrown open. The one who has hope lives differently; the one who hopes has been granted the gift of a new life."

14. Alexy II, as quoted in Janice T. Connell, *The Triumph of the Immaculate Heart* (Santa Barbara, Calif.: Queenship Publishing, 1993), p. 77.

15. *Washington Post*, May 23, 2002, p. A28.

16. From www.zenet.org.

17. Mary's message at Fatima, July 13, 1917. Please see Lucia Marto, *Fatima in Lucia's Own Words,* Vol. III, edited by Louis Kondor (Still River, Mass.: Ravengate Press, pp. 104–105. See also Sandra L. Zimdars-Swartz, *Encountering Mary* (Princeton, N.J.: Princeton University Press, 1991), p. 199, commenting on this message from the Blessed Virgin.

18. Sandra Zimdars-Swartz, *Encountering Mary*, p. 200.

19. Ibid., quoting Jesuit Francis L. Filas, 1959, about Lucia's secrets, pp. 211–212

20. Matthew 24:25.

21. Cardinal Tarcisio Bertone, Foreword by Pope Benedict XVI, *The Last Secret of Fatima* (New York: Doubleday, 2008), p. 53.

22. Ibid., p. 85.

23. Cardinal Tedeschi, Papal Delegate, in his official account to the Pilgrims of Fatima, Portugal, October 31, 1951.

24. Revelation 3:16.

25. Matthew 21:19–20; Mark 11:20–21; Luke 13:6–7.

26. Sister Lucia of Jesus and of the Immaculate Heart, *"Calls" from The Message of Fatima*, English Translation by Sisters of Monsteiro de Santa Maria and Convento de N.S. dp Bon Sucesso, Lisbon. (Secretariado dos Pastorinhos, Fatima, Portugal: Ravengate Press, 2000), p. 51.

27. The following information, disclosing Pope John Paul II's immense dedication to Our Lady of Fatima, is promulgated via Zenit.org. "John Paul II met with Sister Lucia in her Carmelite convent on three occasions: May 13, 1982, and in 1991 and 2000. The first meeting took place exactly one year after the 1981 assassination attempt against the Pope in St. Peter's Square. On that occasion in 1982, the Holy Father went to Fatima to thank the Blessed Virgin for saving his life. He desired that one of the bullets used in the attack be set in the crown of the statue of Our Lady of Fatima, as a sign of his gratitude. The second meeting, in 1991, took place on the tenth anniversary of the attack. The last time that the Holy Father and Sister Lucia met personally was on May 13, 2000. That day, the Pope beatified the two other visionaries, the little shepherds Jacinta and Francisco, and Cardinal Angelo Sodano, Vatican secretary of state, read the text relative to the third secret of Fatima."

28. See Cardinal Tarciscio Bertone, *The Last Secret of Fatima*.

29. See Janice Connell, *Triumph of the Immaculate Heart*, pp. 76–79.

30. See www.bluearmyofFatima.org.

31. Such behavior changes us by opening us to awareness that our Creator loves us, cares for us, and call us onward to sacred peace that passes all understanding.

32. From www.zenit.org, February 12, 2005.

33. Vatican City, February 16, 2005 (zenit.org).

34. Vatican, February 14, 2005

35. www.zenit.org archive ZE06022009

36. Rome, May 13, 2005 (zenit.org). Benedict XVI announced that he will dispense with the five-year waiting period, established by Canon Law, to open John Paul II's cause of beatification. In his meeting with priests of the Diocese of Rome, held today in the Basilica of Saint John Lateran, the Pope read the following announcement in Latin: "The Supreme Pontiff, Benedict XVI, has dispensed with

the period of five years of waiting, after the death of the Servant of God, John Paul II, Supreme Pontiff." Zenit.org. is used with permission.

37. The World Apostolate of Fatima celebrates the feast every year in the Basilica of Saint Mary Major in Rome.

38. See Janice Connell, *Meetings with Mary*, pp. 45–47.

39. A prayer that helps to do so is: "Lord, please give me the grace to change for the better what I can and accept peacefully what I cannot. Please give me the wisdom to know the difference and the strength to live each moment to the best of my abilities. Amen."

40. At Medjugorje, Mary asks the visionaries to fast on bread and water only on Wednesdays and Fridays. All people can fast in some way that is consonant with their individual life journey.

41. See Janice Connell, *Praying with Mary* (San Francisco: HarperSanFrancisco, 1997), pp. 37–54, and *The Visions of the Children*, pp. 349–350 for information about this.

42. Courtesy of the Blue Army of Our Lady of Fatima.

CHAPTER SEVEN: QUEEN OF THE HOLY ROSARY

1. Isaiah 66:18.

2. See Janice T. Connell, *Praying with Mary* (San Francisco: HarperSanFrancisco, 1997) for information about how to pray the Holy Rosary, as well as the prayers of the Holy Rosary.

3. Isaiah 55:8–9.

4. See Janice T. Connell, *The Visions of the Children*, Revised and Updated (New York: St. Martin's Press, 2007), pp 155–183.

5. See www.gracematters.org/interviews/i.llibagiza.html.

6. See Janice T. Connell, *Meetings with Mary* (New York: Ballantine Books, 1995), pp. 234–248.

7. Luke 10:22.

8. I have written about this in several of my previous books

9. Liberia Editrice Vaticana, *Catechism of the Catholic Church,* Second Edition. English Translation for the United States of America (Washington, D.C.: United States Catholic Conference, 2000), p. 867.

10. See Janice T. Connell, *Queen of Angels* (New York: Tarcher/Putnam, 1999), p. 42. See also 1 Corinthians 42–44.

11. Luke 1:26–38; John 2:1–11.

12. Matthew 1:18; Luke 1:26–28.

13. Matthew 1:18–25, 2:14; Luke 2:34, 2:35, 3:51.

14. Luke 11:9–13.

15. Genesis 3:88–10.

16. Matthew 24:30; Mark 13:26; Luke 21:27.

17. Luke 12:40.

18. Luke 12:37.

19. Luke 24:25.

20. Luke 12:34.

21. Matthew 24:21.

22. I have written about this in *Meetings with Mary*, *The Visions of the Children*, *Queen of the Cosmos* (Orleans, Mass.: Paraclete Press, 1990), *Praying with Mary*, and *Queen of Angels*.

23. Teaching of Saint Therese of Lisieux, Doctor of the Church.

24. John 19:25–27.

25. Teaching of Saint Therese of Lisieux, Doctor of the Church.

26. Luke 1:28, 1:42, 1:45.

27. Luke 19:38.

28. Consider how changed the behavior of the three children of Fatima was after their heavenly visions of Mary and the Guardian Angel of Portugal.

29. John 2:1–10.

30. The spiritual world, beautiful as it is, has many traps. A knowledgeable bishop, rabbi, imam, or spiritual director trained in mysticism, and a medical provider should be consulted in such cases. See also Chapters 9 and 11 for guidance from Dr. Theresa of Avila, and Our Lady of the Castle.

31. Luke 2:19.

32. Luke 1:41.

33. Such as Queen of Peace, Comfort of the Afflicted, Help of the Sick—to name only a few.

34. As quoted in René Laurentin, *Messages and Teachings of Mary at Medjugorje* (Milford, Ohio: The Riehle Foundation, 1988), p. 59.

35. Lisa J. Adams, Associated Press, January 16, 2004, as quoted in the *Phoenix Sun*, January 23, 2005.

36. Medjugorje message given August 25, 1987.

37. Matthew 2:16.

38. Consider the following regarding Mary's global call to unity and purpose for peace: Captain Graeme Bicknell, U.S. Army 528th Combat Stress Detachment, while attached to the 10th Mountain Division serving in Afghanistan observed: "Studies have concluded that good leadership and a strong sense of purpose significantly reduce stress." Speaking of the unity among four thousand U.S. soldiers deployed in Afghanistan, he reported: "Stress has to do with unity of purpose and focus. The higher the sense of unity, the less feeling there is of stress." Major Brad Herdon, of the 10th Mountain Division, said of his soldiers: "Their feeling is they are doing the right thing and they are doing it for their country. It [the war, fighting] is not vengeance. It is justice." As quoted in the *Washington Post*, March 24, 2002, p. A20.

39. This account of the Battle of Mons, and the description of the evacuation of Dunkirk are eyewitness oral history through the courtesy of Ishbel McGilvery McGregor, wife of Highlander Black Watch Colonel John McGregor who was among the evacuees of Dunkirk.

40. Ishbel McGilvery McGregor provided much of the eyewitness account garnered from those who served.

41. Excerpts through the courtesy of John Donovan.

CHAPTER EIGHT: QUEEN OF PEACE

1. John 14:1–3.

2. Teaching of Saint Louis de Montfort

3. Hebrews 2:14, 1:17; 1 John 5:20; Titus 2:13; Galatians 4:4; Philippians 2:5–8; John 1:14, 8:58, 17:5.

4. Teaching of Council of Ephesus, A.D. 431.

5. Teaching of Saint Thomas Aquinas

6. These were Archbishops Raymond Burke and Paul Leibold.

7. Archbishop John Carroll, first Bishop of the United States, dedicated the nation to Mary, the Immaculate Conception, perhaps in the presence of President George Washington in 1799. See Janice T. Connell, *The Spiritual Journey of George Washington* (New York: Hatherleigh Press, 2007), pp. 116–117.

8. For more information, consult Our Lady of America at Our Lady of the Nativity Convent, P.O. Box 445, Fostoria, Ohio 44830. Phone 419-435-3838. www.Our-LadyofAmerica.com.

9. www.catholicnewsagency.com, Bogota, March 24, 2008 (CNA).

10. Ibid.

11. Luke 7:43–45, 7:48.

12. Biblical title of God.

13. Zbigniew Brzenski, Comment Section, *Financial Times,* January 14, 2009, p. 9.

14. Pope John Paul II explained how Mary's spiritual motherhood is a light to all people in these times: "What is most important about this motherhood to which she [Mary] gave her free consent is that it places her in union with God uniquely so on a physical level and also, in an archetypical way representative of the whole human race, on a spiritual level through grace. Since all of this happens to her precisely as woman, she also signifies "the fullness of the perfection of what is characteristic of woman, of what is feminine. Here we find ourselves, in a sense, at the culminating point, the archetype, of the personal dignity of women." Message for the XXVIII World Day of Peace, December 8, 1994. January 1, 1995.

15. See Janice T. Connell, *Meetings with Mary* (New York: Ballentine Books, 1995), pp. 234–447.

16. See Janice T. Connell, *Queen of Angels* (New York: Penguin Putnam. 1999; Revised Edition, Orleans, Mass.: Paraclete Press, 2008).

17. See Janice T. Connell, *Meetings with Mary*, pp. 60–66.

18. I have personally heard story after story from visionaries about officials who have disregarded Mary's presence and subsequently experienced most disagreeable consequences. That is not the subject of this book.

19. From the Marian prayer "Hail Holy Queen."

20. Genesis 3:15.

21. Marian Groups are assemblages of people all over the world who pray together for peace in families, cities, countries, the world in response to the Blessed Mother's apparitions. The Blessed Mother asks everyone in the world to form or join a prayer group to pray for peace, which she warns is fragile. She asks all people to pray to overcome the evils of the times by focusing on prayer for peace, conversion of heart, and fasting on Wednesdays and Fridays. The purpose: reconciliation between man and God, and among families, neighbors, coworkers, citizens, tribes, countries and nations. See Janice T. Connell, *The Visions of the Children*, Revised and Updated (New York: St. Martin's Press, 2007), pp. 195–197. 205.

22. John 2:11.

23. Thomas C. Reeves, *America's Bishop* (San Francisco, Calif.: Encounter Books, 2001), p. 1, quoting *The Catholic Almanac*, 2000, published by Our Sunday Visitor.

24. Ibid.

25. Ibid., p. 17.

26. Ibid., p. 26.

27. Ibid., p. 27.

28. See Janice T. Connell, *Meetings With Mary*, pp. 77–80, re Our Lady of Lourdes.

29. Reeves, America's bishop. op. cit. p. 33.

30. Ibid., p. 36.

31. Ibid., p. 37.

32. See entry for Josef Stalin at www.Wikipedia.org.

33. Janice T. Connell, *Meetings with Mary*, p. 38.

34. Fulton Sheen, *Treasure in Clay: The Autobiography of Fulton J. Sheen* (New York: Image Books, 1982). (Society for the Propagation of the Faith.)

35. Genesis 3:24.

36. Cardinal John Henry Newman, *Mary the Second Eve* (Rockford, Ill.: Tan Books and Publishers, 1982).

37. Luke 2:51.

PAGE 171

1. Vatican City, October 17, 2008 (zenit.org).

PART THREE

1. Proverbs 1:5.
2. Proverbs 25:2.
3. John Henry Cardinal Newman said of Mary: "I fully believe that the doctrine concerning Mary has been in substance one and the same since the beginning. *Mary, the Second Eve* (Rockford, Ill.: Tan Books and Publishers, 1982), p. 1.

CHAPTER NINE: MYSTICAL ROSE

1. Ephesians 1:17.
2. Shirley du Boulay, *Theresa of Avila, An Extraordinary Life* (New York: Blue Bridge, 1991, 2004), p. 3.
3. Theresa of Avila, *The Interior Castle.* Trans. K. Kavanaugh (New York: Paulist Press, 1979), p. 191.
4. Shirley du Boulay, *Theresa of Avila,* pp. 82, 83.
5. Theresa of Avila, *The Interior Castle,* p. 192.
6. Ibid., p. 193.
7. Ibid., pp. 194–195.
8. Ibid.
9. Ibid., p. 202.
10. Ibid., p. 199.
11. Ibid., p. 200.
12. Ibid., p. 206.
13. Ibid., p. 208.
14. Ibid.
15. Ibid.
16. The rosary is the chain that binds generations to eternal life.
17. Kevin Kavanaugh, O.C.D., and Otilio Rodrigues, O.C.D., *The Collected Works of St. Theresa of Avila,* Vol. Two (Washington, D.C.: ICS Publications, 1980), p. 430.
18. Never discuss the faults of another. This starts the habit of slander. Try to develop the habit of silence.

19. Beware of the telephone. Beware of chance encounters. These may catch you off guard.

20. Theresa of Avila, *The Interior Castle*, p. 43. "Mutual love is so important that I should like you never to forget it."

21. Ibid., p. 233.

22. Ibid., p. 234

23. Teaching of Pope John Paul II

24. Teaching of Saint Theresa of Avila.

25. I have written about this in *Meetings with Mary* (New York: Ballantine Books, 1995).

26. Luke 10:38–42.

27. Author interview with Mother Teresa.

28. I was a guest of the Honorable M. M. Heckler at the congressional presentation to Mother Teresa.

29. In 1996, Mother Teresa, surrounded by her body guards (to protect her from people seeking relics of her person or clothes), worked her way through a crowd of a thousand or so at her Washington D.C. Home for the Dying to tell me that the Blessed Mother wanted her to write a prayer for my next book, *Praying with Mary* (San Francisco: HarperSanFrancisco, 1997). The prayer she hand wrote at Our Lady's request is: "Mary, Mother of Jesus, help me to be, only, all for Jesus, holy. Amen."

30. Quote from Malcolm Muggeridge, *Something Beautiful for God* (New York: Harper and Row Publishers, 1971).

31. To bilocate is a spiritual phenomenon by which a person is physically present in more than one place at the same time.

32. This phenomenon occurs when demons take on physical shape and engage in physical abuse of their victim. See Janice T. Connell, *Angel Power* (New York: Ballantine Books, 1995), pp. 141–176.

33. Josemaria Escriva, *Christ Is Passing By* (New York: Scepter Publishing, 1974), p. 76.

34. Raymond Arroyo, *Mother Angelica* (New York: Doubleday, 2005), p. 6.

35. A stigmatic bears the physical wounds of Christ in his or her hands, feet, side, and sometimes even upon the forehead. Saint Francis of Assisi had that spiritual gift. Visionary Sister Agnes of Akita, whom I have written about in this book, has the stigmata which I personally observed.

36. Raymond Arroyo, *Mother Angelica*, p. 30.

37. Author interview with Mother Angelica, September 1987.

38. Raymond Arroyo, *Mother Angelica*, p. 42

39. Author interview with Mother Angelica, September 1987.

40. A title assigned to young women who take vows of poverty, chastity, and obedience in the Religious Order of Our Lady of Mount Carmel.

41. Author interview with Mother Angelica, September 1987.
42. Raymond Arroyo, *Mother Angelica*, p. 83.
43. Ibid., p. 108.
44. Author interview with Mother Angelica, September 1987.
45. The Charismatic Renewal traces its origins to a retreat of students and professors in 1967, at Duquesne University in Pittsburgh, Pennsylvania.
46. Raymond Arroyo, *Mother Angelica*, p. 127.
47. The Eternal Word Television Network was officially founded by Mother Angelica on August 15, 1981.
48. Raymond Arroyo, *Mother Angelica*, p. 248.

CHAPTER TEN: TOWER OF IVORY

1. John 14:21.
2. Nicholas II, Emperor and Autocrat of All the Russias, and canonized by the Russian Orthodox Church as Saint Nicholas the Passion Bearer, ruled Russia from 1894 until his abdication on March 15, 1917. He, his wife, son, four daughters, medical doctor, personal servant, the chambermaid of the empress, and the family's cook were murdered together on the night of July 17, 1918. The multiple assassinations occurred in their prison basement at the Ipatiev House in Yekaterinburg, Siberia.
3. The story of missionary Walter Ciszek, S. J., in Russia follows in this chapter.
4. Current conditions in Russia through the courtesy of Victor Potopov, USIA, Russian Desk, Voice of America.
5. Martin Cruz Smith, *National Geographic*, 214, no. 2 (August 2008): 107.
6. Ibid., p. 116.
7. German born princess Alix of Hesse-Darmstadt, was the fourth daughter of Louis IV, Grand Duke of Hesse and by the Rhine, and Princess Alice of the United Kingdom, second eldest daughter of Queen Victoria and Prince Albert. Though baptized Lutheran, Princess Alix was required to convert from Lutheranism to Russian Orthodoxy to marry Nicholas II. Her conversion ceremony occurred shortly before her wedding to Czar Nicholas II on November 26, 1894, and she took the name Alexandra. Henceforth she was known as Empress Alexandra.
8. Pisma Imperatristsi, I, p. 615, as quoted in Hugo Mager, *Elizabeth Grand Duchess of Russia* (New York: Carroll & Graf Publishers, 1998), p. 311.
9. March 1, 1917, was the day Nicholas II relinquished his autocratic, anointed authority. On March 15 he abdicated the sacred throne of Holy Russia.

10. Walter J. Ciszek, S.J., *He Leadeth Me* (Garden City, N.Y.: Doubleday, 1973; San Francisco: Ignatius Press, 1995), p. 38.
11. Ibid., p. 58.
12. Ibid., pp. 42–43.
13. Walter J. Ciszek, *With God in Russia* (Garden City, N.Y.: Doubleday Image Books, 1966).
14. Ibid., pp. 214–215.
15. Kim Murphy, "A Spiritual Icon Returns to Russia," *Los Angeles Times*, June 26, 2004.
16. Times staff writer Alexei V. Kuznetsov contributed to this report Copyright © 2004 Los Angeles Times.
17. Courtesy of Archpriest Victor Potopov.
18. Richard Stengel, "Choosing Order Before Freedom," *Time*, January 7, 2008, p. 44.
19. *Time* magazine, January 7, 2008.
20. Ibid., p. 48.
21. Ibid., p. 51.
22. Ibid., p. 49.
23. Jason Horowitz, *New York Times*, Friday, August 27, 2004.
24. Copyright © 2004 The International Herald Tribune, www.iht.com: "In all probability, it is the most significant copy among the extant ones, after the destruction of the original by thieves in 1904, as stated in czarist police documents. According to these sources, it is the copy that Czar Peter the Great could have ordered in the 18th century for the Cathedral of St. Petersburg, the new capital, dedicated to the Mother of Kazan. It is said that it was taken out of Russia in 1917, at the end of the October Revolution."
25. On July 12, 2005, I had the privilege of standing before the recently returned holy Icon of the Mother of God of Kazan in the Cathedral in Saint Petersburg. It was a moment never to be forgotten. Few were in the vast Cathedral. Viewers of the icon were, for the most part, elderly, some with small children. There was little information available in any language describing the history and lure of the Icon of the Mother of God of Kazan.

CHAPTER ELEVEN: HOUSE OF GOLD

1. Luke 1:68.
2. Acts 1:14.
3. See Janice T. Connell, *Queen of Angels* (New York: Jeremy P. Tarcher/Putnam, 1999), pp. 6–9.

4. Waltraub Herbstraith, *Edith Stein, a Biography*, translated by Bernard Bonowitz, OCSO (San Francisco: Harper & Row, 1971), p. 5.

5. Ibid., p. 15.

6. Ibid., p. 19.

7. Ibid., p. 30.

8. Ibid., quoting Saint Augustine, p. 31.

9. Ibid., quoting Saint Theresa of Avila, p. 32.

10. Ibid., p. 43.

11. Ibid., quoting Edith Stein, p. 52.

12. Ibid., p. 67.

13. Colossians 1:24.

14. Luke 2:5.

15. Luke 6:27.

16. Luke 1:43.

17. Teaching of Saint Bernard of Clairvaux.

18. Teaching of Saint Alphonsis Liquiri.

19. Teaching of Saint Maximilian Kolbe.

CHAPTER TWELVE: REFUGE OF SINNERS

1. John 3:16.

2. Psalm 25:14.

3. Luke 1:28.

4. Courtesy of Professor Robert Faricy, S. J., Pontifical Gregorian University, Rome.

5. The Divine Mercy Novena and Chaplet of Divine Mercy herein are used with permission and excerpted from *Diary of Sister Maria Faustina Kowalska, Divine Mercy in My Soul,* copyright © 1987. Congregation of Marians of the Immaculate Conception; all world rights reserved.

6. See Janice T. Connell, *Prayer Power* (San Francisco: Harper, 1998) for the story of the Divine Mercy, the Chaplet, and the Novena.

7. Maria Faustina Kowalska, Saint, *Diary of Saint Maria Faustina Kowalska: Divine Mercy in My Soul,* Third Edition with Revisions (Stockbridge, Mass.: Marian Press, 2007.

8. Ibid., p. 264.

9. Ibid., p. 42.

10. Ibid., pp. 374–375.

11. Ibid., pp. 342–849.

12. Ibid., p. 342.

13. Ibid., p. 559.
14. Ibid., pp. 563–564.
15. Ibid., p. 631.
16. John 20:33–34.
17. See Janice T. Connell, *Meetings with Mary* (New York: Ballantine Books, 1995), pp. 234–248, for information about Our Lady's apparitions in Kibeho.
18. For information about the Divine Mercy World Apostolic Congress, visit www .world apostoliccongressonmercy.org. In the United States, contact the Shrine of Divine Mercy: Stockbridge, Massachusetts. Phone 1-800-462-7426.
19. See *Diary of Saint Maria Faustina Kowalska: Divine Mercy in My Soul.*
20. I wrote about this in *Meetings with Mary,* pp. 188–195.
21. From Fr. Rene Laurentin-Fayard, *Dictionary of Apparitions* (*Le dictionnaire des Apparitions*) (Paris: Editions Fayard, 2007) 2006.
22. Vatican City, May 13, 2005, www.infoenglish@zenit.org.
23. *L'Osservatore Romano*, front page.
24. John 2:11.
25. Teaching of Saint Therese of Lisieux.
26. Teaching of Saint Louis de Montfort.
27. Teaching of Saint Maximilian Kolby.
28. John 15:23.
29. Author's interview with Professor Robert Faricy, S.J. in Rome, October 1989.
30. Pope Benedict XVI.
31. Author interview with Medjugorje visionary Ivan Dragicevic during the Gulf War, January 1991, Washington, D.C.
32. Numbers 6:23–26.

AFTERWORD

1. Acts 2:17–21.

APPENDIX ONE: SPECIAL PRAYERS TO MARY

1. The Miraculous Memorare Prayer to Mary.

APPENDIX TWO: SOME REPORTED APPARITIONS OF
THE BLESSED VIRGIN MARY

1. Not all of these apparitions have been authenticated by the Roman Catholic Church. For more information see Campus.udayton.edu/Mary//resources. Marian Apparitions.

APPENDIX THREE: CONSECRATION TO JESUS
THROUGH MARY

1. As practiced by the late Pope John Paul II.

Selected Bibliography

Alacoque, Saint Margaret Mary. *The Autobiography of Saint Margaret Mary.* Trans. V. Kerns. Westminster, Md.: Newman Press, 1961.

Aquinas, Thomas. *Summa Theologica.* Five Vols. Westminster, Md.: Christian Classics, 1981.

Arroya, Raymond. *Mother Angelica.* New York: Doubleday, 2005.

Augustine, Saint. *The Confessions,* Garden City, N.Y.: Doubleday Image Books, 1960.

Benedict XVI, Pope (Joseph Ratzinger). *Jesus of Nazareth.* New York: Doubleday, 2007.

————. *Deus Caritas Est.* Encyclical Letter. Boston: Daughters of St. Paul, 2007.

Bertone, Cardinal Tarcisio. *The Last Secret of Fatima.* New York: Doubleday, 2008.

Blackbourn, David. *Marpingen: Apparitions of the Virgin Mary in Nineteenth-Century Germany.* New York: Alfred A. Knopf, 1994.

Bojorge, Horatio. *The Image of Mary According to the Evangelists.* New York: Alba House, 1978.

Boulay, Shirley du. *Theresa of Avila, An Extraordinary Life.* New York: Blue Ridge, 1991, 2004.

Boylan, M. Eugene. *This Tremendous Lover.* Allen, Tex.: Christian Classics, Inc., 1987.

Brigid, Saint. *The Magnificent Prayers of Saint Brigid of Sweden.* Rockford, Ill.: Tan Books, 1983.

Brigitta of Sweden, Saint. *Brigitta: Life and Selected Revelations.* New York: Paulist Press, 1990.

Bryant, Christopher. *The Heart in Pilgrimage.* New York: Seabury Press, 1980.

Cataneo, Pascal. *Padre Pio Gleanings.* Sherbrooke, QC: Editions Paulines, 1991.

Catherine of Geona, Saint. *Purgation and Purgatory: The Spiritual Dialogue.* New York: Paulist Press, 1979.

Catherine of Sienna, Saint. *The Dialogue.* Ramsey, N.J.: Paulist Press, 1980.

Caussade, Jean-Pierre De. *The Joy of Full Surrender.* Orleans, Mass.: Paraclete Press, 1986.

Ciszek, Walter J., S.J. *He Leadeth Me.* San Francisco: Ignatius Press, 1997.

———. *With God in Russia.* Garden City, N.Y.: Doubleday Image Books, 1966.

Connell, Janice T., *Angel Power.* Introduction by Robert Faricy. New York: Ballantine Books, 1995.

———. *Meetings with Mary.* Introduction by Robert Faricy. New York: Ballantine Books, 1995.

———. *Prayer Power.* Introduction by Robert Faricy. San Francisco: HarperSan Francisco, 1998.

———. *Praying with Mary.* Introduction by Robert Faricy. San Francisco: HarperSanFrancisco, 1997.

———. *The Spiritual Journey of George Washington.* Long Island City, N.Y.: Hatherleigh Press, 2007.

———. *The Triumph of the Immaculate Heart.* Introduction by René Laurentin. Santa Barbara, Calif.: Queenship Publishing, 1993.

———. *The Visions of the Children.* Introduction by Robert Faricy. New York: St. Martin's Press, 1992: Revised, 1997, Revised and Updated, 2007.

———. *Queen of Angels.* Afterword by Robert Faricy. New York: Jeremy P. Tarcher/Putnam, 1999, Revised Edition Orleans, Mass.: Paraclete Press, 2008.

———. *Queen of the Cosmos.* Introduction by Robert Faricy, Orleans, MA: Paraclete Press, 1990; Revised, 2005.

Danielou, Jean, S.J. *The Angels and Their Mission According to the Fathers of the Church.* Westminster, Md.: Christian Classics, 1988.

Delaney, John J. *A Woman Clothed with the Sun.* New York: Doubleday Image Books, 1961.

DeRobeck, Nesta. *Padre Pio.* Milwaukee: Bruce Publishing Co. 1958.

De Waal, Ester. *Seeking God: The Way of St. Benedict.* London: HarperCollins Publishers, 1996.

Dubay, Thomas, S.M. *Fire Within.* San Francisco: Ignatius Press, 1989.

Dupre, Louis, and James A. Wiseman, editors. *Light from Light: An Anthology Of Christian Mysticism.* New York: Paulist Press, 1988.

Dziwisz, Stanislaw. *A Life with Karol: My Forty-Year Friendship with the Man Who Became Pope.* New York: Doubleday, 2007.

Emmerich, Anne Catherine. *The Life of the Blessed Virgin Mary.* Rockford, Ill.: Tan Books, 1954.

Escriva, Bl. Josemaria. *The Way.* Manila: Sinag-Tala Publishers, Inc., 1982.

Estrade, J. B. *My Witness, Bernadette.* Springfield, Ill.: Templegate, 1946.

Faricy, Robert, S.J. *The Lord's Dealing: The Primacy of the Feminine in Christian Spirituality.* New York: Paulist Press, 1988.

Faricy, Robert, S. J., and Lucy Rooney, S.D.N. *The Contemplative Way of Prayer.* Ann Arbor, Mich.: Servant Books, 1986.

Fernandez-Carvajal, Francis, and Peter Beteta. *Children of God.* Princeton, N.J.: Scepter Publishing, 1997.

Francis and Clare. *Francis and Clare, The Complete Works.* Trans. R. J. Armstrong and I. C. Brady. New York: Paulist Press, 1982.

Francis of Assisi, Saint. *The Best From All His Works, Christian Classics Collection.* Nashville, Tenn.: Thomas Nelson Publisher, 1989.

Fukushima, Mutano (Francis). *Akita: Spiritual Oasis of Japan.* Santa Barbara, Calif.: Queenship Publishing, 1994.

Gertrude of Helfta. *The Herald of Divine Love.* New York: Paulist Press, 1993.

Griffiths, Bede. *Sacred Wisdom of the World.* London; HarperCollins, 1994.

———. *The Cosmic Revelation: The Hindu Way to God.* Springfield, Ill.: Templegate Publishers. 1983.

Groeschel, Benedict, C.F.R. *A Still Small Voice.* San Francisco: Ignatius Press, 1992.

Groeschel, Benedict, C.F.R., and James Monti. *In the Presence of Our Lord.* Huntington, Ind.: Our Sunday Visitor Press, 1997.

Hahn, Scott. *Hail Holy Queen.* New York: Doubleday, 2005.

———. *Lord Have Mercy.* New York: Doubleday, 2003.

———. *The Lamb's Supper.* New York: Doubleday, 1999.

Hebblethwaite, Peter. *Pope John XXIII.* New York: Doubleday, 1985.

Heine, Max. *Equipping Men for Spiritual Battle.* Ann Arbor, Mich.: Servant Books, 1993.

Herbstrith, Waltraub. *Edith Stein; A Biography.* Trans. Bernard Bonowitz, OCSO. San Francisco: Harper & Row, 1971.

Hickey, James Cardinal. *Mary at the Foot of the Cross.* San Francisco: Ignatius Press, 1988.

Huber, Georges. *My Angel Will Go Before You.* Introduction by Cardinal Charles Journet. Westminster, Md.: Christian Classics, 1988.

Ignatius of Loyola, Saint. *A Pilgrim's Journey, the Autobiography of Ignatius of Loyola.* Collegeville, Minn.: The Liturgical Press, 1991.

———. *The Spiritual Exercises.* Trans. Anthony Mohola. New York: Doubleday Image Books, 1989.

Jelly, Frederick M. *Madonna, Mary in the Catholic Tradition.* New Huntington, Ind.: Our Sunday Visitor Publishing Division, 1986.

John of the Cross, Saint. *Selected Writings.* Trans. Kieran Kavanaugh, O.C.D. New York: Paulist Press, 1987.

John Paul II, Pope. *The Splendor of Truth*, Encyclical Letter. Boston: Saint Paul Books and Media, 1993.

———. *Crossing the Threshold of Hope.* New York: Alfred A. Knopf, 1994.

———. Apostolic Letter *Dies Domini.* Boston: Daughters of St. Paul, 1998.

———. Encyclical Letter *Fides Et Ratio.* Boston: Daughters of St. Paul, 1998.

———. *Mary: God's Yes to Man.* Encyclical Letter *Mother of the Redeemer.* Introduction by Joseph Cardinal Ratzinger. San Francisco: Ignatius Press, 1988.

———. *Theotokos: Woman, Mother, Disciple.* Boston: Pauline Books and Media, 2000.

Johnson, Francis. *Fatima, The Great Sign.* Rockford, Ill.: Tan Books, 1980.

Johnson, William, ed. *The Cloud Of Unknowing.* New York: Doubleday Image Books, 1973.

Julian of Norwich. *Showings.* Introduction by Edmund Cooledge, O.S.A., and James Walsh, S.J. New York: Paulist Press, 1978.

King, Thomas M., S.J. *Teilhard's Mass.* New York: Paulist Press, 2005.

Kondor, L., ed. *Fatima in Lucia's Own Words.* Trans. Dominican Nuns of the Perpetual Rosary. Fatima, Portugal: Postultion Centre, 1976.

Kowalska, Blessed M. Faustina. Diary of Saint Maria Faustina Kowalska: *Divine Mercy in My Soul,* Stockbridge, Mass.: Marian Press, 1987.

Langford, Joseph, MC. *Mother Theresa: In the Shadow of Our Lady.* Huntington, Ind.: Our Sunday Visitor Publishing Division. 2007.

Langsam, Jude, managing ed. *Welcome to Carmel.* Washington, D.C.: Teresian Charism Press, 1982.

Laurentin, Rene, O.S.B. *Bernadette at Lourdes.* Minneapolis, Minn.: Winston Press, 1979.

————. *The Church and Apparitions—Their Status and Function; Criteria and Reception.* Milford, Ohio: The Riehle Foundation, 1989.

Laurentin, Rene, and H. Joyeux. *Scientific and Medical Studies on the Apparitions at Medjugorje.* Trans. L. Griffin. Dublin: Veritas, 1987.

Laurentin, Rene, and Lejeune. *Messages and Teachings of Mary at Medjugorje.* Milford, Ohio: The Riehle Foundation, 1988.

Lewis, C. S. *The Screwtape Letters.* New York: The Macmillan Company, 1943.

Liguori, Saint Alphonsus de. *The Glories of Mary.* Rockford, Ill.: Tan Books, 1977.

Lucia, Visionary of Fatima. *Fatima in Lucia's Own Words.* Fatima, Portugal: Postulation Centre, 1976.

Lymann, Sanford M. *The Seven Deadly Sins: Society and Evil.* New York: St. Martin's Press, 1978.

Maloney, George A., S.J. *Called to Intimacy: Living in the Indwelling Presence.* New York: Alba House, 1983.

Margaret Mary, Saint. *The Autobiography.* Rockford, Ill.: Tan Publishers, 1952.

Martin, Thomas F., OSA, *Our Restless Heart: The Augustinian Tradition.* Maryknoll, N.Y.: Orbis Books, 2003.

Mary of Agreda, The Venerable. *Mystical City of God.* Four Vols. Washington, N.J.: Ave Maria Institute, 1971.

McHugh, Rosita. *The Knights of Malta: Nine Hundred Years of Care.* Dublin: The Irish Association, SMOM, 1996.

Michel, Frère de la Sainte Trinité. *The Whole Truth About Fatima.* Buffalo, N.Y.: Immaculate Heart Publications, 1989.

Miravalle, Mark. *Introduction to Mary.* Santa Barbara, Calif.: Queenship Publishing, 1993.

————. *Mary, Coredemptrix Mediatrix Advocate.* Santa Barbara, Calif.: Queenship Publishing Company, 1993.

————. *The Message of Medjugorje.* Lanham Md.; University Press of America, 1986.

Montfort, Saint Louis Grignon De. *God Alone: The Collected Writings of St. Louis De Montfort.* Washington, N.J.: The Blue Army, 1989.

————. *The Secret of the Rosary.* Washington, N.J.: The Blue Army, 1951.

————. *True Devotion to Mary.* Edit. The Fathers of the Company of Mary. Trans. F. W. Faber. Rockford, Ill.: Tan Books, 1941.

Most, William G. *Our Father's Plan.* Manassas, Va.: Trinity Communications, 1988.

Mowatt, Archpriest John J. *The Holy and Miraculous Icon of Our Lady of Kazan.* Fatima, Portugal: Domus Pacis, 1974.

Mullins, Peter. Foreword by Janice T. Connell. *Shrines of Our Lady.* New York: St. Martins Press, 1998.

National Conference of Catholic Bishops. *Behold Your Mother, A Pastoral Letter on the Blessed Virgin Mary.* Washington, D.C.: United States Catholic Conference, November 21, 1973.

Neumann, Erich. *The Great Mother.* Trans. Ralph Manheim. Princeton, N.J.: Princeton University Press, 1955.

Newman, John Henry. *Mary the Second Eve.* Rockford, Ill.: Tan Books, 1982.

Nikodimos, Saint, and Saint Makarios of Corinth. *The Philokalia.* Four Volumes. London: Faber and Faber, 1984.

Northcote, J. *Celebrated Sanctuaries of the Madonna.* London: Longmans Green, 1968.

O'Carroll, Michael, C.C.Sp. *Medjugorje Facts, Documents, Theology.* Dublin: Veritas, 1986.

———. *Theotokos: A Theological Encyclopedia of the Blessed Virgin Mary.* Wilmington, Del.: Michael Glazier, 1982.

O'Daly, Gerald. *Augustine's City of God.* New York: Oxford: Oxford University Press, 1999.

Pelletier, Joseph. "The Fatima Secret in 1960?" *Messenger of the Sacred Heart* 95 (January 1960): 18–22.

———. *The Sun Danced at Fatima.* Garden City, N.Y.: Image Books, 1951.

———. *The Queen of Peace Visits Medjugorje.* Worcester, Mass.: Assumption Publications, 1985.

Pius XI, Pope. *Ineffabilis Deus,* December 8, 1854.

Pius XII, Pope. *Munificentissimus Deus,* 1950; *Signa Magna,* 1948.

Pius XII, Pope. *Signa Magna,* Encyclical Letter, 1948.

Ratzinger, Joseph Cardinal (Pope Benedict XVI). *The Ratzinger Report.* San Francisco: Ignatius Press, 1985.

Reeves, Thomas C. *America's Bishop: The Life and Times of Fulton J. Sheen.* San Francisco: Encounter Books, 2001.

Rengers, Christopher. *The Youngest Prophet.* New York: Alba House, 1986.

Roberts, Cokie. *We Are Our Mothers' Daughters.* New York: William Morrow, 1998.

Rouvelle, Alexander De. *Imitation of Mary in Four Books.* New York: Catholic Book Publlishing, 1985.

Salles, Saint Francis De. *The Sermons of Saint Francis De Salles on Our Lady.* Edit. Lewis S. Fiorelli, Rockford, Ill.: Tan Books, 1985.

Sanford, Agnes. *The Healing Gifts of the Spirit.* Philadelphia: Harper and Row, 1966.

Sanford, John A. *The Kingdom Within.* San Francisco: Harper and Row, 1987.

Scanlan, Michael, T.O.R. *Appointment with God.* Steubenville, Ohio: Franciscan University Press, 1987.

Scanlon, Michael, T.O.R., and Randall J. Cirner. *Deliverance from Evil Spirits.* Ann Arbor, Mich.: Servant Books, 1980.

Schlessinger, Laura, and Rabbi Stewart Vogel. *The Ten Commandments.* New York: Cliff Street Books, 1998.

Schouppe, F.X., S.J. *The Dogma of Hell.* Rockford, Ill.: Tan Books and Publishers, 1989.

Scupoli, Dom Lorenzo, *The Spiritual Combat and a Treatise on Peace of Soul.* Rockford, Ill.: Tan Books and Publishers, 1990.

Shamon, Albert. *The Power of the Rosary.* Milford, Ohio: The Riehle Foundation, 1989.

Sheen, Fulton J. *Three to Get Married.* Princeton, N.J.: Scepter Publishing, 1951.

———. *The World's First Love.* Garden City, N.Y.: Garden City Books, 1952.

Silvestrini, Achille. *The Life of the Madonna in Art.* Boston: Daughters of Saint Paul, 1985.

Sreavinskas, Oeter M.J., ed. *Catholic Encyclopedia.* Huntington, Ind.: Our Sunday Visitor, 1991.

Terelya, Josyp, with Michael Brown. *Josyp Terelya Witness.* Milford, Ohio: Faith Publishing Company, 1991.

Testoni, Manuela. *Our Lady of Guadalupe.* New York: Alba House, 2001.

Theresa of Avila, Saint. *Collected Works.* Three Volumes. Trans. K. Kavanaugh and O. Rodriguez. Washington, D.C.: ICS Publications, 1985.

———. *The Interior Castle.* Trans. K. Kavanaugh, New York: Paulist Press, 1979.

———. *The Way of Perfection.* Trans. and edit. Allison Peers. New York: Doubleday Image Books, 1964.

Therese, Saint of Lisieux. *The Autobiography: The Story of a Soul.* New York: Doubleday, 1957.

Tissot, Joseph. *How to Profit from One's Faults.* London: Scepter, 1996.

Two Friends of Medjugorje. *Words from Heaven.* Birmingham, Ala.: St. James Publishing, 1990.

United States Catholic Conference. *Catechism of the Catholic Church,* Second Edition, revised in accordance with the official Latin text promulgated by Pope John XXIII. Citta del Vaticano: Libraria Editrice Vaticana, 1994, 1997.

Van Kaam, Adrian, C.S.Sp. *The Mystery of Transforming Love.* Denville, N.J.: Dimension Books, Inc., 1981.

Wagner, E. Glenn. *The Awesome Power of Shared Beliefs.* Dallas, Tex.: Word Publishing, 1995.

Walsh, Michael, ed. *Butler's Lives of the Saints.* Foreword by Cardinal Basil Hume. San Francisco: Harper and Row, 1984.

Walsh, William J., ed. *The Apparitions and Shrines of Heaven's Bright Queen.* Four Volumes. New York: T.J. Carey, 1904.

Weigel, George. *Witness to Hope: The Biography of Pope John Paul II.* New York: HarperCollins. 1999.

Weil, Simone. *Waiting for God.* New York: Harper and Row, 1951.

Werfel, Franz. *The Song of Bernadette.* Trans. Ludwig Lewisohn. New York: St. Martin's Press, 1970.

Whelan, Sister Ellen, O.S.F. *The Sister' Story: Saint Mary's Hospital–Mayo Clinic 1889 to 1939.* Rochester, Minn.: Mayo Foundation for Medical Research, 2002.

———. *The Sister' Story: Part Two. Saint Mary's Hospital–Mayo Clinic 1939–1980.* Rochester, Minn.: Mayo Foundation for Medical Research, 2007.

Wright, John Cardinal. *Mary Our Hope.* San Francisco: Ignatius Press, 1988.

Wuerl, Archbishop Donald W. *The Catholic Way.* New York: Doubleday. 2001.

Yasuda, Teiji. *Akita: The Tears and Message of Mary.* Eng. Trans. John Haffert. Asbury, N.J.: 101 Foundation, 1989.

Zimdals-Swartz, Sandra L. *Encountering Mary from LaSalette to Medjugorje.* Princeton, N.J.: Princeton University Press, 1991.